# The Theology of Grace

# THE THEOLOGY OF GRACE

MARTIN ANGELO RECIO

TATE PUBLISHING
AND ENTERPRISES, LLC

The Theology of Grace
Copyright © 1986, 2012 by Martin Angelo Recio. All rights reserved.

No part of this publication may be reproduced, stored in a retrieval system or transmitted in any way by any means, electronic, mechanical, photocopy, recording or otherwise without the prior permission of the author except as provided by USA copyright law.

Scripture quotations, unless otherwise indicated, are taken from the *Holy Bible, King James Version*, Cambridge, 1769. Used by permission. All rights reserved.

Scripture quotations marked (RSV) are from *Revised Standard Version of the Bible*, copyright © 1946, 1952, and 1971 National Council of the Churches of Christ in the United States of America. Used by permission. All rights reserved.

This book is designed to provide accurate and authoritative information with regard to the subject matter covered. This information is given with the understanding that neither the author nor Tate Publishing, LLC is engaged in rendering legal, professional advice. Since the details of your situation are fact dependent, you should additionally seek the services of a competent professional.

The opinions expressed by the author are not necessarily those of Tate Publishing, LLC.

Published by Tate Publishing & Enterprises, LLC
127 E. Trade Center Terrace | Mustang, Oklahoma 73064 USA
1.888.361.9473 | www.tatepublishing.com

Tate Publishing is committed to excellence in the publishing industry. The company reflects the philosophy established by the founders, based on Psalm 68:11,
"The Lord gave the word and great was the company of those who published it."

Book design copyright © 2012 by Tate Publishing, LLC. All rights reserved.
*Cover design by Rodrigo Adolfo*
*Interior design by Jake Muelle*

Published in the United States of America

ISBN: 978-1-62147-033-5
1. Religion / Christian Theology / General
2. Religion / Christian Theology / Soteriology
12.12.19

# Dedication

Dedicated to our son, Stephen Juan Recio

# Preface

Today, more than ever, we need a living, vital theology for the Christian faith. The great doctrines of Christianity seem all but forgotten in our modern age. Still, they are the life-breath and heartbeat of our religion. We do not wish to have them forgotten and buried in the past. We believe that the teachings of the apostles and the ancient church fathers, especially those of St. Augustine, are as meaningful and necessary to a vital and strong Christianity today as when they were first written. We do not really propose anything new, but we do intend to lay out the great teachings of the church in a clear and simple style and to bring the great doctrines of our faith to light once more.

# Table of Contents

**Faith and Reason: Faith and Epistemology** .............. 13
The Current Uncertainty ............................. 13
Our Faith and the Past .............................. 14
The Birth of Our Faith .............................. 17
Our Basic Beliefs: Our Presuppositions ................ 18
Modern Epistemology: The Modern Theory of Knowledge ... 23
Sartre and Existentialism ........................... 29
The Theological Encyclopedia ........................ 33

**Christian Hamartology: The Doctrine of Sin** ............ 37
The Chief Good: With All Thy Heart .................. 37
With All Thy Soul ................................... 38
With All Thy Mind ................................... 39
Sin ................................................. 41
Savior and Salvation ................................ 42

**Satan: The Doctrine of Evil** .......................... 45
The Origin of Satan and Evil ........................ 45
His Entry into the World ............................ 46
Evil and the Dividing Force of Faith ................ 48
The Narrative Situation ............................. 49
The Divine Force of Faith ........................... 51
Satan's Power Is Temporal and Can Be Broken ......... 51

**Soteriology: The Doctrine of Salvation** ............... 53
Salvation: A Manifestation of the Grace of God ...... 53
Salvation: Essentially a Process of
    Redemption and Restoration ..................... 58
The Proto-Evangel: Through the Seed of the Woman .... 60
The Promise of the Indwelling of the Holy Spirit .... 61
The Promise of the Outpouring of the Holy Spirit .... 65

The Annunciation of Jesus . . . . . . . . . . . . . . . . . . . . . . . . . . . . . 65
From the Threshold of Heaven . . . . . . . . . . . . . . . . . . . . . . . 68
The Fullness of Time. . . . . . . . . . . . . . . . . . . . . . . . . . . . . . . . . . 71
Your Faith in Christ Jesus . . . . . . . . . . . . . . . . . . . . . . . . . . . . . 73
The Atonement of Jesus Christ . . . . . . . . . . . . . . . . . . . . . . . 81
The Saving Passion . . . . . . . . . . . . . . . . . . . . . . . . . . . . . . . . . . 84
Justification. . . . . . . . . . . . . . . . . . . . . . . . . . . . . . . . . . . . . . . . . . 88
The Reality of Adult Conversion . . . . . . . . . . . . . . . . . . . . . . 98
Adult Conversion. . . . . . . . . . . . . . . . . . . . . . . . . . . . . . . . . . . 102

**Christology: The Doctrine of Christ** . . . . . . . . . . . . . . . . . . . 113
God the Son: The Incarnation . . . . . . . . . . . . . . . . . . . . . . . 114
The Temptation . . . . . . . . . . . . . . . . . . . . . . . . . . . . . . . . . . . . 122
The Transfiguration: A View of His Glory . . . . . . . . . . . . . . 128
The Transfiguration in Glory. . . . . . . . . . . . . . . . . . . . . . . . . 131
The Afterglow of Glory. . . . . . . . . . . . . . . . . . . . . . . . . . . . . . 134
The Humiliation: The Golden Passional. . . . . . . . . . . . . . . 136
The Crucifixion: The Cross and the Crown . . . . . . . . . . . . 140
The Cross, the Crown, and You . . . . . . . . . . . . . . . . . . . . . . 143
The Resurrection. . . . . . . . . . . . . . . . . . . . . . . . . . . . . . . . . . . 144
Alleluia He Is Risen: Jesus Christ Is Lord . . . . . . . . . . . . . . 153
The Ascension of Christ . . . . . . . . . . . . . . . . . . . . . . . . . . . . . 158
The Exaltation of Christ . . . . . . . . . . . . . . . . . . . . . . . . . . . . . 163
The Second Advent of Our Lord . . . . . . . . . . . . . . . . . . . . . 168

**Pneumatology: The Doctrine of the Holy Spirit** . . . . . . . . 170
The Promise of the Father . . . . . . . . . . . . . . . . . . . . . . . . . . 174
When the Day of Pentecost Had Come . . . . . . . . . . . . . . . 177
The Power Pentecost. . . . . . . . . . . . . . . . . . . . . . . . . . . . . . . 179
Thou Hast Stricken My Heart . . . . . . . . . . . . . . . . . . . . . . . . 185
The Holy Spirit Working in Human Lives . . . . . . . . . . . . . . 188
The Morning Star in Their Work. . . . . . . . . . . . . . . . . . . . . . 190
The Ebb and Flow of the Spiritual Life . . . . . . . . . . . . . . . . 193
The Healing Presence . . . . . . . . . . . . . . . . . . . . . . . . . . . . . . 196
The Lord and Giver of Life. . . . . . . . . . . . . . . . . . . . . . . . . . . 199

Responding to the Presence ........................... 201
The Presence Encountered ........................... 202

**Ecclesiology: The Doctrine of the Church** .............. 204
The Church: Its Nature ................................ 204
The Church: Its Composition .......................... 212
The Church: Its Structure ............................. 219
The Church: Its Mission .............................. 220
The Kingdom of God Is Within ....................... 221
The Growth of the Kingdom .......................... 223
The Church: Endurance ............................... 225
The Church: Its Ministry ............................. 228
The Church: The Sacraments .......................... 230

**Eschatology: The Doctrine of the Last Things** .......... 238
The Resurrection of the Body ........................ 247
The Second Advent of Our Lord Jesus Christ ............ 250
The Final Judgment .................................. 254
The New Heaven and the New Earth ................... 257

**Grace for Successful Living** ......................... 259
Grace in Our Daily Lives ............................. 260
Grace and Our Spiritual Life ......................... 261
Grace and Inner Renewal ............................. 262

# Faith and Reason: Faith and Epistemology

## The Current Uncertainty

As we look at our faith in the modern world, we express our concern because we are living in an age of doctrinal aversion and deterioration. The cardinal teachings of our religion are only half-heartedly presented, if at all. There is vagueness and an uncertainty in the delivery of the message that was once proclaimed in the power and spirit of the living God. There is a lack of definitive expression, simple reasoning, and spirit-filled emotional directness that is so essential in striking at the heart and making men and women conscious of God's existence and turning them to the Lord Jesus.

We acknowledge that much has changed since the birth of our faith—Christianity. Modern man appears confused and disorientated, and the voices that should ring out with the strong Gospel evangel are nearly silent. Knowledge has continued to increase in all fields of human endeavor in medicine, in space science and astronomy, in transportation, in communications, and in advancing technology. The average man and woman may well wonder whether there is any validity left in the faith that was born two millennia ago. Men and women may wonder whether the current vast accumulation of knowledge runs counter to the concepts of their traditional beliefs, and they question whether historical Christianity can still speak effectively and intelligently to modern man. Can our faith still address itself to man's most urgent and poignant needs?

Is it still possible for the Spirit of the living God to touch man's soul and cause him to come alive with a quickening power? Does the grace of our Lord Jesus Christ still apply to man and to his family? How can God, who keeps a million galaxies and their trillions of stars in their course, hear man's prayers, understand the anguish of his soul, and answer the petitions of his child?

In view of the babble of the many strange and alien voices, we can understand modern man's perplexity. We would assure him that he to whom we look for strength and spiritual life has lost none of his power to redeem and uplift the human soul. Jesus Christ is the same yesterday, today, and forever. Christ our Lord, with the quiet suffusing power of the Holy Spirit, can still bring a spiritual awakening to man's soul. And our religion can still challenge the best thought of our day.

In truth, the concepts of historical Christianity alone offer the basis for reasoning, for intelligent direction, and for the acquisition of knowledge. Its teachings have always been the underlying foundation for the moral and spiritual qualities of life. Its influence continues to inspire all who embrace it to the good and noble and best in life. Our religion is linked with strong ties to the past, but the past is not prologue. It is the foundation upon which we live and move and have our being.

I am an Augustinian, and like St. Augustine, I will endeavor to maintain an organic unity of thought and concept throughout. The essence of St. Augustine's writings is their organic wholeness. His mental activity (philosophy), his view on the nature of God's dealing with men (theology), and his faith are all deeply interfused. This is one of the reasons why his writings preserve and express a strong, spiritual inheritance so profoundly vital to the Protestant expression of the Christian religion.

## Our Faith and the Past

Let us look for a moment to the past, because Christianity grew out of the far distant yesterday. In looking at the Heavens, at stars in untold millions, at star clusters, galaxies, and distant island universes, we are looking at the past. Can we even imagine that the light from a distant star has been traveling through space since the days of Abraham and that it has been doing so at the speed of light? In seeking to solve the mystery of the universe and its origins, astronomers look up into the far-distant Heavens. They are looking into the past. They know, as we must surely know, that all has grown out of the past.

God's redemptive promises, although grown out of his lovingkindness toward us through Christ Jesus, from our perspective, were made in the past. They were brought into realization in time—in the past, in the present, and in the future. When we read about the promises of God in the book of Jeremiah, or in some other passage of the scriptures, we are looking to the past. We look back to the origins of the promises of God; we look back to his creation of the universe and to his creation of man in his own image.

We look back, especially, to the promise about the coming Redeemer of men and to his incarnation. We look back to the origins of the only Righteous One, a Branch from the Stem of David—the Lord Jesus Christ, who is also the Lord our Righteousness. As we become aware of it, we see God's dealings with us and that his dealings with men would lead to man's ultimate good. It is in his dealings with men that God reveals himself and his character. As these promises relate to our ultimate good, they acquire a redemptive perspective. These promises reveal God's desire to turn us to himself to awaken our spiritual life and to redeem us from selfishness, envy, hatred, and sin.

God's purpose of mercy began as a very faint light and gradually broke out into a broad avenue of splendor, glory, and hope. We see God's love, patience, and understanding in his dealing with our limited and frail nature. Our faith is a historical religion, and we see God working in the history of nations and in the growth and development of man and his societies. In the historical perspective, we are enabled to see God's kindness and providence manifested in his relationship with Abraham when he called him out of Ur of the Chaldees.

God was present with Abraham and led him in all his wanderings. Abraham received the promise of the land in which he moved as a stranger, the enlargement of his seed, and that through his seed would come the promised Redeemer in whom the whole world would be blessed. The marvel of Abraham's faith in God was that it endured so many years without fulfillment, for there were times when he had only his trust in God to cling to.

Still, in the mystery of providence, when we look back to the time when God's Spirit spoke to our hearts with the assurance of his love, our souls are revived. We can look back to that moment when, in answer to our prayers, our heavenly Father touched our souls with the gentle impulse of his grace. Then the grasp of our beliefs becomes firm and strong once more. It was as though deep inside of us there was released an incipient river of strength. If the past teaches us anything at all, it is that our God is faithful. In his good time, he will work out his purpose of good for our lives and for the life of his church.

As it concerns our faith, the past is not to be buried and forgotten. Nor is it meaningless—quite the contrary, it is rich with meaning and with reference of faith and belief. The history of our religion is a storehouse of wealth, of lessons in spiritual growth and inspiration, and of lives lived in sacrifice and devotion to the cause of the Kingdom. It is replete with heroes and martyrs of our religion, and their lives shine for us as the bright and morning stars of faith, hope, and love. They dreamed dreams and were heroic in the realization of those dreams. They exemplified the care and providence of the Lord our God. In being full of meaning, the ages past give us a solid foundation for the present and for the future.

We do not build, nor do we grow, on thin air. Nor do we build on doctrinal beliefs that have not been tried and tested through the centuries. We are linked with strong bonds of faith with all who have ever walked in the way of the Lord. We build on the expressions of their religious experiences, on their work, and on their writings. We build on the comfort, assurance, and instructions they have preserved for us. They left us a wealth of spiritual devotion and made our religion all the richer for it.

But there is more. The foundations and the promises of the past move with us as a universal redemptive constant. They become a part of us and enable us to make our faith stretch out. Our religion is a living faith that is strong enough, deep enough, and broad enough to meet the challenges of every age. It must remain alive and flexible enough for the lives and conditions of men and women of all times and of all societies. It must not become so rigid that it applies only to one part of society or to a prescribed number of people. We can make as broad an application of our faith as men can imagine and as the Holy Spirit would lead. It is in the past promises realized that we see displayed the grandeur, glory, and immensity of the grace of God and of his never-failing and everlasting love.

## The Birth of Our Faith

The birth of our religion occurred in the time of the Roman Empire. But that ancient civilization was dying, for already it was in a sure and steady process of decline. Human thought, as expressed through its writers and men of letters, had long ago exhausted itself, had strangled itself, and had ended up in despair and hopelessness. In the arena, human life was counted as naught. The universal realization was that the human race had become so hopeless that it was incapable of saving itself. Might is not right, and this was true even though the Roman Empire was overly massive and armed with physical strength. The moral and spiritual imperatives of their religion had long ago waxed old and faded away.

As if in a distant cloud, the birth of our faith was nearly hid in obscurity. There were so many provinces to govern—so many legions on the move—and the multiplicity of religions throughout the empire were all contending for recognition. The time was one of near universal peace all over the land in the rule of Caesar Augustus. In a far country, distant from the capital city of Rome, in the Roman province of Judea, Jesus Christ was born in the humblest of circumstances. His days on earth were not long, for about thirty three years later he was cut off in the midst of his life. He was brought to capital punishment under Pontius Pilate and died on a cross—a cruel Roman instrument of torture and death.

When Christ met his untimely death, his name was hardly known beyond the limits of Palestine. He was rejected by his people in favor of a murderer and robber and hung between two thieves. The cross ended his brief tenure of earthly ministry. Years later, Tacitus, a Roman historian, wrote that Jesus was put to capital punishment by Pontius Pilate.

Yet in the mysterious working of the providence of God, faith in the Crucified One, through his resurrection, became faith in a risen and living Lord. Christianity refused to die on the cross of its founder. He did not sleep. He was not in the tomb, for it had been impossible for the pangs of hell to hold him. In the belief that our Savior arose after the power of an endless life in the Spirit of holiness, the Christian faith grew as if endowed with a supernatural power of propaganda. It burst its bounds asunder. Within three hundred years, it had conquered the then known civilized world and even the Roman emperor, Constantine, on his death bed.

This was no small achievement. Still, the men of the church had to contend for its growth and existence, and they had to do it against the best thought of their day. They had to develop and justify their doctrines before the world at the bar of spirit, truth, and reason—and they succeeded. Our faith is still able to contend with the best thought of our day, and it can do so quite well. Let us look at our basic presuppositions.

## Our Basic Beliefs: Our Presuppositions

### God as Self-contained and Sovereign

We maintain that God is self-contained and sovereign and that he only is sovereign in creation. We believe him to be the ultimate creator of both the universe and man. We hold that all creation is subject to him and that it is dependent upon his providence for its continued existence. We hold that from the beginning, God created with intelligent purpose and design. We attribute ultimate power and energy only to God.

## As God is Sovereign in Creation, He Is Sovereign in Knowledge and Revelation

All creation is the subject of knowledge, and since God is sovereign in creation, he is also sovereign in knowledge. This applies both to the physical world as well as to spiritual realities. Since only God can reveal God and his spiritual provisions for man, God is also sovereign in revelation—in the revelation, communication, and interpretation of spiritual truths.

## The Reality of God's Eternal Counsel

We believe in God's eternal counsel. God's eternal counsel is that which alone gives definitive meaning and expression to the whole of reality. We further believe that his counsel is solely legislative for reality—for what can be possible. We are well aware that this concept has been called determinism by the very dogmatic. However, determinism simply means intelligent purpose and design. Concerning creation of the universe and all that it contains, we mean that God created with intelligent purpose and design from the very beginning.

## Complete and Exhaustive Knowledge with God

Since it is conceived that God is the sole creator and that his eternal counsel gives definitive meaning and expression to the whole of reality, then there is complete and exhaustive knowledge with God. How does this affect man's unity and coherence? We are created in God's image, a part of his creation. We are related to God and to the objects of creation—by creation. Therefore, we have unity and coherence in our knowledge—because all is related to God's eternal counsel.

## Our Knowledge Is Partial

As finite creatures, our knowledge could only be partial. But although our knowledge is partial, it is nonetheless true. It is precisely because we are aware that our knowledge is partial that we seek to understand more about our subject in every matter that we undertake to deal with. Our study is always an endeavor to learn more and more about the objects of knowledge. And when we think and reason, we do so against the background of the intelligent purpose and design of God: against the unity and coherence of God's eternal counsel.

# The Acquisition of Knowledge

## Because All Is Creation, Both the Subjects of Knowledge and the Objects of Knowledge are God Created Entities

The sorts of atoms that compose the nuclear furnace in the most luminous quasar far out in space also compose a part of my being. The same God who created the Heavens also created the human mind. The universe and all existent data of creation are the objects of knowledge that are accessible to the human mind. These objects of knowledge are also understandable by the human mind because both are created with intelligent purpose and design.

## Relating Knowledge

We can relate one thing to another, and we can reason about them because all is creation. And we can respond to one another for the same reason. For man was created in the image of God—in the image of God created he him; male and female created he them. The knowledge acquiring facilities are implanted within us by reason of the Creator's hand. God made us a little lower than the angels and has crowned us with the glory and honor of his

Spirit residing in us. He has given us dominion over the works of his hands and has shed abroad his love in our hearts through the Holy Spirit that was given us.

## God Is Sovereign in Revelation

While we are aware that Christianity is a supernatural religion, we must be aware that it is also a revealed religion. As God is sovereign in the realms of creation and knowledge, we maintain that God is also sovereign in the realm of revelation.

## The Supernatural

The distinguishing features of the Christian religion are also its greatest miracles. These are the incarnation of God in Jesus Christ, the resurrection of Christ, and the indwelling and outpouring of the Spirit upon the Church of Jesus Christ. These are the cardinal incidents of our faith and man's redemption, and they are all supernatural events.

## Only God Can Reveal God

The simple reasoning of our mind, and all its intellectual powers, lead us to believe that only God can reveal God. And only God can reveal his purposes of mercy for man. It is he alone who reveals his redemption for the human race and by what means he chose to effectuate that redemption. Only God can reveal his Christ, and only the grace of the Holy Spirit can cultivate the human heart and make one receptive to the word of the God and to Jesus Christ as Savior and Lord.

In this realm of revelation, God is sovereign, and the Word of the Lord alone is what gives definitive expression and meaning to the incidents involved in man's redemption. In our own personal experience, as in the personal experience of millions of others, we have learned to understand that when the Holy Spirit makes the human heart receptive to the word of the Lord and to his Christ, the mental assent will always follow.

## Man Is Finite

Because man is finite, and because his acquisition of knowledge is partial, man needs to be told about God's purpose of mercy and about the incidents God has laid out for his redemption. Man is told about that redemption in the canons of scripture and in the preaching of the Gospel.

## Revelation Is Objective

While the revelation of God in Scriptures is objective, man's reception of revelation is subjective. Whether or not man chooses to accept that revelation has nothing to do with the reality of its existence. The revelation of God in the Old and New Testaments is there as an objective reality, and all who wish to do so may pursue it. To keep our thinking clear and precise, we must maintain the objective reality of God's revelation distinct and separate from its reception by man. This in no way obscures the fact that the Holy Spirit gives us understanding of the word of God.

## All Men Are Confronted by God

Since all men are created by God, all men are confronted by their Creator. The knowledge of God is within man because it was implanted there by the Creator's hand. Men everywhere are also confronted by God in creation because there are only God-created facts. We believe most acutely that man is confronted by God as both his Creator and Redeemer. We realize that because man may be at moral enmity with God, and subsequently morally estranged from God, knowledge of God within and without him may be suppressed. St. Paul tells us that this is so. The natural man suppresses the knowledge of God in unrighteousness. And though suppressed, the knowledge of God is still there, and it is there forever. It is only the enabling power of the Holy Spirit that can break through that suppression, awaken his soul to spiritual realities, and turn his heart to the Lord Jesus.

# Modern Epistemology: The Modern Theory of Knowledge

We are interested in the following questions. How do we know? How is knowledge possible? Why are we able to reason? How do we recognize truth from falsehood? Does Christianity make life meaningful and explainable? And how can we achieve rational certitude? How can we know that the knowledge we have acquired is true? We have given our answer in the brief review of our basic presuppositions. Our epistemology—theory of knowledge— is simple and direct. We believe that the concepts of modern man, estranged from having God in his thinking, leave much to be desired. We have said that Christianity has always been able to contend with the best thought of its day. To challenge the best thought of our day, we must be aware of the principles involved in the modern theory of knowledge—postmodern epistemology.

The quest for knowledge begins where it has always begun since time immemorial. Modern man asks the same old question: "How is knowledge possible?"

Actually, modern man brings nothing new to this issue. However, we believe that Justin Martyr takes a much better approach to the search for knowledge. Justin Martyr stated the issue positively. He said that as a philosopher, "He sought for the knowledge of truth and the perception of reality." This is our approach and we distinguish it from the approach of modern man—because our reference point is God and the concept of creation.

## The Current Trend: Time Is the Ultimate Reference Point

Whether he chooses to admit it or not, the present-day man is embedded in the current trend, and though it is not always explicit in his thinking, he reasons on the premise that time is the ultimate reference point. Time and man are the first and final reference points; *this means that man is the final arbitrator of reality*—of what is and what is not possible. When this concept is in the foreground of his consciousness, he will acknowledge that he perceives time as ultimate. When he is intellectually honest with himself, he readily admits that his perspective ability is limited to time-orientated categories. This means that should he perceive any sort of god, his god would also be limited and controlled by the categories of time. In trying to be consistent with his perception, modern man refuses to acknowledge any god that exists beyond his ability to reason. He does this in the mistaken belief that this attitude gives him the attribute of being rational. What modern man believes is this: that because he is limited to that reality which he perceives, and because God is infinite or lives in infinity, man cannot reach him or know him by reason—by the human mind alone. A time centered theory of knowledge, rejects the eternal council of God and God's description of creation.

Moreover, this means, precisely, that God as conceived by historical Christianity and delineated in the Scriptures—God as a Spirit, infinite, eternal, and unchanging in his being, wisdom, power, justice, truth, and holiness—could never come within the scope of a human mind limited to time-orientated categories. This brings into focus that one's starting point also determines his methodology and his conclusion. His method and mind are controlled by time; and man determines what can or cannot be. Since we believe in the created universe and in the creation of man and that both were created by God, then time in our estimation can never be the ultimate reference point. *Time can only be a created mode of finite existence, and as such, it can never be ultimate.*

The implication of the current trend is that the God of historical Christianity could never speak to man effectively in his sovereign revelation unless God was subject to man's time-orientated categories. The only god he could possibly have would be one made in his own image. But from the beginning, Christianity has maintained that it is man who is made in the image of God. "For God created man in his own image; in the image of God created he him." Our faith rejects a god made in man's image. And we understand that since we conceive God as self-contained, he could never be subject to man's accretions. Nor could he be made after the art of man's devices.

## Existence Precedes Essence

When present-day epistemology states that existence precedes essence, the meaning is that what exists existed before any definitive description of its nature and meaning were conceived in the eternal counsel of God. This means that what exists does so independent of God and independent of Christianity's concept of creation. As we apply the simple reasoning of the human mind to these concepts, it means that what exists came into existence independent of intelligent purpose and design conceived in the mind of God.

Modern man claims that this is so because only man can determine that which is within the scope of his knowledge. For example, only man can determine the existence of any part of reality within the category of time. This is the only place that he will acknowledge the confrontation of the objects of knowledge. This meaning and presupposition stance of modern epistemology has far reaching consequences.

## The Rejection of the Eternal Counsel of God

Present-day epistemology rejects the concept of the eternal counsel of God. Later in our critical evaluation of Sartre, we will come to understand that this is true. Sartre bases his theory of knowledge on the absolute rejection of the concept that both man and reality are, or ought to be, the realization of certain concepts in the divine intelligence. This means that the objects of knowledge are not related to a comprehensive system of thought.

## Independent Entities

So stated, facts and all objects of creation are only independent entities. They are without any definitive expression and meaning that the God of historical Christianity might give them.

## No Coherence

Being unrelated to a comprehensive system of knowledge, these separate entities would lack true coherence. Coherence then would appear to be no more than one's personal preference, taste, or convenience. What present-day thought has done is this: it has set itself in direct opposition to God and creation as conceived by historical Christianity. Most lack the intellectual honesty to admit this, but not Sartre. He immediately sees the point and readily admits it. This will be further illustrated later on. Although being an atheist and absolutely wrong, Sartre has intellectual honesty and courage.

## The Law of Contradiction

Since he has rejected the eternal counsel of God as being determinative of the whole of reality, how does present-day man order the objects of knowledge? Modern thought does so by the law of contradiction. In logic, this means that one proposition is so related to the second that it is impossible for both to be true or both to be false. For example, since man is a finite, limited being, he can never know about God, who is infinite and transcends creation. Man cannot know about God because man is limited to the temporal phenomena.

The point is that modern man attempts to control the objects of knowledge—what may or may not be possible and whether the God of Christianity exists—by limiting his reach to all that is temporal. He uses law of contradiction to order his world of knowledge. Any God he would admit would have to be penetrated in his essential nature by the finite mind of man. From the

Christian point of view, this could never happen, since the ways of God are past finding out and beyond our limited understanding.

## All Is Possible

Since the eternal counsel of God is rejected, not only as giving definitive expression and meaning to all of reality but also to the possibility of its existence, then anything is possible. This is the hallmark of modern epistemology, of Sartre's philosophy, and of the concept called chaos. Having rejected the eternal counsel of God as the originator of all that is possible, then pure possibility means pure chance.

This gives modern epistemology a "chance universe." However, a contradiction in a chance universe is a contradiction in terms. None of this is really new. It has just been ignored. The implication is this and was so stated in the scriptures long ago; if the eternal counsel of God and the divine intelligence is rejected as determining all of reality, then all is not only possible, but "Each will do that which he deems to be right in his own eyes." And where have we heard this before? The simple fact remains that the mind of man is incapable of being legislative for reality—of determining what may or may not be.

## The Principle of Interpretation

Modern thought insists that the principle of interpretation and the facts of reality are related to each other. Specifically, for modern thought, that principle is man and his finite limitations. We are aware that one's principle of interpretation, his method, and his conclusion all stand or fall together. And we agree, for this is true.

## Beginning with Man

Modern thought begins with man as limited to time-orientated categories. He will accept nothing beyond his ability to perceive physically. Hence, his method and his conclusion must also end with him here—in time.

## Beginning With God as Creator

Historical Christianity begins with the concept of God as Creator, that he created all with intelligent purpose and design from the beginning, and that he did so according to his will and eternal counsel. We maintain the distinction between the creature, man, and God as Creator. We hold that our knowledge about man's redemption comes by way of revelation because God is a God who reveals his purpose of mercy for the human race. And finally, we maintain that God's revelation is sovereign.

## Reality as a Process of Flux

Since modern thought concludes that all becomes possible, then reality becomes nothing more than a process. Man is a part of this process, and so is any god that he will admit. His god becomes limited—finite and subject to time and the law of contradiction.

His god, of course, is made in his own image. This thing called "Process Theology" is a product, allegedly profound, of modern thought. What should be pointed out is that it is divorced in presuppositional standing and meaning, and in its terms, from historical Christianity.

## Difference in Conceptions

Having rejected the eternal counsel of God and his sovereignty in creation, God is also rejected as sovereign in revelation. This means that God's description in his revelation as to the incidents and events germane to man's redemption—and restoration to fellowship with God—is also rejected. Therefore, Christianity and modern thought will have different conceptions about God, about Christ, and about the Holy Spirit. They ascribe different meanings and implications to the Atonement of Jesus Christ and to his cross; and they will also differ in the essential meaning of redemption. So we ought not to be surprised when this, in fact, does occur.

## Only Two Alternatives

From all that has proceeded, we can see that only two alternatives are really possible. When all the philosophers have expounded their theories, when all the books have been written, and when every voice is silent, there are still only two alternatives. Either a process of undetermined flux is the ground for all that is possible, or it is God the Creator of Heaven and earth who is the ground for all that is possible in this universe. We believe it is better to do our reasoning based on the province of God on his eternal counsel with intelligent purpose and design than on a concept of pure possibility and a chance universe. This is the one true God, and his revelation gives meaning to life and to life's ultimate destiny. This alone makes human reasoning and understanding possible.

## Our God Is Active

Neither God nor his creation nor his revelation has ever been conceived as static by the thinking men of the church. Creation is ever unfolding and expanding. God's is a living, active, and operative presence through the entire universe. We maintain that the universe and men are both dependent for their existence on the grace and providence of God. Moreover, revelation has always been considered as developing in an historical process. We find it is so from Genesis to the Revelation of St. John. Let us look at Sartre.

# Sartre and Existentialism

In our evaluation of modern thought, we have remained critical rather than dogmatic, since we believe that this is only fair. After all, no seeker after truth should fear the primacy of the intellect. We will not deal with Christian Existentialism, for this is only a mixture of concepts and of basic presuppositions. None of the Existentialists actually state the doctrine in its pure form as simply as does Sartre. And we will deal with him lightly. Sartre is bold. He makes no pretense of being a Christian or even of believing in God. He tells us that he is sorry that there is no God. He states quite frankly that he is an antitheist. He even labors a bit to explain his philosophy.

Existentialism, Sartre informs us, is a doctrine that makes human life possible. But human life was not only possible; it was an existent reality hundreds of years before Sartre was born. Now, it is possible that Sartre may have implied that his doctrine may make life meaningful or explainable, but than he would have to tell us how we can know this. Why are we able to reason? How do we know the truth from the falsehood? And he would have to tell us how we can achieve rational certitude? This, however, he is unable to do.

Sartre informs us that Existentialism makes human life possible because his doctrine presents a possibility of choice. The following are his basic concepts:

(1) Existence precedes essence.

(2) Subjectivity must be our starting point.

(3) Sartre proposes the absolute rejection that both man and reality are the realization of certain concepts in the divine intelligence.

(4) God does not exist; therefore, everything is possible.

This ought not to strike us as strange. There have always been men who seek God, who wish to know and understand him, if only in part. And there have always been those men, who, for whatever reason, seek to be free of any concept of God or to have such a concept influence their thinking.

## The Theology of Grace

According to Sartre's philosophy, if existence precedes essence, if reality preceded any concept of what it should be and why it was brought into being, then there is no need to explain it by way of a fixed or given nature conceived in the mind of God. This would mean that there is no such thing as creation by a Creator with intelligent purpose and design. Because he has pre-supposed this concept—that existence precedes essence—man and the universe are not perceived as intelligent creations by God, nor are their nature and course determined by God. Hence, man is now declared to be free.

Man, asserts Sartre, is freedom personified. He tells us that man exists, first of all, and that man exists without any definitive characterization. Only afterward is it that man defines himself regardless of what the sovereign God of the universe may have said about man and his nature in his revelation. There is no God, as held by historical Christianity, who conceived man and created him. Man, as the subject of knowledge, must be aware of himself and take full responsibility for the current course of his existence. We certainly agree with this last thought for our Christian literature since its inception holds man responsible.

Sartre insists that man must choose what he will make of himself, but it is impossible for man to transcend human subjectivity. He affirms, "We make our own man and we create our own image." St. Paul wrote that for the natural man at moral enmity with God; this is all too true. When man makes a choice, Sartre instructs us, he has affirmed the value of what he has chosen. But making an evaluation of a certain thing or of a certain action involves a thought process. Some thoughts must fly before such a choice is made. But what does Sartre say?

As to values, we must trust our instincts. We have certain feelings, and the feeling is realized by performing the act. Instinct, then, not intellectual activity or the simple reasoning of the human mind, is determinative as to judgments or value.

Feeling, for Sartre, then, is the final motive power; but this would make the basis of all human action and choices irrational. These feelings are realized as man struggles to conceive his own image; and thus, man is nothing more than his own plan.

We do not imply that Sartre is the deepest or most profound thinker in this school of thought, but only that his expression is typical of what has developed out of modern thought. He is clear and direct and makes an effort to have himself understood. We are not going to go into the details of his philosophy. We simply wish to indicate the distinction between the acme of the modern thought process and the Christian faith. Sartre denies creation and the existence of God. The denial of creation according to the eternal counsel of God means that there is no intelligent purpose and design as to the creation of the universe or the creation of man. In epistemology, this means no intelligent purpose as to the objects and subjects of knowledge. Since Sartre postulated that God does not exist:

(1) All things are possible.

(2) Man is now free and free to choose.

(3) Sartre rates the value of man's choice according to the intensity of the feeling given expression in the act'

(4) And, finally, subjectivity controls.

We do not believe that one can build a Christian philosophy or theology on the concept of individuals who have consciously renounced all belief in God, especially who have renounced belief in a personal God. Nor will we surrender the simple reasonableness of the human mind to the pure subjectivity of Existentialism, to the impulse of feeling, and to the concept of mere possibility. We stand firm in our belief that as our Creator and Redeemer,

God is sovereign in the realm of being, sovereign in the realm of knowledge, and sovereign in the realm of revelation.

We hold to our belief that both man and the universe have come into their existence and definitive meaning by reason of the eternal counsel of God. We maintain that the course and conduct of the universe are dependent upon the grace and providence of God. We hold that as long as man remains at enmity with God because of moral estrangement, he is in need of redemption and restoration to spiritual fellowship with God.

We hold that this redemption must be of God, and that it is according to his grace. The nature of this redemption is revealed in our Christian literature and in the doctrinal teachings of our faith. We further believe that the ultimate nature of this redemption was revealed in Jesus Christ our Lord. In systematic theology, we endeavor to lay out the concepts of God's redemption in an orderly manner, that is to say, in an abbreviated system of though called the theological encyclopedia. The theological encyclopedia is laid out in several main divisions. These divisions are described below.

## The Theological Encyclopedia

### Hamartology: The Doctrine of Sin

This division deals with the origin of sin and its invasion of man. We will discuss its nature and effect on the mind and soul of man. We point to the moral estrangement and enmity with God caused by sin's effect on the soul.

### Satan: The Doctrine of Evil

We will deal with the origin of Satan and evil, his entry into the world, and his opposition to God's purpose, to the church, and to the believer. We will discuss his nature and acts; we will bring out his use of lies, murder, and deception. Satan is still a creature and he will be judged as such.

## Soteriology: The Doctrine of Salvation

Salvation is seen as a manifestation of the grace of God, and, essentially, it is a process of redemption and restoration. We will discuss the Proto-Evangel: the promise of hope and redemption given to Eve. This is also known as the Mother Promise. We will discuss the promise of the indwelling and outpouring of the Holy Spirit. We tell about the promise of a Redeemer, which was fulfilled in Christ.

## Christology: The Doctrine of Christ

We view Christ as the eternally existing Son of God. We conceive of Christ as God and man in one person—the Incarnation Christ's humiliation, the temptation, the transfiguration, and the atonement of Jesus Christ. We will discuss his crucifixion, his resurrection, and his ascension. We will discuss his exaltation and headship of the Church, which bears his name. And finally, we will discuss his second advent.

## Pneumatology: The Doctrine of the Holy Spirit

We will discuss the nature of the Holy Spirit. We will discuss his proceeding from the Father and the Son, his function and purpose, his indwelling presence in the believer, and the outpouring of the Holy Spirit upon the Church of Jesus Christ. We will discuss the Spirit's presence and effect upon the church and upon the individual believer.

## Ecclesiology: The Doctrine of the Church

The church is conceived as a body in fellowship with Christ in Spirit and with each other. Christ is present as her head and as central in worship. We will discuss the purpose of the church and its objective and the promise given to the church by Christ of his presence and power. We will discuss the sacraments and the eternal testimony of the church.

## Eschatology: The Doctrine of the Last Things

This division involves the resurrection of the body, immortality, the second advent of our Lord, the final judgment, and the new Heaven and new Earth.

In the theological thought process and in the development of the encyclopedia, we shall endeavor not to get immersed in too much detail. We shall strive to present a living, doctrinal development. We acknowledge that all the variations and some details may not even be touched. We are working for a general conceptual presentation and a basic framework for reference to major theological doctrines.

We acknowledge that many individuals are inclined to ask, "Why Systematic Theology? Why not just preach Christ? Why not simply preach the Gospel message?" The truth of the matter is that every time one explains an act or function of our Lord in his life and mission, he is speaking in the field of theology. Every time a minister makes a spiritual application of the word of the Lord to the heart and soul of the believer, he is making a spiritual application from a theological premise. On every occasion that Holy Communion is celebrated or the sacrament of baptism is administered and the celebrant or recipient is told the meaning of the act, the information discussed is theological. This is true whether the individual is a minister of the Assemblies of God or an Episcopalian priest. In a membership or communicant class, the entire encyclopedia is generally touched upon, however lightly. This occurs even though the teacher is intellectually unaware that he is giving instruction in theology.

God, having given us minds and having touched our hearts with his grace, causes us to reflect on the great teachings of the church. We systematize these thoughts because we are reasonable men and because reason and order are applied to all the activities of our daily life and in all fields of study. We endeavor to make our views in this field unified and consistent. We also attempt to remove uncertainty, for who can possibly see any merit in being uncertain about everything essential to the great doctrines of the church? The time has long since passed for pious agnosticism. And in this age of doctrinal aversion, we can keep our faith vital, energetic, and strong by bringing to light once again her living and articulate doctrines. Thus, we are in a position where we are adequately stating our faith, and we are also in a position to challenge consistently and intellectually the best thought of our day.

# Christian Hamartology: The Doctrine of Sin

## The Chief Good: With All Thy Heart

> Moses has summoned all Israel and said to them: Hear, O Israel, the statutes and ordinances which I speak in your hearing this day, and you shall learn them and be careful to do them. The Lord our God made a covenant with us in Eden and in Horeb…with all of us here alive this day. The Lord spoke with you face to face at the mountain, out of the midst of the fire, while I stood between the Lord and you at that time, to declare unto you the word of the Lord; for you were afraid because of the fire, and did not go up into the mountain.
>
> Deuteronomy 5:1-5 (RSV)

> Here, therefore, O Israel…that it may go well with you, and that you may multiply greatly, as the Lord, the God of our fathers has promised you: a land flowing with milk and honey… The Lord our God is one Lord; and you shall love the Lord your God with all your heart, and with all your soul, and with all your mind.
>
> Deuteronomy 6:3 (RSV)

Of all the things that invigorate the soul and mind, there is none greater than the love of God. This is the chief good of all. We do this that it may go well with us, and that we may find fulfillment and happiness in life. Happiness means good fortune, pleasure, joy, and contentment.

Though we seek to understand God's dealings with us through our minds, the matter of our faith in God is a matter of the heart. Following after God expresses the desire of happiness. We follow after God by loving him. We come near to him in the immaterial aspect of our communion. In following after him and in loving him, the Holy Spirit quickens our hearts, souls, and minds. We cannot help to follow after God if we love him and seek to serve him.

Still, to follow after him and to worship him, we must see a vision of him. We see him not really with our eyes but with the mind. We sense him in our soul, and we feel him in our heart. Loving him with all our hearts means that we love God without any reservations. It means that we place no other gods before him. Loving with the heart implies that we desire him only as our God. The main complaint voiced through the narratives of the prophets was, "You praise me with your mouths…but your heart is far from me."

It was not the sacrifice of rams but of a broken and contrite heart that was acceptable to God. The prayers in the Psalms express the thought, "Create in me a clean heart and renew a right spirit within me." We believe in God, we place our faith in him, and we behold him in spirit and in truth. We learn to move at the impulse of his love. God desires the affection of our whole heart.

## With All Thy Soul

"With all thy heart" was not enough. Moses added, "And with all thy soul." The soul is the essence of our being—that part of us that is immortal. When God breathed into man's nostrils the breath of life and man became a living soul, the soul was clothed with immortality. It is the soul that gives life to our bodies, and when awakened toward God, spiritual life ensues. The soul is the residence of God's grace wherein resides the Spirit of our Lord Jesus Christ. Our soul is the harbor of our spiritual life and of the love of God that was shed abroad in our hearts through the Holy Spirit that was given to us.

Volition ensues from the soul, and the spiritual quality of our soul determines our behavior. Most acutely, the spiritual sensitivity of the soul determines our responsiveness. Thus, it is that loving God with all our souls implies that the very seat of our being will be wholly motivated toward God and that we respond to his love and grace. It involves the surrender of our wills to the leading of his Spirit and to his love and care with absolute trust. Is it not true that man is conformed to that which he loves?

The apostle Paul encouraged us in the cultivation of God's love when he wrote in his letter to the Romans that "all things work together for good to them that love God; to them that are called according to his purpose" (Romans 8:28). By expressing the enduring worth of the love of God extended to us in Christ Jesus, St. Paul asked, "What then shall separate us from the love of Christ? Shall tribulation, or distress, or persecution, or nakedness, or peril or sword?" No, they cannot separate us from the love of God. By his grace and faithfulness in all things, we are more than conquerors through Jesus Christ who loved us. As the Holy Spirit cultivates our response, we shall learn to love God with the essence of our being—with all our soul.

# With All Thy Mind

"With all thy heart," Moses instructed the people; and knowing that this was not enough, he added, "And with all thy soul." But God wanted the whole person, so Moses included, "And with all thy mind." The mind does our thinking for us. It can turn our thoughts to God and to spiritual realities. The mind and the intellect give assent to the intent of the heart, and to the feelings of the soul. But there is more than this.

The mind forms the words of our confession and reasons that it is good to so love the Lord our God. In saying that we are not to love the world more than God, we mean that the mind is not to depart from God in affection. We are not to depart from the love of God as our chief affection. Although the mind may wander, through the necessity of being busy with other things, it will return to God. It will return because the pull of the heart strings is there. It is from our souls and the seat of our emotions that the cry for the living God ensues. They call the mind away from the noise of the world, and we return to the thoughts of God and worship.

As our love of God grows, the mind tends to become like God in affection (at least in part and in a created mode). With the spiritual attraction of the soul and God's love tending the emotions, the mind surrenders to God for enlightenment. In so doing, it will go well with us in the land of the living, and in so loving him, all things will issue to our good. Our chief good is in loving God with heart and soul and mind.

St. John wrote, "We love him because he first loved us." St. Paul wrote of God's kindness and grace.

> The kindness of God, and his love have appeared toward us in Christ Jesus…According to his mercy he saved us: through the cleansing of regeneration, by the renewing of the Holy Spirit which he poured upon us richly through Jesus Christ our Savior; and being justified by his grace, we have been made heirs to the hope of eternal life.
>
> Titus 3:4-8

Hence, we learn to love God because he first loved us. He loved us according to his mercy and grace. And in love he saved us through the cleansing grace of regeneration as his kindness appeared, renewing our souls with the Holy Spirit, which was given us richly in Christ Jesus our Lord. With heart, soul, and mind, we acknowledge that his grace has justified us and made us heirs to the hope of eternal life. He is our hope, our glory, and our good.

And yet one more grace we would ask of our heavenly Father. In the words of St. Augustine, our petition is, "That thou may give what thou commandest." This is our plea, that the Lord God be pleased to give us that grace by which we may be enabled to love God with all our hearts and with all our souls and with all our minds. In this manner, we were meant to have communion and fellowship with the Lord God and to worship him only as our God and Creator.

## Sin

While that is how it was meant to be, it is not the true picture of man's spiritual life. We sense a moral estrangement from the Father of our spirits. Most men are at enmity with God, and some of us have missed the mark of our high calling in the grace of our Lord Jesus Christ. Sin, *hamartano*, means I have missed the mark. It simply means to commit an offense or a fault of any kind. It means to break spiritual law and to remain separated and estranged from God. If we linger in this condition long enough, it results in the spiritual death of the soul. This occurs because of the noetic—cumulative effect—of sin and estrangement from God.

Both the soul and mind are affected by the noetic and cumulative effect of sin and estrangement from God. By noetic, we mean that it has an adverse bearing on all our faculties and especially on our intellectual activity. As this relates to God and knowledge of spiritual things, it dims perception and distorts understanding and reasoning. The longer man remains morally estranged from God, the farther he moves from God until spiritual death ensues. Then man may become more like an animal than like the bearer of the image of God.

We hear as an echo from Old Testament times, "The soul that sinneth, it shall die." The soul is that part in us that is regarded as immortal, and which is the spiritual entity of our nature. The soul also has influence on the functions of thinking and willing, and hence, the spiritual condition of the soul is determinative of our behavior. The soul is adversely affected by sin. The sense of God within and without us becomes suppressed. We seek even to avoid the concept of God, and all that such a concept rationally and logically implies. Behavior is determined by how real and close the concept of God is to us by what we conceive his nature to be and by our relationship with him.

## Savior and Salvation

How then shall he who has been created in the image of God be rescued and delivered from spiritual death into which sin has brought him? We give only a brief answer here, but we will go into more depth under the division of soteriology, the doctrine of salvation. To save means to rescue or to preserve from harm, to make and keep safe, and to preserve for future use. To save also means to deliver a person, a soul, from sin and punishment and to redeem him from spiritual death.

We have a Savior. We call him Christ Jesus, the Son of God. If we are to trust Christ our Lord, and if we are to have our faith rest in him, we must have some relationship with him. There must be a need and a relationship. We must come to the Lord personally, and come to him for the need of our soul, that entity of spiritual life within us.

Christ, the Son of God, can exercise the power to redeem our souls from the consequences of moral fault. He can deliver us from spiritual death, awaken the soul toward God, and restore us to fellowship with himself and the Father. We call this salvation. It means to rescue from spiritual death and to restore the now awakened soul to spiritual realities through the Atonement of Jesus Christ. These simple words (sin, salvation, and Savior) ought not to frighten anyone. We can understand them quite readily. And they come to us with love, grace, and glory. They come with spiritual healing, and they come with hope and expectation.

It is well known to those versed in this area that the Law, the "Old Schoolmaster" with its many ancient ritualistic requirements, made men despair because of their faults, failures, and sins. And who among us, we ask, is without some sin, some fault, or some past failure? Even now, we must admit that we have not loved the Lord our God with all our hearts and with all our souls and with all our minds. And we confess that we have not loved our neighbors as ourselves. We have left undone those things that we ought to have done, and in those things that we have done we cannot always say that the love of our Savior has been our primary motive.

Yet all true work of grace must spring from the heart and from the soul of the person. While the soul is immortal, it is also our spiritual heart. It is from the heart and soul that the will and motive must ensue toward God. The soul has a deep and constant spiritual need that must be met. If we acknowledge that our faith is one of spirit and truth, then our souls and hearts have a spiritual need that must be met. It is our souls that most stand in need of the redemption that Christ our Lord brings.

It is the soul that cries out for the living God—the Father of our spirits. At times, the cry emerges from a misty perplexity through a fog that tends to obscure the vision. And before the vision clears, the soul must be redeemed from the fault of moral estrangement from God. The soul must also be redeemed from spiritual death. It must be redeemed from the failure to seek after God with a pure heart. Hence, the soul and mind must be redeemed from the moral obscurity that seeks to make its own way in the world without faith in God. Our souls and hearts have the need of being redeemed from their way of wondering where they can be lost in the babble of many voices and where they can only die a slow and lingering spiritual death. Truly has the prophet spoken, "The soul that sinneth, it shall die."

Moreover, the soul has need of faith for a spiritual awakening. Our faith is immersed from beginning to end in spiritual realities. In its need for spiritual manna, the soul cries out to the heart and mind; it expresses the need to commune with the Father. In the need of our soul for a Redeemer, for our Savior-God, it is the consciousness that we have not loved God with all our hearts, with all our souls, and with all our minds. This need also brings to light that we have not loved our neighbors as ourselves and that we have left undone those things that we ought to have done. There is the awareness that we have sinned.

We have discussed the soul, redemption, and Redeemer. We have acknowledged that our soul is the first part of us that must be redeemed, reclaimed, restored to spiritual life, and renewed in the image of him who created us. It must be awakened to the love of God, which is in Christ Jesus our Lord. Christ our Redeemer redeems from the consequences of sin, and he restores us to spiritual fellowship with him and God the Father. "In Christ Jesus, the grace of God that bringeth salvation hath appeared to all men" (Titus 2:11).

We call our Redeemer Jesus Christ, the Son of God and Savior. In his office as a priest, he comes to us with love and absolution and with reception into his Kingdom. His Holy Spirit in our hearts awakens our soul to his glory and grace. What more can we say but, "Come then, Almighty, to deliver"? Deliver our hearts, souls, and minds, from all that is estranged from thee. In the multitude of thy mercy, let us all, even now, thy grace receive; and thou, "Soul of my soul, I shall see thee again." (Robert Browning).

# Satan: The Doctrine of Evil

What is evil? Is it real, and does it exist? Yes, it is real. It exists throughout the entire world and throughout the human race. Evil is anything that is morally bad or wrong. It is anything that is wicked and depraved. It is also that which causes pain or trouble, which is harmful and injurious. All this and more is evil. Satan, throughout the history of the church, has been considered the greatest enemy of man and goodness. Scripture identifies the devil as Lucifer, the son of the morning, and the chief of the fallen angels. He was cast out of Heaven by the archangel Michael at the direction of God. He is identified as the head of all that is evil, morally bad, wicked, and depraved.

## The Origin of Satan and Evil

Lucifer, the son of the morning, was once an archangel with glory, position, and power. He had angels who served under him and did his bidding. He had more honor than most of the hosts of Heaven. He should have been content and filled with satisfaction at serving God in that exalted position. But he became vain in his imagination, and his foolish heart became darkened. He became envious of the divinity of God. He became futile in his thinking. He rejected the glory of the immortal God for the greed and lust of his own being. In the progression of his futile thinking, he would, in a very short time, refuse to worship and serve his God and Creator, for he had already refused to do so in his heart. Not content with his own personal high estate, he sought to become supreme even over the Almighty, even over God, his Creator. In the vain imagination of his thoughts, he would ascend beyond the Heavens and ascend to the highest crown of glory and be as God.

We trace the process of Satan's fall through St. Paul's concept of man's fallen condition. We do so because as the originator of evil, Satan, works his evil in man—in opposition to God and goodness. We trace evil to its origin.

Satan had exchanged the truth of God for a lie; he no longer saw fit to acknowledge the Almighty as his God. And God gave him up to a base mind. Lucifer was given up for rebellion and opposition to God, who had given him everything. Satan would, in time, be filled with all manner of wickedness, evil, covetousness, and malice. He would be full of envy, murder, strife, deceit, and malignity. He would become a hater of God—insolent and boastful. He would become an inventor of evil—heartless and ruthless. He would become a corrupter of man, and the corrupt creature was hurled out of Heaven.

## His Entry into the World

Satan became the Prince and Power of the Air. He is that spirit that now works in the children of disobedience—those who refuse to have God in their thinking and do evil. He became the usurper and prince of this world. When the sons of God (those who looked to God as their heavenly Father) came to present themselves before God, Satan also came among them. Lucifer's coming among them was for only one purpose—to accuse, to deceive, to delude, and if possible, to destroy man's religious affinity toward God. He had come from going to and fro on the earth and from walking up and down upon it.

In the form of a Serpent, he moved up and down in the Garden of Eden on that fatal day so long ago. He would oppose God's hope for man, for none should obtain the glory that the son of the morning had lost. Satan would cast doubt, suspicion, and division between God and man. Satan looked closely at man. Created in the image of God was he? Made a little lower than the angels? Crowned with glory and honor? What a frail thing this living soul was. Walking and talking with his Maker? Let's check him out—such, we imagine, were Satan's thoughts.

## The Theology of Grace

Scripture informs us that the serpent was more subtle than any other wild creature that the Lord God had made. Then, and even now, he would lure man to any other path as long as it was away from God. Lucifer always begins by indirection and subtlety. Satan's rebellion and opposition to God in Heaven had come down to earth. It is now manifested in opposition to the Kingdom and in opposition to God's redemption for mankind. Lucifer still goes about like a roaring lion, seeking whom he may destroy or devour. As to Christian men and women, Satan's sole aim is destruction—to deceive by whatever means he can employ. All his devices are foul. We note the dialogue in the garden, its subtlety, doubt, and deception. The serpent said to the woman, "Did God say this? Really? Did God say that?" He cast doubt, causing the woman to waver and become uncertain.

Satan cast doubt about God's purpose and motives. "For God doth know that... you will be as gods" (Genesis 3:5). He planted the seed of doubt about the consequences of her actions. "You shall not surely die" (Genesis 3:4). He used deception. "You shall be as gods." Satan beguiled man that he should not obey the word of God and deceived him into disobedience. Man had paradise before him should he obey. But being influenced by Satan, man chose to disobey God. And through the first Adam, sin and its noetic effect came upon the human race. There occurred moral estrangement from God, and man everywhere would be at enmity with God.

The soul that sinned would die a slow, lingering, spiritual death. The spiritual heart of man would die out. And the image of God in man, created with such high expectations, would be suppressed.

Satan, the devil, the evil one, is the personification of all that is ugly and distorted, of all the harm and evil in the world. He seeks to dominate man through his malevolent influence and spirit. Satan's endeavor is to suppress caution and prudence in man's acts. He strives to bring out the uncultivated, unredeemed nature, in man and to identify it with himself. There is nothing of good in Satan's influence. He brings nothing of redeeming value. He seeks to bring out only hatred, suspicion, lies, injury, and uncontrolled revenge in men and women. He does it quite simply by anything that will suppress the image of God in us, by anything that will weaken our spiritual vitality, and by anything that will cause the spiritual life of our souls to die out. He acts to make man in his own image. Satan seeks to make man vain in his imagination, darkening his foolish heart. He does this in order that man may reject the glory of the immortal God for the greed and lust of his own being. Lucifer desires that mankind be given over to a reprobate mind.

Always, like in the Garden of Eden, man must choose. He acts in free agency. He has the intellectual capacity to think, reason, and to evaluate. And he is responsible for all his voluntary acts. He must choose between the voice of God and the vague subtleties and false promises of the devil. Satan always comes this way. "Do as I say. Follow me, and you will become like unto the gods." He never mentions that it will lead to spiritual death and to moral estrangement from God. He never tells us that it will place us at enmity with the Father of our spirits. It was so in the Garden of Eden, in the day of our Lord, and it is so now.

In himself, man is really no match for the devil and his legions of demons. He needs the strength of one who has broken the power of Lucifer. Man needs the Holy Spirit to keep him spiritually strong. He must rely on his Redeemer, Jesus Christ. We in ourselves are frail human beings.

## Evil and the Dividing Force of Faith

An incident manifesting the divine force of faith is found in the Gospel of Mark.

In the days of our Lord, we are given the story of a father who was in a desperate situation. He was distressed because his child was gravely ill. Scripture attributes the child's illness to demonic influence. The father pleaded with Jesus to have mercy on him. Jesus responded and said, "If you can believe, all things are possible to him that believes" (Mark 9:23). The father cried out, "I believe: help my unbelief" (Mark 9:24).

It is a marvelous thing that faith in Christ can bring a response to common human needs. We believe this because God is still active in the world, and our Lord Christ Jesus is still in the midst of it. Faith is a divine force, and it is a power for good. There is no real barrier that can possibly stand against the energy of Christ's Spirit. It is not so much our human weakness that prevents our Lord's grace working in us but our doubt about his ability. The father in the New Testament story acknowledged his desperate situation together with his weak and imperfect faith. Then he cast his faith upon the Lord Jesus without reservation. And Jesus cast out the evil spirit and healed the child.

## The Narrative Situation

The child had a dumb, unclean spirit, causing him to fall down, foam at the mouth, grind his teeth, and become rigid. The disciples were unable to cast it out. And Jesus alleged they could not do so because of unbelief. When the dark spirit saw Jesus, he caused the child to convulse. Jesus rebuked the unclean spirit, and after crying out and convulsing the child, it came out. Scripture states that Jesus healed the child by exercising his power and authority over the demon. The demon could not stand in our Lord's presence.

In this working out of the divine power, the narrative brings us face to face with unclean and evil spirits that recognized Jesus and yielded to his command. Evil spirits and demons must yield to the divine force of faith. Demonic control and possession is a strong bondage. In this instance, we have a direct confrontation with evil. We must deal with the narrative because it implies the existence of Satan and his legions of demons. We can do one of two things. We can disbelieve the narrative or we can believe it. What is revealed here comes within God's counsel for man's redemption. There is both instruction and warning in it. Along with the historical teaching of the church, along with the church fathers and reformers, we choose to believe the narrative. We take our Lord at his word.

The Lord Jesus stood and opposed evil in this world. He knew that we are continually exposed to illusions mingled with reality. He knew that in this world we are exposed to distorted perspectives, to twisted and hidden motives, and to uncertain hopes. Concerning the evil in the world and against which the kingdom of God must contend, St. Paul wrote, "For we are not contending against flesh and blood, but against the principalities, against the powers, against the world rulers of this present darkness, against the spiritual hosts of wickedness in the heavenly places" (Ephesians 6:12, RSV).

We are confronted with the biblical concept of Satan, the devil, and the personification of all evil. We are confronted with God's revelation of this concept and with Christ's concept of the Devil. And we are given a picture of our Lord's fight against demonic and evil spirits. We only wish to point out that intellectual contempt and disdain of these incidents narrated in scripture implies contempt and disdain for the teachings of the church and for the teachings of Christ. This is not a medieval concept. It goes back to creation, when Lucifer and all his supporting evil angels were hurled out of Heaven because of rebellion and opposition to God.

How do these forces of darkness oppose the kingdom of God and its growth? They do so with anything that will diminish the value, power, and redemptive significance of the church's great beliefs. The powers of darkness, the devil, and all his evil spirits will do anything at all to make the individual lose his hope and all the high expectations of his belief in Christ. Every encounter with evil seeks to dim our aspirations, weaken our faith, and dash our hopes to the ground. They seek to suppress the reality of the image of God in us.

## The Divine Force of Faith

In the temptation of Christ, Satan failed in his purpose to defeat and destroy Christ. This leopard does not change his spots. His purpose is to deceive and to destroy every child of God. There is only one thing that Satan cannot stand against. That is the divine force of our faith in Christ Jesus. We attribute ultimate power only to God and to our Lord Jesus Christ. Satan is but a fallen creature, and so are the fallen demons. They cannot stand against the outpouring of our Lord's Spirit and power. True, our faith may be weak. It may be imperfect, and at times it may be only a faint glimmer. But if we call on the Lord, he will come to be our helper. He will come with all his grace, love, and redemptive power. He can still set the prisoner free. And he can still cause hope to spring eternal in the human heart.

## Satan's Power Is Temporal and Can Be Broken

Lucifer, the fallen son of the morning, has become the Prince and Power of the Air—the prince of this world. That is part of the problem. He is a fallen prince. Although he may act as if he has all the power, and though he may promise to give all the kingdoms of the world, he is unable to do so. He is not the ultimate reality. Satan acts as if the world is his because he goes to and fro upon it. But the perception of truth and reality is far otherwise. The truth is that Lucifer is nothing but a trespasser. He is in adverse possession and claiming title. His influence, while it is deceptive and destructive, is finite and temporary. His power, as he discovered in his confrontation with the archangel Michael, is limited. He must yield and obey the command of Christ and be submissive to his will.

Finally, Satan's power can be broken. He may seek to suppress the image of God in us and cause death to overwhelm as many as he can, but the battle does not end there. Lucifer is also called the tempter, and when Jesus comes, the tempter's power is broken, and bondage to his influence is broken asunder. Our Redeemer's Spirit can pierce this thin veil of woe and strike at the heart. His grace can quicken man's soul and restore the image.

Christ's is the ultimate creative power in the universe. With a simple prayer to him, the commitment of a life to him as Lord and Savior and the pangs of hell are shattered. The divine force of faith in Christ Jesus will give each child of God supremacy over Lucifer. We ought to remember that he is but an unrepentant, self-deceived, fallen creature. And Lucifer shall be judged as such. He will suffer the consequences of his rebellion, opposition, and disobedience to God. God has made our Lord Jesus to be the judge of both the quick and the dead. God has committed the final judgment to him. And then who shall stand when he appears?

# SOTERIOLOGY: THE DOCTRINE OF SALVATION

None of us really questions that we have missed the mark of our high calling in the grace of our Lord Jesus Christ. Hence, we are need of redemption. A little review is in order. Sin, *hamartano*, means I have missed the mark. It simply means to commit an offense or a fault of any kind. It means to break spiritual law and to remain estranged from God. And if we linger in this condition long enough, it results in the spiritual death of the soul.

To save means to rescue or to preserve from harm or danger. To save means to make and keep safe and to preserve for future use. In the context of historical Christianity, to save means to deliver a person, a soul, from sin and punishment, and it means to redeem from spiritual death. When we speak about the ability of our Lord and the Holy Spirit to preserve for future use, we are talking about the concept of sanctification. When we speak about the ability of Christ to keep us safe (from falling), we are talking about the ancient church doctrine of the Perseverance of the Saints. Presently, our main interest is in the concept of salvation as deliverance from sin and punishment and as deliverance from spiritual death.

## Salvation: A Manifestation of the Grace of God

Essentially, salvation is a gift of the grace of God

> God who is rich in mercy, through his great love wherewith he loved us; even when we were dead in sin, hath quickened us together with Christ (for by grace are you saved), and has raised us up together and made us sit together in heavenly places through Christ: in order that

in time to come, He might show the exceeding riches of his grace, in kindness towards us in ChristJesus.

Ephesians 2:4-8

What is grace? In Psalm 84, we read, "For the Lord God is a sun and a shield; the Lord will give grace and glory...Blessed is the man who trusteth in thee" (Psalm 84:11-12). Grace is favor—God's lovingkindness toward us in Christ Jesus. It is mercy that falls from Heaven like the gentle rain. It is a state of being favored while God is ours and we are his. Grace also means exemption from penalty. And it is attractiveness, a charm, and a natural elegance. And finally, grace means divine forgiveness and assistance in human life. Grace reveals the heart of God in the person of Jesus Christ: "in Christ Jesus the grace of God appeared, bringing salvation to all men."

> The Lord is merciful and gracious, slow to anger and plenteous in mercy. He will not always chide: neither will he keep his anger forever. He has not dealt with us after our sins; nor has he rewarded us according to our iniquities. For as Heaven is high above the earth, so great is his mercy toward them that fear him. As far as the east is from the west, so far has he removed our transgressions from us. Like as a father pitieth his children, so the Lord pitieth them that fear him. For he knoweth our frame: he remembereth that we are dust.
>
> Psalm 103:8-14

God's grace and mercy are manifestations of his love for his creation and his creatures. His grace and mercy spring from his universal Fatherhood of the entire human race. Although many are estranged from him and suppress the image and knowledge of God within them, God is still their creator. Of all men, he would be their Redeemer-God. The greatest grace in this concept is that he knows our frame. He remembers that we are made from the dust of the ground.

## The Theology of Grace

In Christ Jesus, we have the supreme revelation of the character of God and of his purpose of mercy toward men. On one occasion, Pharisees questioned our Lord about his Father. Christ said, "If you had known me, you should have known my Father also" (John 8:19). Philip the Evangelist also wanted to see the Father. Then he would be satisfied. Seeking hearts in every generation have voiced the same desire; they would like to catch a glimpse of God or to know what God is like. Our spiritual entity, our soul, seeks rest in God. The desire to know him comes from the heart. Augustine expressed his feelings on this matter. "Oh, Lord, our God, thou hast created us for thyself, and our souls are restless until we find our rest in Thee" (*Confession*—Augustine).

Man has been created differently from every other creature on earth. He is different from the birds of the air and from the beasts of the field. He is restless. At times, he appears to be a bundle of passions, drives, and desires. And deep in his soul is the strong desire to know and search out the mysteries of life.

In our quest, we also would like to see God or at least to know what he is like. Our hearts are restless. Questions remain; some are unanswered, and some are answered only as through a glass darkly. Indeed, when we consider the marvels of the Heavens, we echo the thoughts of the Psalmist, "What is man that God should show concern for him?" How can God, who created the universe and all its vastness, think of me, of my family, and of my little child? In his management of the universe, will he have time to hear my little daughter's prayers or to tend his watchful hand over my little boy?

Yet I consider this thought: what good is his management of the universe if I have no assurance that God cares and understands the inmost longings of my heart—that he knows the way I take? There are things I must know about Him. At least I need to know what God is like. Where can I see or feel and sense this grace—this emanation of his love? How can I know "that he knoweth our frame, he remembers that we are dust?" On some occasions, our need to know is greater than at other times. In the midst of the tragedy that struck his life, leaving him destitute, Job gave expression to his anguish of heart and to the longing of his soul.

> Then Job answered and said: today also my complaint is bitter... and his hand is heavy upon me: oh, that I might know where to find him, that I might come even to his seat. Behold, I go forward, but he is not there; and backward, but I cannot perceive him; I turn to the right hand, but I cannot see him, and yet, he knoweth the way that I take.
>
> Job 23:1-10

Job asked, "Can man, by searching, find God? Can he find out what God is like? Can he find out about God's grace, glory, and love and about his redemptive purpose for man?" Since God has chosen to reveal himself, the answer is yes. If we look where God has revealed himself, there will come light and understanding. Still, however much we see and understand of what he has revealed, it can only be a fragmentary ray of light from the incredible brightness of his majesty and splendor.

God has revealed himself to his people through his prophets. God has revealed himself to nations through judgment and blessing. He has revealed himself in nature and in the course of human lives. In his Spirit, God spoke to holy men of old. He spoke in his Son, Christ Jesus, in the days of his incarnation. And all was not darkness even in Old Testament times. God spoke in diverse ways and in sundry times. He revealed his character, purpose, and promises of grace and redemption. The prophet Isaiah wrote:

> In the year that king Uzziah died, I saw the Lord sitting upon a throne, high and lifted up; and his train filled the temple. Above it stood the seraphim...and one cried unto another, and said: Holy, holy, holy is the Lord of hosts; the whole earth is full of his glory...And I said, Woe is me!

> For I am lost...for my eyes have seen the King, the Lord of hosts.
>
> Isaiah 6:1-5 (RSV)

At the beginning of his ministry, Isaiah obtained a vision of the glory of God. He felt so unworthy that he thought he would die. But he survived. By God's act of absolution, God manifested his grace to Isaiah.

"Then flew one of the seraphim to me, having in his hand a burning coal which he had taken with tongs from the altar. And he touched my mouth, and said: Behold, this has touched your lips; your guilt is taken away, and your sins forgiven" (Isaiah 6:6-7, RSV).

Isaiah was covered over by the grace of God—his disposition to deal in kindness toward us in Christ Jesus. Isaiah was the recipient of God's mercy. God's grace is exemption from penalty, for it means divine forgiveness, absolution, and reception into his kingdom. What is God like? This is what God is like. "Thus saith the Lord, the king of hosts: I am the first and I am the last; besides me there is no God" (Isaiah 44:6). Does God care for me? Does he understand my need to know and my need of assurance?

> But now thus saith the Lord, he who created you, O Jacob, he who formed you, O Israel: Fear not for I have redeemed you; I have called you by name and you are mine. When you pass through the waters I will be with you; and through the rivers of waters, they shall not overwhelm you: when you walk through the fire you shall not be burned, and neither shall the flame kindle upon you. For I am the Lord your God, the Holy one of Israel and your Savior.
>
> Isaiah 43:1-3

Through the ministry of Isaiah in his prophetic office, God revealed his grace and himself as the Redeemer and Savior of his people. God revealed himself as one who delivered from sin and punishment and as one who delivered from spiritual death. Seven hundred years later, the Lord Jesus said to Philip, "He who has seen me has seen the Father" (John 14:9, RSV). Christ meant it not only for Philip but for all of us in ages to come. In his life's work and mission and in our Savior's death on the cross, resurrection from the dead, and exaltation, we are given to understand that he was full of grace and truth.

He, our Redeemer and risen Lord, is Lord of the ages and the creator of the ends of the universe. Scripture reveals that he is "the express image of his (God's) person" (Hebrews 1:3). In him the fullness of God was pleased to dwell. As the only begotten Son, he has made God known. The passage of the centuries does not matter. The vast distances of space do not matter. If you have known the Son, you have known the Father. He is wherever you may be. His is a living, active, and operative presence throughout the universe.

I believe, and I want you to believe, that God will hear the prayers of my child, that he knows the longings of my heart, and that he directs the way I take. He has searched me and known me. He understands every thought of my heart and all the imaginings of my mind. And there is not a word in my heart, but that the Lord knows it altogether. Such knowledge is too wonderful for me. It is high and I cannot attain unto it. Now we see through a glass darkly. We know in part, and we understand in part. But then it shall be face to face, and I shall know even as I am fully known of God. Meanwhile, until our final goal and rest be attained, we are satisfied. For in having known the Son, we will have known the Father, the God of grace and glory.

## Salvation: Essentially a Process of Redemption and Restoration

If the Christian religion is anything at all, it is a religion of redemption and restoration. To redeem (as used in our concept of salvation) means to recover, to set free, to rescue, and to deliver from sin and its penalties by the sacrifice of Christ on the cross. To redeem implies that a promise of deliverance will be fulfilled. And finally, it means that all our faults, failures, and sins will be atoned for and that a Redeemer will render compensation for us.

To restore means to bring back to a former or normal condition. It means to be brought back to spiritual life and fellowship with God the Father. Again, we may say that when used alone, redemption refers to the entire concept of salvation. When so used, it implies the doing of what was necessary to restore and to give a ransom for or to pay the price of making atonement.

We have a Redeemer who left the splendor and glory that he had with the Father to inhabit a body like ours. The Lord Jesus came to bring about that redemption by his teaching, his death on the cross, and his resurrection from the dead. Our Redeemer is Jesus Christ our Lord. And the hallmark of our faith is that it is one of redemption and restoration. This is its goal, purpose, and reason for being. All other aspects of our religion are outgrowths of its main theme.

## The Words of Delivery

The Gospel of the grace of our Lord Jesus Christ comes in plain, simple words. And yet it is utterly profound. It has the power of the Spirit to strike at the heart and to turn men, women, and children to the Lord Jesus. It has done so in every generation. We deny all allegations of sheer credulity. When we embrace our faith, we do so because we have been nurtured in the church and have come to accept its doctrine as true. Our acceptance is a focus of intellectual activity. When we believe on hearing the proclamation of the Gospel, it is because the Holy Spirit has opened our hearts to be receptive to the word of the Lord. When Christ, in love and grace, has won our hearts, the assent of the mind will surely follow.

We acknowledge that the words of redemption are common, everyday words—love, grace, truth, spirit, soul, God, man, Jesus

Christ, Savior, the cross, the Son of Man, fellowship, life everlasting, and faith. They are simple words, yet absolutely beautiful and eternally significant in their meaning. There are also forgiveness, absolution, and reception into the kingdom. These are simply beautiful words and unending in their meaning—these words of truth and grace. But unless these simple words of the Gospel message speak to our hearts, they may not have touched us at all.

# The Proto-Evangel: Through the Seed of the Woman

In the Garden of Eden, our progenitors became susceptible to the malevolent influence of Lucifer. They chose to believe his false promises rather than the truth of God. The first Adam broke spiritual law in direct disobedience to his creator and chose to believe the lie, and mankind became subject to spiritual death. The close spiritual communion that he had enjoyed with God was severed, and moral estrangement ensued. If permitted to remain in this condition, then there would follow enmity toward God and spiritual death. But God would not so leave his children—his own creation.

In dealing with man's failures and sins, God chose to manifest his grace, and he did so at the inception of creation. He extended his promise of grace and redemption to our progenitors in the Proto-Evangel, and God extended his promise to the whole human race.

The Mother Promise has been called the Proto-Evangel because it was like the first small grain of the promise. It was the promise of redemption given in capsule form. Like a small seed, it was planted in their hearts, souls, and minds. And like a seed in the passage of time, it would grow. It would become progressively clearer and more explicit. God would redeem his people and deliver them from spiritual death. Since their frame was subject to dust, the redemption would be of God. The Redeemer himself would come from the heart of God.

"And the Lord God said, I will put enmity between thee and the woman, and between thy seed and her seed; it shall bruise thy head and thou shall bruise his heel" (Genesis 3:15).

The promise of grace was the promise of a Deliverer. The Deliverer, in his redemptive power, would bruise the head of the Serpent, destroying his works and power over man. The promise was to be embraced in faith and hope. And when she left Paradise, Eve carried with her the promise of a Redeemer. This Redeemer is designated throughout scripture as the Second Adam, Christ Jesus our Lord. As in Adam all were to die spiritually, even so in Christ all would be made alive spiritually. "And as we have born the image of the earthly, we shall also bear the image of the heavenly" (1 Corinthians 15:49). In the first Adam, man became a living soul. But in Christ, man receives a quickening spirit.

# The Promise of the Indwelling of the Holy Spirit

As God's redemptive dealings with man unfolded, he made a new covenant with man. The covenant of stone was done away with. God's children were no longer able, if they ever were, to walk before God as with the tablets of stone. The tablets became a slave master and more like a coffin of stone. The new covenant involved the promise of the Holy Spirit. In the mystery of God's redemptive counsel, the incidents, factors, and agency involved gradually unfolded. As the history of the nation played out amidst all its changing fortunes, so did the redemptive aspect of revelation unfold in its historical development. At each stage in its progress, more light was added as man was able to bear it. The promise is narrated in the prophetic books of Ezekiel and Jeremiah.

In the book of the prophet Jeremiah, the promise of the indwelling presence is narrated at follows.

> Behold, I will make a new covenant: not like the covenant which I made with their fathers when I took them by the

hand to bring them out of the land of Egypt: my covenant which they broke, though I was their husband, said the Lord. But this is the covenant which I will make with the house of Israel: I will put my law within them, and I will write it upon their hearts; and they shall know me: for I will forgive their iniquity, and their sins I will remember no more.

Jeremiah 31:31-34

In Ezekiel, the promise of the Holy Spirit is narrated as follows.

A new heart I will give you, and a new spirit will I put within you; and I will take out of your flesh the heart of stone and give you a heart of flesh. And I will put my Spirit within you, and cause you to walk in my statutes and to be careful to observe my ordinances.

Ezekiel 36:26-27

God proposed a new covenant with man, not like the one which he made with his people when he had led them out of Egypt. Moses had descended the mountain of God with the tablets of stone. In Jeremiah and Ezekiel, the old covenant, the tablets of stone, referred to the whole body of minute ritualistic procedure. St. Paul acknowledged that even our fathers were unable to bear it. It had become too oppressive. The old covenant was done away with because it was broken. It was broken because man found it impossible to keep. They were unable to walk before God with the tablets of stone.

What had occurred? It became a weight of stone, dragging men down and making them despair of their ability to be what God intended them to be. They also despaired of their own ability to approach God in the proper manner. What the stone coffin really brought home to men who sought after God was that any concept of redemption would have to be wholly of God. It would be a pure outpouring of his grace. When it did come, this manifestation of grace was so abounding that it permitted both the saint and sinner to approach and worship God. It enabled those who knew that of themselves they were not ritualistically clean—through he beauty of divine compassion and forgiveness—to approach God in worship.

Men were to appropriate and accept this divine compassion through the exercise of faith in God. Even Abraham, the father of the faithful, was not righteous as such or ritualistically clean. What does Scripture say? It says that Abraham believed God. And because of his faith, God accounted (imputed) him as righteous.

Under the new covenant, where would men find the essential knowledge of God? They would find it in their hearts, in their souls, and in their minds. It would be put there through the Holy Spirit, which God would send to men. Impelled by the Spirit, the heart of man would incline toward God. This would occur because the Spirit of God would dwell with them. When Samuel urged the people to rededicate themselves to God before the battle marked by the Stone of Ebenezer, he urged the people to turn to the Lord with their whole heart. Samuel knew that true religion was a matter of the heart, and this incident was a foreshadowing of the promise that God would manifest his Spirit in the heart of his people.

In the Old Testament, generally only the outward influence of the Spirit was experienced, not the indwelling presence. The indwelling presence of the Holy Spirit is God's special gift to the Church of Jesus Christ. The law written in our hearts refers to the law of the Spirit. We are to understand the abiding and sanctifying presence of the Holy Spirit as dwelling in the hearts of God's people as though dwelling in a temple. This is so even if the temple be made of clay.

Being written on the heart refers to the inner springs of our being and of life, thoughts, feelings, and purpose. Though it may not always be apparent, the moral effect of the indwelling presence of the Holy Spirit is direct, primary, and permanent.

This is true even though there occur moral lapses in the life of the believer. The remorse he feels for the moral lapse and the sorrow he senses are the Spirit touching his conscience. The Holy Spirit also bestows spiritual gifts and understanding.

Through the proceeding of the Holy Spirit, Christ is in our hearts and at the right hand of God. He makes intercession for his people above, and he covers us over with the righteousness of his grace. He warms our hearts in our inner being by the grace of his Spirit. The Holy Spirit is also the Paraclete and the Comforter, and he is an intercessor for the temple in which he dwells.

We agree with St. Paul and St. Augustine that the believer has a warring in his members. As the grace of God prevents those who are morally estranged from him from acting consistently in a perverse and evil way, so the natural man in us prevents us from consistently manifesting a spiritual life. Even so, where sin does abound, the grace of God does much more abound. Although on some occasions evil may wholly surround us, the morally wrong do not dominate us. It is not predominant or the controlling influence in our lives. Though Satan may have bruised our heels, the bruises will heal in time. None of this detracts from the promise or the reality of the indwelling presence of the Holy Spirit in the life of the believer. What does it prove? It proves that, alas, the Spirit in us resides in the temple of clay.

Two promises made possible man's salvation. The first was the promise of a Redeemer, our Savior-God. The second was the promise of the indwelling and outpouring of the Holy Spirit. The Father promised to send his Son, and in his name he would send the Spirit. In each instance, it was a further manifestation of the grace of God. In the New Testament, the promise came to full realization. The Annunciation of the birth of Jesus broke forth in hopeful expectation. Those who heard and saw God's issue come forth, who beheld the birth of their Savior, could only utter, "Lord, now lettest thy servant depart in pace" (Luke 2:29, RSV).

# The Promise of the Outpouring of the Holy Spirit

The promise of the indwelling presence of the Spirit refers to the Spirit residing in and dwelling with the individual believer. The promise in the book of Joel is that of the outpouring of the Holy Spirit upon believers as the church of Jesus Christ. It is the special gift of the Holy Spirit given to the church. We will discuss it further under the division of Pneumatology, the Doctrine of the Holy Spirit.

In the book of the prophet Joel, the promise is as follows.

> And it shall come to pass that I will pour out my spirit on all flesh; and your sons and your daughters shall prophesy, and your young men shall see visions, and your old men shall dream dreams. Even upon the menservants and the maidservants, in those days, I will pour out my spirit.
>
> Joel 2:28-29

It was the outpouring of the Spirit upon the church that gave it growth, which guides and protects it. This outpouring of the Spirit upon the church keeps it alive and moving with spiritual life.

# The Annunciation of Jesus

The promises that we have discussed, of a Redeemer and the gift of the Holy Spirit, were incidents of revelation when given. In the unfolding of God's counsel for man's redemption, God manifested his sovereign grace in the realm of revelation. He also revealed the promise of the coming Redeemer, which occurred in the Annunciation of Jesus. All Israel, from the least to the greatest, knew that the redemption of the human race depended on the coming of a Redeemer—the advent of God's holy Word. Quite simply, men knew that without a Savior-God, there could never be redemption for the human race. The angel of the Annunciation spoke the words every heart and soul had waited to hear.

Hail, thou art highly favoured, the Lord is with thee: blessed are thou among women. Thou shall conceive in thy womb and bring forth a son, and thou shalt call his name Jesus. For the Holy Ghost shall come upon thee, and the power of the Highest shall overshadow thee: Therefore also the holy thing which shall be born of thee shall be called the son of God.

Luke 1:28-35

Immediately, we are concerned with the first advent of the Lord Jesus. Advent means the coming, the appearing in time, of the Lord Jesus Christ, the Son of God and Savior of the world. It means the coming of God in human form—the incarnation of God in Jesus Christ. This "holy thing" that was born of Mary was called Jesus. He would be great and be called the Son of the Most High. God would give him the throne of his father David. And he would reign over the house of Israel forever.

This was the beginning of the incredible interlude of the promised Savior-God come to earth. It was the angel of God's presence, which God sent to Mary to make the Annunciation of the birth of Jesus. The angel of God's presence and the heavenly greeting could only have spoken of a further revelation of God—another outpouring of grace. The angel told of the child's greatness. His name would be called Jesus. The name Jesus means *he who would save his people*. The angel depicted Christ's eternal reign, his acknowledgement as the Son of God, and his never-ending kingdom. The Annunciation, as all new revelations, brought with it a spirit of renewal and an awakening of the longing heart in the knowledge that God would do great things. We can only imagine that there was a sense that God was near.

Even in our time, as Advent draws near, we feel and sense the increased intensity of the Spirit. There is also, in these days, a deep stillness in the Heavens. There is a silence that portends the doing of great things, of wonder, of heavenly hosts, and of angel visitants. There is the aura of the glory of the Lord and of the

## The Theology of Grace

grace of God revealed to men on earth. The flame of faith and hope will be rekindled once more because the Spirit of the Savior's coming pervades these days. And if we let it, it can pervade our hearts, also. Like Simeon, we will confess our need of him. He is our Savior who comes to us with transforming and strengthening power. Advent comes with gentle strength. Advent tells us that the Mother Promise was fulfilled.

We will note two things before moving from the Annunciation—Mary's reply to the revelation given her, and God's outpouring of grace to our acceptance of his Word.

Mary displayed a heart willingness to be of service for the grace of God and for the glory of the kingdom. She was willing to become a vessel fit for the Master's use. The teaching of scripture is that God works his wonders of grace through men and women who are not disobedient to the heavenly vision. He works through those who answer his call to service. Having understood and accepted the knowledge given her, Mary's own spirit issued forth in a psalm of praise.

> My soul does magnify the Lord, and my spirit rejoices in God my saviour, for he has regarded the low estate of his handmaiden: for behold, from henceforth all generations will call me blessed: For he that is mighty hath done to me great things: and holy is his name. And his mercy is on those who fear him from generation to generation… He has helped his servant Israel, in the remembrance of his mercy; as he spoke to our fathers, to Abraham and to his posterity for ever.
>
> Luke 1:46-55

Since one humble maiden of Nazareth willingly chose to serve God's purpose, the promise of the coming Savior was fulfilled. One woman surrendered her heart and soul to furthering God's grace, and God's grace was extended to all the nations of the world. One maiden responded to the Annunciation of the birth of Jesus, and the whole human race has benefited.

God's grace is shed upon those who answer God's call for service. God's word to Mary was, "The Holy Ghost will come upon you; and the power of the Most High will overshadow you." It is the presence and bestowal of the Savior's Spirit that ensures success in any work undertaken for the Kingdom. Generally, all work undertaken for the Kingdom will be blessed, and the individual himself will be blessed with an outpouring of God's grace.

Advent is the season when the Spirit of God moves over the face of the land, searching for a place of abode. Like the winds coming from the four corners of the earth, the Spirit seeks lodging in the hearts of men, women, and children. If we look for him with expectation, there will be a moment during the advent season when the Holy Spirit will break a silence through it all, and God, in the birth of the infant Savior, will be speaking to our souls. And we will know beyond a shadow of a doubt that this is the moment for us. The Annunciation of the Lord Jesus will have a special meaning and call for us. For then, like Mary, our souls will magnify the Lord, and our spirit will rejoice in God our Savior. For he that is mighty will have done great tings. He will have blessed us with his mercy—even to us and to our posterity for ever. Let us look as he who came from the threshold of Heaven.

## From the Threshold of Heaven

In the city of David in that first advent season, devout souls retained in their hearts one great hope—the promise of God in the coming Redeemer. From the writings of the prophet Isaiah, we understand that it was the consolation of Israel that was viewed through the prophetic future. They had the temple as the central place of worship. It had grown out of the past, out of the Tabernacle in the wilderness, which Moses had made according to the pattern given to him on the Mount. It spoke of the time when the Lord God had worded wonders with his people. For all the devout of Israel, there was only one temple—the temple in the holy city of David. It was the dwelling place of the Most High, for it spoke of the presence of God. It was here that the God-appointed priesthood could offer sacrifice.

In the temple stood the Ark of the Covenant, containing the tablets of the law and the manna. There was also Aaron's rod that once budded and blossomed. Then, too, there was the incense that rose toward the Heavens from the golden altar as the symbol that God accepted their prayers and worship. Finally, there was the seven-branched candlestick, indicative of God's presence. Although it spoke of the past, the temple service, in all its elements and symbols, pointed to the future and to the hope and consolation of Israel. That hope was in the manifestation of the Kingdom of Heaven, wherein would dwell righteousness peace and joy in the Holy Spirit. The hope of the Kingdom was centralized in God's promise of the coming Redeemer.

Isaiah had foretold it. "His name shall be called Wonderful, Counselor, the mighty God, the everlasting Father, the Prince of peace" (Isaiah 9:6). God the Son became the Lord's Christ for righteousness and peace. The Kingdom speaks of the inner and spiritual life that Christ brings. Every advent season denotes the time when from Heaven's threshold he came and sought us and when God the Son assumed human form and when the mighty God, through the overshadowing of the Holy Spirit, did a great wonder.

For this, the world had waited. The world dreamed and prayed for the grace that loves, calls with patience, and redeems. This is what fills the advent season with expectation—the riches of our Redeemer's grace that falls from the very threshold of Heaven like the gentle rain. And like the still drops of dew, it awakens the soul and heart to God's salvation.

From Heaven's threshold to the human threshold is not as far a journey as it may seem. When he was born, the infant Savior crossed the human threshold, and he became one of us. "Blessed be the Lord God of Israel," said Zechariah, "for he has visited and has redeemed his people" (Luke 1:68). The Lord Jesus, having become a part of our experience and moved our very souls, seeks a new dwelling place. His dwelling place would no longer be a sanctuary made of stone but those of flesh and blood. The divine presence would no longer be attested solely by the golden altar of incense and the seven-branched candlestick, but by the Spirit's presence in humble souls and contrite hearts.

When the Savior's presence crosses a human threshold, it is always a redeeming experience. Whether that crossing occurs during the advent season or at any other time of the year, he comes to abide. For it is his abiding with us that touches the heartstrings of our souls and causes the conscious acceptance of his grace. His words come to us with quickening power, for they come carried on the breath of the Spirit. "Abide in me, and I in you."

With his abiding, our Savior brings his assurance, which is a feeling of confidence and security. We know that with many there is a misdirected searching after an assurance of faith. At times, our hold to spiritual things grows tenuous and seems to be hanging by a slender thread. But let our Savior's Spirit abide with us, and the doubts vanish. A quiet peace takes possession of us, that peace that "passes understanding," and our souls are at rest.

The human soul has a threshold of realization. It is that point at which one awakens with a response. We understand that, for many, the realization of spiritual things is difficult to awaken. There comes a dull insensitivity to the person of Christ, to his claim upon our hearts and to things of the Kingdom. Unless we come to the threshold of realization, to the point at which we are receptive to the message of his coming, the redemption that is in Christ Jesus together with the peace and joy of the Holy Spirit will never come upon us. During the advent season, we must be spiritually sensitive to the signs of the times.

The Holy Spirit that overshadowed the Annunciation and the advent of our Savior was meant to reveal the glory of the Lord. The Spirit strives to touch our souls, bringing us to an awareness of his abiding presence and to respond with an acceptance of our

Redeemer's grace. What, we may ask ourselves, does it take to awaken a response in our hearts? Will we be able to abide the moment of his coming to respond to his love and grace and to the redemption that he brings? We must welcome and accept the touch of the Spirit. And if we respond and believe in him, then Christ will cross the threshold of our hearts. He will visit us and redeem our souls for his Kingdom, and he will abide with us now, always, and forever. It is already the fullness of time.

## The Fullness of Time

With God, a promise is as good as done. In the fullness of time, when angels sang and a star traversed the skies, and when shepherds watched and wise men marveled, the promise was fulfilled. God sent forth his Son. And in him, God the Son, all the promises were realized. Both Roman history and Christian literature record the time. It was in those days when Caesar Augustus levied the tax, when the whole world was ruled from the city on the Tiber. In those days, each came into his own city to be enrolled. It was the time that the prophets had spoken of, of which young men had dreamed dreams and of which old men had seen visions. It was the season when snow covered Mount Hermon and King Herod ruled in Jerusalem and all the inns in Bethlehem were filled.

In those days, Joseph also went out from Galilee to the city of David. He went in accordance with the imperial decree. And during the time he was there, Mary, his wife, brought forth the Child of the Holy Spirit. She wrapped him in swaddling clothes, laid him in a manger, and called him Jesus. The Lord God of Israel had visited his people. And in peace and mercy, we receive the birth of the Christ child.

Christmas, the day of the birth of the infant Redeemer, is a day of wonder. The birth of a baby is always a thing to marvel. It is the mystery of a new life given. We have this marvel of birth amidst bells and stars and amidst shepherds and wise men. We are reminded of the inn and the manger and of the expectant eyes of little children. A marvel is something to wonder about and is more like a miracle to an act of God. For the Word was made flesh and dwelt among us, and there was no place for him even in the lowliest of inns. Within the overshadowing of the Spirit, the simplicity of God was seen as wiser than the wisdom of men.

All the world's hopes are centered in one new birth. And are not always the hopes and fears of the family centered on every newborn child? We see visions in our minds' eyes and dream dreams of the future. We fear for his safety. We pray that the child will grow in stature and in wisdom. And all the while we wait and watch the miracle of growth taking place before our eyes.

Although Christmas is a day of wonder, it was not until the shepherds came and the wise men brought gifts that adoration was given the child. In adoration we worship and pay homage. The shepherds came to worship when they knelt before him whom the angels had made known to them. The wise men came to do homage as they laid their gifts at his feet. Ever since, the Savior has been to us an object of adoration and worship. We worship him because unto us the Son was given. We worship Christ because in him the glory of God assumed the form of human flesh, and we look to him as Savior, for in him dwells all the fullness of God bodily. This was the miracle.

We pay Christ homage because, like the wise men, we know what he came to do. From the beginning, he came to give his life as a ransom for many, as a ransom for sins.

"Behold, there came wise men from the east to Jerusalem, Saying, 'Where is he that is born king of the Jews? For we have seen his star in the east, and are come to worship him'" (Matthew 2:1-2).

"The King" is one of the divine titles of Christ, and in his divine title, the wise men ascribed worship to the infant Redeemer. From the perspective of our present day, we know that the manger envisioned in the future a cross. The infant Savior would be depicted by the Holy Ghost as the Lamb of God who takes away the sins of the world.

And so it was that the humble shepherds knew that in the city of David was born a Savior who was Christ the Lord (Luke 2:11). They made known the saying that had been told them concerning this holy child, for the shepherds knew that it was the time of God's appointing. Softly, as on the wings of the wind, the Spirit had spoken to their souls.

The work that the Holy Spirit can do in any human life is always a marvel and a miracle of grace. The Holy Spirit, the Lord and giver of life who spoke by the angels and the prophets, was active over all the events of the advent season. And in the giving of a new life, even in his birth, there was a foreshadowing of the indwelling of the spiritual life, which the infant Savior brought to the people of earth. Asleep in the manger, the infant Redeemer may not have appeared as the Son of God who has eyes like a flame of fire and whose feet were like burnished brass. For now, the stillness of the winter night had settled over the land. But on the day of Pentecost, the overwhelming power of the Spirit would be revealed. And all those endowed with the Spirit would seem to speak as with tongues of fire. Yet it was the birth of Christ that brought the new era of the reign of the Spirit in human souls. Only where the Spirit reigned, born in the human heart, would there be the beginning of the Kingdom of Heaven.

## Your Faith in Christ Jesus

> For the grace of God hath appeared...in Christ Jesus... bringing salvation to all men. That we should live soberly and righteously and godly, looking for the blessed hope: The appearing of the glory of the great God and our Savior Jesus Christ: Who gave himself for us that he might redeem us from all iniquity.
>
> Titus 2:11-12

The passage from Paul's letter to Titus quoted above is known as "The Epiphany of Grace." Epiphany means revelation and manifestation, in this case a manifestation of the grace of God in Jesus Christ. And how does Christ brings salvation to all men? "Christ Jesus…gave himself for us that he might redeem us from all iniquity." That was how he did it. He gave himself for us. And that is why we believe in him and accept him as our Savior and Lord. That is why we place our faith in him because of who he is, what he did for our salvation, and how he did it.

## The Primacy of Christ

The apostle Paul wrote in his letter to the Colossians, "we give thanks to God and the Father of our Lord Jesus Christ, praying for you always, since I heard of your faith in Christ Jesus" (Colossians 1:3-4).

The apostle prayed for a people he had not seen as yet. He was glad. His heart rejoiced because some individuals in a distant city, unknown to him, had obtained faith in Christ. Their faith in Christ received Paul's attention. Their worship and love of Christ lingered in Paul's mind. He prayed for them because the Son of God was the object of their faith and worship.

Paul brought out an important feature found in the Gospels and in all our Christian literature. In the New Testament, we find more frequently than not that all the writings designate as the object of our faith, not God the Father or God the Holy Spirit, but God the Son. Although the New Testament truly speaks of faith in God, its main redemptive voice speaks more often of faith in Christ. And before we can desire him, we must believe in him and love him.

We recognize this simple fact that no one can have faith in Christ who does not have faith in God the Father and in God the Holy Spirit. What we now stress about our faith in Christ is that our faith in Christ is based on historical fact, on knowledge, on revelation, and on the influence of the Holy Spirit. Faith in the Lord Jesus involves intellectual activity. Some thoughts must always pass through our minds, and they must always precede the giving of our assent.

Why is this so? It is so because in the narrative of the New Testament, the mission of our Lord is laid out as a life and work that occurred at a specific time in history—during the rule of Tiberius Caesar. Christ, as the founder of the Christian movement, drew the major attention of the Latin writers Pliny the Younger and the Roman historian Tacitus. Tacitus wrote, "He was…a certain Christ who lived in Judea in the reign of Tiberius, and brought to capital punishment by the procurator Pontius Pilate. (cf. Tacitus, *Annals*, xv44) Christ was worshipped by the Christians of Pontus and Bithynia as their God. (Pliny, *Epistles*, xcvi [Pliny's letter to Trajan])

These writers saw in the growth of the infant Church, and in its literature, the depiction of the primacy of Christ as the object of faith and worship. In Christ, the redeeming grace of God became visible on earth. In the Lord Jesus Christ, grace obtained our salvation through his life and ministry that ended on the cross. Thus, in the New Testament, it is Christ the Son of God who is generally seen as the object of worship.

## Our Faith Is Based on Knowledge

Before we can desire the Lord Jesus, we must believe in him and love him. And we cannot believe in him until we know him, nor can we love him until we know about him. St. Augustine reminded us that intellectual activity always precedes belief. Some thoughts must turn in our minds before we give our assent. And those thoughts are always based on some kind of knowledge about the person of Christ. This knowledge centers on who he was, what he did, and how he did it. We must know this before we place our faith in him or before we can truly love him.

We realize that we are separated from his physical presence and ministry on earth by centuries. But the passage of centuries means little because Christ is Lord of the ages. Nevertheless, even though his Spirit can always touch the human heart, there is still the need to know. We need to know that we have a risen and living Savior. This means that we need to know about the crucifixion and resurrection. We need to know that he can touch our lives and cover us over with his grace. We need to know that he awakens our spiritual lives and restores us to fellowship with the Father. And this means that we need to know that Christ has promised to abide with us always even unto the ends of the earth. We need to know that he has promised us his power and his presence.

We need to know that Christ is able to keep that which we have committed unto him against that day. We need to know that as our High Priest, he is able to present us faultless before his Father's throne of grace. Most of all, we need to know that his love and grace forgive all our faults, failures, and sins. We feel that we have good standing to plead the issue of the need to know and the need for some knowledge about the person of Christ. From the book of the prophet Isaiah, we read, "Come now, saith the Lord our God, let us reason together" (Isaiah 1:18). This gives us good standing indeed.

Let us reason. Let us think on this. We commit to Christ the most precious things we possess: our loved ones, hopes, dreams, and expectations for this world and the next. We commit to him our hope of immortality, the consummation of all the spiritual realities that exist for us now, and that will exist for us in eternity. What more can we say but that for us, this is the supreme expression of our faith in Christ. It is a glorious act of trust in Christ. It expresses nothing less than our ultimate confidence in Christ as our Redeemer and Savior. So then, quite simply, we ought to know in whom we have believed. He is the strong Son of God.

In holding that some knowledge is a condition precedent to faith, we are saying that some knowledge about Christ necessarily precedes faith in him in the order of time.

We acknowledge that on some occasions, faith in Christ and knowledge about him may occur at the same time. Although the Holy Spirit does indeed open the eyes of our understanding, the Holy Spirit deals with the whole person: with our hearts, souls, minds, and emotions. And this is the height of intellectual activity. As our knowledge of Christ increases, we will realize that our understanding of him involves knowledge of his pre-existence in glory with the Father. We learn that in the Son, the fullness of God was pleased to dwell. We learn about his humiliation—how he emptied himself and assumed human form.

In time, our understanding of Christ will involve some knowledge of his life and ministry on earth—his temptation, transfiguration, and his atonement on the cross. We will acquire knowledge of his resurrection, ascension, exaltation, and the promise of his second advent. Our faith and knowledge of it involve implications for time and eternity. It is for this reason that the church has held that real faith in Christ embraces him as the eternal Son of God who at a certain point in the history of the world became man. He came to earth for us and our salvation and manifested his glory, grace, and truth. And now as the risen Savior, Christ holds mystic sweet communion with all who commit their lives to him.

## Knowledge in the Psalms

The knowledge found in Scripture portrays Christ in the function of his three offices: Prophet, Priest, and King. All three offices are germane to his stereological function. They are necessary to his ministry as the Savior of those who place their faith in him. Again, we would note that as we characterize our Lord in the function of one of his three offices, we are dealing with conceptions. These conceptions are mediated to us through the divine revelation in the canons of the Old and New Testament.

As far back as Genesis, we find the concept of the Priest-King Melchizedek. He gave bread and wine to Abraham when the latter returned from the successful encounter with the kings of the north. We should note that the essence of this concept is that of an endless life; the new high priest will have a ministry like the Priest-King Melchizedek after the power of an endless life. Moses delineated the promised Redeemer as a prophet who would be greater than he who was but a servant of the household. Christ would be the Son of the Father and the Lord's anointed. He would be greater by reason of his "glory that excelleth." These revelations, whether to the psalmists or prophets, were always high moments of the Spirit for those through whom they came. In the Psalms, where the spiritual heart of the people is revealed, it expressed the full glory of the Lord. The Psalms are full of the knowledge of Christ. We will touch on this only lightly.

## The King

In coming to earth, our Lord founded his kingdom of love, righteousness, and peace. His kingdom came running over with streams of glory and grace. He has been portrayed as a King of peace and righteousness. When the Spirit of the Lord stirred his soul and moved his heart, David wrote.

> My heart is [thinking about] a good matter: I speak of the things which I have made touching the king: my tongue is the pen of a ready writer. Thou art fairer than the children of men; grace is poured into thy lips: therefore God has blessed thee for ever...Thy throne, O God, is for ever and ever: the scepter of thy kingdom is a right scepter. Thou lovest righteousness, and hatest wickedness: therefore God, thy God, hath anointed thee with the oil of gladness above thy fellows.
>
> Psalm 45:1-7

Christ, as King, is characterized as a King of peace and righteousness. He is given a throne and a spiritual kingdom over which he is to reign. It is a kingdom of peace and righteousness and joy in the Holy Spirit. He is the King of righteousness.

## A Priest

In the Psalms, Christ is also portrayed as our High Priest. This portrayal is also found in the Epistle to the Hebrews. As a priest, Christ makes intercession for his people. He comes into the presence of God on their behalf. He makes atonement for the sins of the people. Christ presents his body as a living sacrifice that has been nailed to the cross. He suffered, was abused, and endured pain and humiliation. He died and was buried, even though it was impossible for the pangs of hell to hold him. As a priest after the power of an endless life, Christ broke all bonds asunder, especially the bonds of death.

After the power of an endless life, Christ rose victoriously over death. He ascended to Heaven to continue his ministry. He entered into the holy of holies. As our High Priest, Christ serves in making intercession for us. God's purpose in this is immutable.

"The Lord hath sworn and will not repent. Thou art a priest, forever, after the order of Melchizedek" (Psalm 110:4).

## A Prophet

A prophet is one who speaks the word of the Lord God to us. A prophet is also one through whom the Lord God is pleased to speak. He both tells and foretells the Word of the Lord. Through the Spirit of Christ that was in David, Christ uttered, in prophesy, the humiliation of his passion.

"They pierced my hands and feet; they counted all my bones, Yea, they looked and stared at me. They parted my garments among them; and over my vestures they cast lots" (Psalm 22:16-19).

As a prophet, Christ reveals God's will and purpose for our lives. He brings us the Word of the Lord. He proclaims the Gospel of grace and calls into his Kingdom. As our High Priest, Christ offers us forgiveness and absolution for our sins. He removes the handwriting on the wall that was against us and so makes peace for our souls. He covers us over with his grace, keeps us from falling, and presents us faultless before the Father's throne of grace. As King he reigns in our hearts with his love and presence, endowing us with the Holy Spirit. His Spirit in us makes us desire him because we know about him and come to love him. Our hearts awaken to the realization that in Christ Jesus the grace of God appeared, bringing salvation to all men.

## Faith in Christ Jesus and You

In the Gospels and Epistles, Jesus of Nazareth is portrayed as an object of faith. He is so represented because of who he was, what he did, and how he did it. The concepts of Christ as Redeemer, Prophet, Priest, and King became obscured in the latter part of this century. When Christ as the object of our faith and Head of the church become obscure, one's faith is not as strong and vital as it should be. And the church loses power and growth.

Have we not sensed this? Do we love him enough to place our faith in him? Do we really worship Christ as our Savior-God? We cannot really say that all of our Churches resound with the saving and atoning Christ of the cross. Is it possible that the grace of God that appeared in Christ Jesus is once again buried in the past and forgotten like a concept time out of mind? Let us hope that the light as merely grown dim.

We are aware that this is not the first time in the history of the church that Christ, the object of faith and worship as Redeemer and head of the church, has become obscured. This occurred in the middle ages and also in the centuries before the Wesleyan revivals. But when the measure of iniquity became full, as immediately prior to the Protestant Reformation, the Gospel of

Jesus Christ burst forth in power, grace, and redemptive might once more. It moved the kingdoms of world. This gospel, which had such a telling effect, was the same gospel preached by Paul and defined by Augustine.

When the reformation comes again in our mainline churches, it will come through those upon whom God has laid his hand. It will come through those to whom the gospel has become a burning fire within and who speak and write because they are compelled to do so by the Spirit of the Lord God. With heart, soul, and mind, we believe in the great teachings of the Church. They must be proclaimed with the heartwarming strength of conviction, in the power of the Spirit, till they strike fire in the human heart. We must acknowledge Christ as our Redeemer-God; head of the church that bears his name, and as our faithful High Priest.

This is the Savior I bring to you in these writings—the Savior-God of our faith and worship. And I so bring him to you that you may believe and rejoice in your faith in Christ Jesus. His love and Spirit can awaken your soul like the blooming flowers of spring. He can make you sensitive to his grace, glory, and the Love of God that is in Christ Jesus our Lord. He will come to you if you love him, and he will come to you if you desire him. He will come like a whispering hope, making your heart in its sorrow rejoice.

## The Atonement of Jesus Christ

Where do we meet God Incarnate in all his redemptive power? Where do we behold the Lamb of God who takes away the sins of the world? And where do we know Christ as Savior? We so know him and meet him at the cross. And unless we accept the Christ of the cross, we may not really have known him as Savior and Lord. On the cross we see him at the height of his priestly office. Here he gave his body to be broken and his blood to be shed for many for the remission of sin. On the cross we have the atonement of Jesus Christ.

Atonement means concord, reconciliation after estrangement and enmity. It means having made satisfaction for moral wrong. It is expiation for sin. And as it relates to our redemption, the atonement on the cross by Christ is the expiation of all our faults, failures, and sins. Christ achieved our reconciliation to God through his obedience, suffering, and death on the cross. *The cross is the primary symbol of the Christian faith because it reminds us just exactly how and where atonement was made.*

Ultimately we are reconciled to God the Father through the suffering and death of Christ on the cross. St. Paul, in his first letter to the church in Corinth, included the atonement in the summation of the Gospel that he preached. He was trying to arouse them to the heart of their faith by reminding them of the essence of the Gospel.

> Now I would remind you, brethren, in what terms I preached to you the Gospel: and by which you are saved; For I delivered unto you as of first importance that which I also received: That Christ died for our sins in accordance with the Scriptures; that he was buried, and that he rose again the third day according to the Scriptures.
>
> 1 Corinthians 15:1-4

We must constantly remind ourselves that we have a risen and living Savior worthy of our faith and trust and that we come to him for the needs of our souls. We believe that his love and grace can touch our lives. Most of all, our Lord Christ touches our hearts, souls, and minds through his cross. There he blotted out our transgressions and nailed them to the cross. This is the heart of the Gospel that we preach; Christ made peace for us with God through his cross.

When we think of Christ as Savior and Redeemer, we have in mind the Christ of the cross. When the Holy Spirit touches our hearts, we place our faith in him, and we accept Christ and his cross. What we have just said about Christ, faith, and the cross is known as the Church's historical doctrine of the atonement of Jesus Christ. It is not a complex doctrine. It is quite simple. A little child can understand it and place his faith in Christ. He can trust the Son of God to be his Savior. On the cross, he died for us and took our blame and our guilt. God saw the travail of his soul and was satisfied. From its beginning, the Church has held to this great teaching.

Knowing about Christ does not place a barrier between us and faith in him. Our faith in Christ is a saving grace wherein we receive and trust upon him for our salvation as he is offered to us in the Gospel. In the Gospel, Christ is offered to us as the eternal Son of God, our Savior-Redeemer, and our Prophet, Priest, and King who, in the climax of his redemptive mission, tasted death on the cross for every man.

When writing about the cross, the apostle Paul told his readers that the cross was an offense to the wisdom and sophistication of the world. He was speaking from personal experience. An offense is a thing that causes resentment, hurt feelings, and even anger. In the time of the Roman Empire, the cross was a cruel instrument of death. We can understand why, as a means of salvation, it would cause a great deal of resentment. The world may well have sought for a way of salvation it could have deemed profound and highly cultivated. The simplicity of the cross may have offended the ancient society because it saw in the cross no great human meritorious achievement.

Why should the cross be deemed offensive? Who does it offend? And why should the love and grace and sacrifice God displayed on the cross seem as so much foolishness to the world at large? Why should a world at enmity with God relegate the gift of God's Son merely to a childhood faith or to rustic believers?

In this confused, perplexed, deluded, and spiritually destitute society, why should Christians be ashamed of the simple Gospel of Jesus Christ? The Cross, the Atonement, the Crucified One, this is our salvation? Yes, this is our Salvation. This is what the

Church of Jesus Christ has taught in all ages. The concept is not obscure. It is open and direct. Here our Lord extends his very heart and life with a love that surpasses knowledge. He offers us the consummation of our spiritual reconciliation through his body that was broken and through his blood that was shed for the remission of sins. We should note that acceptance of the Lord Jesus Christ as he is offered to us in the Gospel of his redeeming grace is really not an offense but a saving grace.

## The Saving Passion

There is a story about Philip the Evangelist narrated in the eight chapter of the book of Acts. And it is noteworthy that this incident took place on a desert road.

> An angel of the Lord said to Philip, Rise and go toward the south, to the road that goes down from Jerusalem to Gaza. This is a desert road. And he rose and went. And behold, an Ethiopian, an eunuch, a minister of Candace, Queen of The Ethiopians, in charge of all her treasure, had come to Jerusalem to worship and was returning. Seated in his chariot, he was reading in the book of the prophet Isaiah. And the Spirit said to Philip, "Go up and join this chariot." So Philip ran to him and heard him reading the prophet Isaiah; and Philip asked, "Do you understand what you are reading? And the Ethiopian eunuch answered, "How can I, unless some one guides me?" And he invited Philip to come up and sit with him. Now the passage of Scripture that he was reading was this:
> 
> 'As a sheep led to the slaughter, or a lamb before his shearers is dumb, so he opened not his mouth. In his humiliation justice was denied him. Who can describe his generation? For his life is taken from the earth.'
> 
> 'About whom, asked the eunuch, does the prophet speak: about himself, or about someone else?' And Philip began from this Scripture and preached Jesus.
>
> Acts 8:26-35

## The Theology of Grace

The eunuch was reading from the passage of Scripture known as the Golden Passional. A Passional is a book describing the suffering of saints and martyrs. The Golden Passional is the fifty-third chapter of the book of the prophet Isaiah, where the prophet, in a vision, foretold the sufferings of Christ. It was here that the eunuch had read.

## On a Desert Road

Philip the Evangelist was led by the Spirit to preach the fulfillment of prophecy in Christ to an Ethiopian eunuch. And it was away from the crowds, away from the cities and the marketplace, that the Spirit led Philip. The place was far removed from the academies, the seminaries, and the places of intellectual attainment. It was removed from the grace and culture of the universities and the preoccupation with refinement. The Spirit led him out into the solitude where nothing existed but Heaven and earth, man and God, and the leading of the Spirit. It was out on desert road with nothing to distract contemplation.

It was in the wilderness of Midian that Moses learned obedience and trust in God through the things he had suffered. It was there that the angel of God's presence appeared to him as a flame of fire in the midst of the burning bush. And once again, in the wilderness on this desert road, the fulfillment of the promise was revealed to the eunuch. It was revealed that the passion of our Lord was according to all that the prophets had written. In many and various ways, God spoke to the fathers of the Savior's passion, even as by the Spirit of the Lord.

## Our Lord's Passion

Philip the Evangelist preached Jesus from the Golden Passional in Isaiah where the passion of our Lord was foretold. The Ethiopian understood the meaning of the passage quite clearly. His only question was to whom this passage applied—to the prophet

Isaiah himself or to some other person? Philip well understood the eunuch's uncertainty. Philip may have been one of our Lord's disciples or surely a close follower of our Lord. When Jesus pointedly told his disciples that he would be delivered over to the Gentiles, be mocked scourged, abused, and put to death, they became confused. It is narrated in the Gospel that the disciples understood none of these things.

On the way to Emmaus, two of our Lord's followers were also confused about his passion. As Jesus drew near to his followers, he said,

> O fools, and slow of heart to believe all that the prophets have written: Ought not Christ to have suffered these things, and to enter into his glory? And beginning at Moses and all the prophets, he expounded unto them in all the scriptures the things concerning himself.
>
> Luke 24:25-27

These followers of Christ were slow of heart to believe all that the prophets had written, but this was not so for the Ethiopian. He believed the prophets that, according to the will of the Father, the Redeemer should suffer and die. Philip told the Ethiopian about the passion of Christ, and he began reaching for the Ethiopian's heart.

The Spirit has led the Evangelist out to the desert road. As Philip preached Christ, the gentle grace of the Holy Spirit warmed the eunuch's soul and opened up his heart to be receptive to the Word of the Lord. The Ethiopian believed and he turned to the Lord Jesus. And when all had become clear to him, he stopped the chariot. Out on that desert road he stopped, for even in the desert, God had provided. Here was water—water like the stream of God's grace. What was to prevent his baptism? And Philip and the eunuch went down into the water and Philip baptized the eunuch.

## Our Lord's Passion and You

At times, life can be like this: a desert road in the midst of a wilderness, void of all spiritual significance, and dry and barren of all spiritual grace. Although surrounded by countless people, one can still be isolated and alone. Life has taught us that flesh and blood can endure only so much before the soul cries out for grace, for God, and for the renewal of the Spirit. The grace and love of our Lord Jesus Christ, the remedial touch of his passion, can do some of its best work for you out in the desert when you find yourself wandering in a wilderness.

Like his Savior, John the Baptist was led out into the wilderness to be nourished. Away from the crowds and into the quiet solitude of life he was led by the Spirit. There in the desert, God spoke to his soul, strengthened his spirit with divine fortitude, and made him like a mighty wind that could rend the rocks in pieces. John called for repentance and was ready to lay the axe to the root of the tree. Out in the wilderness, he was formed into a strong man of the Kingdom.

God in Jesus Christ will meet you when you are out on some desert road. You and he will be there, and the encounter will come as if face to face. For the moment, nothing else will really matter. When isolated or alone and flesh and blood can endure no longer, we can turn to the Lord Jesus. When the heart cries out for grace, for God, and for renewal of the spirit, our Savior will be there. He, too, was led by the Spirit into the wilderness for forty lonely days. There he struggled with truth and reality. There he fought for the kingdom and for you. And worthy is he as the Lamb that was slain to receive honor and power and glory forever.

Christ is your way into the Kingdom and your peace with God. He is the Crucified One—the sacrifice on the golden altar. His Spirit can lead you from any place on a desert road to truth and light and to spiritual grace once more. In the quiet stillness of a desert night at the early dawn of the new day or during the first rays of light from the east, look for the coming of the Spirit.

Like the wind, it blows where it will. Like the still, small voice of the morning, he will speak to your heart. See and know at the cross the Lamb of God who takes away the sins of the world for you and for your children forever. You will know the reality of our Lord's atonement his saving passion, and his love.

# Justification

Since man is unable to walk perfectly before God, the question arises: "How can a man be just (made right) with God?" The issue is that of justification. Justification means being made right with God. One of the cardinal doctrines of the Protestant expression of the Christian religion is "justification by faith." In his letter to the church in Rome, the apostle Paul wrote,

> But now is the righteousness of God manifested, being witnessed by the law and the prophets...*Even the righteousness of God which is by faith in Jesus Christ. Being freely justified by his grace through the redemption which is in Christ Jesus.*
>
> Romans 3:21-24

Again, we remind you that when we refer to faith in Christ as Lord and Savior, we also mean faith in his redeeming work. When we acknowledge Christ as our Redeemer, God bestows his grace upon us, his favor, and his lovingkindness toward us in Christ Jesus. He deems us accepted in the Beloved. We are covered over by the righteousness of Christ. We are made right with God, being freely justified by his grace. On what basis are we justified?

We are justified (made right with God) through the redemption in Christ Jesus. We may ask the question in another way. With all my faults, failures, and sins, how can I still be right with God? The answer given in the New Testament is a simple one. We are made right with God through faith in our Redeemer, Christ Jesus. This includes faith in his redeeming work. Then we may ask, "How is Christ's redeeming work applied to our souls?"

The mediation comes through the Holy Spirit. The Spirit moves over the face of the waters and over the length and breadth of the land. He applies the efficacy of the redeeming work of Christ to our souls. Even though we are separated from the cross by centuries, the atonement of Jesus Christ applies to all who place their faith in him. In ages past, in the present, and in all time still to come, it is still the redeeming work of Christ that is vital to our souls. It is still the Holy Spirit that applies the work of the crucified Christ to our spiritual heart. And justification by faith means exactly that. Being justified, we are made right with God through the one in whom our faith is reposed. It is so by the love of God the Father—and through the grace of our Lord Jesus Christ.

When all is said and done, the efficacy of our faith, its surety, depends upon him in whom we have believed—Jesus Christ our Lord. In faith we receive him. We embrace him. We avail ourselves of his love and grace, and we accept the gift of his salvation. Only he is the Savior of our souls yesterday, today, and forever. We will not listen to those who advocate salvation by character. It can never happen. According to the prophet, those who seek to stand in God's sight on the basis of their own merit have nothing to offer but filthy rags. They cannot stand. They cannot abide the day of his coming. We must rest under the shadow of the cross as under a great rock and upon the sacrifice that Christ offered on the cross.

In the knowledge of the atonement of Jesus Christ, we have the gift of peace with God and rest for our souls. Faith and trust are two simple words, but they have profound significance and come with the gift of eternal redemption. According to God's promise, the righteousness of God becomes our very own in and through the grace of our Lord Jesus Christ. Our fellowship is with him and with the Father. The fellowship of the redeemed is founded on a personal trust in our Lord's ability to save and on our faith that he will do so if we come to him with our whole heart.

The Christ of the cross is our salvation who, when we come to him with believing hearts, will impart unto us forgiveness, absolution, and grace for all of our sins. With that will come the relief of conscience from all our burdens, no matter how heavy laden our souls may be. When we come to him, he will cover us over with his grace and righteousness. How simple, how beautiful, and how far reaching. We are justified, made right with God through our faith and trust in Christ Jesus, and by being justified by his grace, we have become heirs of eternal life.

In our time, in our churches, and in the hearts of our people, the seasons of refreshment must come once again. The enabling power of the Holy Spirit must come once again and speak to our hearts, souls, and minds of things unseen, of the saving grace of our Lord Jesus Christ, and of personal faith that we must place on him. The teachings of St. Paul are needed today more than ever. The world is still inclined to believe that man can work out his own salvation. But he is far, far from the millennium of peace and even farther from peace with God. Though the desire for universal peace is strong in every one of us, a warless world is not our first vocation. We must seek first the Kingdom of God and his righteousness, for even the law and the prophets so instruct us. And so will every man of God.

"Now the righteousness of God is manifested, being witnessed by the law and the prophets, even the righteousness of God which is by faith in Christ Jesus. Being freely justified by his grace which is in Christ Jesus" (Romans 3:21-24).

"Therefore we conclude that a man is justified by faith" (Romans 3:28).

With the enabling power of the Spirit, the season of refreshment will come. And with it will come the assurance of grace and pardon. There will be the lifting of the burden for those who are heavy laden. And the doors of the Kingdom will open wide once more. The church will once again witness streams of our Savior's grace and glory. Not only will the hearts of the people be strangely warmed, but also their souls will be quickened and made alive unto God. We will sense his presence and feel his love, and we will have obtained our own personal assurance of the reality and certitude of our faith in Christ Jesus. And that can be real glory.

## Adoption

In one of his letters, St. Paul wrote that we are heirs of the kingdom through the adoption that we have in Christ Jesus. In our seeking to understand God, we find him as our heavenly Father through Christ our Lord. In Psalm 89, the author wrote, "My steadfast love shall be with him. He shall cry to me, 'Thou art my Father, my God, and the Rock of my Salvation'" (Psalm 89:26). The apostle Paul wrote to the Galatians, "For in Christ Jesus you are all sons of God" (Galatians 3:36). And because we are sons and daughters of God, "God has sent the Spirit of his Son into our hearts, crying, my Father, my Father" (Galatians 4:6).

From a state of enmity and alienation, we have been reconciled to God as our heavenly Father through the adoption that we have in Christ Jesus. We have become the sons and daughters of God in our spiritual essence. We are heirs of God's kingdom of grace and truth and are joint heirs with Christ. In a very true sense, through his act of creation, God is the universal Father of all men. But the vast majority is still in moral estrangement from him. They remain at enmity with God. They refuse to acknowledge him as their creator whom they should obey. In Scripture, the concept of adoption is simplicity itself.

The people of Israel were adopted by God to be a kingdom of priests and a holy nation. Through them, as spiritual heirs, the Gospel of grace and knowledge of God would be brought to all the peoples of the world. On the night of the Passover, Israel had been redeemed from the bondage of Egypt. And at Mount Sinai, they were adopted as God's people when God made a covenant with them. It was the spiritual implication of that covenant that was essential. They would be his people, and he would be their God.

In the New Testament, adoption refers to those who have acknowledged God as Father, Son, and Holy Spirit and have placed their faith in Christ Jesus. Being adopted into the Kingdom of God, they have become members of the household of faith. They are those who with patience and hope wait for the appearing of our great God and Savior the Lord Jesus Christ. God, in his grace, has received us into the relationship of sons and daughters through the redemption and adoption that we have in Christ Jesus. As spiritual heirs of the Kingdom of grace, we are the heirs of God on earth. And because of this, we have direct access to God in prayer.

## Sanctification

Israel was born as a nation on the night of the Passover when they were redeemed from the land of Egypt. They were sanctified at Mount Horeb when God made a covenant with his people. In its spiritual essence, Israel was to be a kingdom of priests and a holy nation. Sanctified by their spiritual relationship as God's people, Israel was to act as God's redemptive agency. They would be a light unto the Gentiles. When redeemed, adopted, and sanctified by God, Israel was to be the mediator of God's grace and purpose of mercy. They were the people through whom God mediated the knowledge of himself in the law and the prophets. It was through them as concerning the seed of David that Christ our Lord was born as the Son of God and Savior of the world.

It was Israel's spiritual relationship with God that mattered. They were to grow spiritually and conduct themselves righteously before God. Although Abraham was told to walk and be perfect before God, none of them were perfect, and neither are we.

As long as human beings struggle in the body, no one will be perfect. Perfection or righteousness is not a condition precedent to the redemption that we have in Christ Jesus. Our righteousness and standing before God, according to the Christian faith, is in Christ Jesus. He is the "Lord our Righteousness." If we cannot expect to be perfect, what then are we to do? Like Israel was expected to do in its relationship with God, we are expected to grow spiritually. Again, as with Israel, it is our spiritual relationship with God that matters.

The actual progress of the Christian life is to be conformed to the image or to the likeness of Christ. We should attempt to achieve this at least in some traits of his personality. It can also be an attempt to be attuned to the fruit of the Spirit. But if we struggle to achieve this in our own strength, it will never occur. It must be something else: the silent, unseen working of the Spirit in our members. Even so, through it all there will be a "warring" in our members, and while the spirit is ever willing, the flesh is ever weak. The spirit struggles against the flesh and the flesh against the spiritual life.

The Holy Spirit works in our souls, in our wills, in our motives, and in our reasons for doing what we do. In a word, the true concept of sanctification refers to spiritual growth in the life of the believer. We know that there is an ebb and flow in our spiritual life. We wonder at this. Why should it be so? At times, like David, we agonize over it. David prayed, "Take not thy Holy Spirit from me" (Psalm 51:11). And yet God chose to shed abroad his love in our hearts through the Holy Spirit. Again, on occasion, we may ask, "Why is it necessary for us to become more spiritual? How is this achieved? Is a deeper spiritual life only the gift of a few?" Let us look at Jacob, Israel, a prince with God, after whom the people were named. Scripture states that he had power with God and man.

It was not until he had tired of twenty years of contest with his uncle Laban that Jacob decided to return home. It was on his return to the land that had been promised that Jacob became Israel. At the Ford of Jabbok, when he wrestled with the Angel of the Lord, the real Jacob was born. This occurred only after "Jacob after the flesh" had been wounded deeply and disabled in the hallow of his thigh. During his struggle with the angel of the Lord, Jacob recognized him—for whose favor he had previously wrestled with cunning and deception as a supplanter.

Does it seem so strange that God's ways will never be through the cunning or deception of man's devices? Jacob, after recognizing the angel, asked to be blessed. He was blessed, and his name was changed to Israel—a prince with God. What had occurred? The old Jacob was wounded and disabled because the arm of flesh was stricken. Henceforth, the influence of the Spirit would more and more assume control over Israel's actions, desires, and motives. In his new spiritual character, Jacob was given power with God and man. God blessed him there, and Jacob called the name of the place Peniel, for he had seen God face to face and his soul recovered. He halted upon his thigh. On that day, Israel, a prince with God was born but only after "Jacob after the flesh" had been wounded and disabled.

The teaching from the Ford of Jabbok is this: all his life, Jacob had wrestled for the promise with Isaac his father, with Esau his brother, with Laban his uncle, and even with God. He hoped to inherit the spiritual blessing in his own strength through device and cunning. After the Ford of Jabbok, he could no longer contend in his own strength because he was deeply wounded and disabled. His reliance would now be completely on God and on God's ability to carry out his own purpose. In prayer, he would persevere and endeavor to move under the leading of the Spirit.

It seems as though before the spiritual influence of God's grace can have an effect on us, the old man in us must first be deeply wounded and disabled. At what cost must we learn that when strong in ourselves, our seeming strength is nothing but weakness? When weak in ourselves, it is Jesus Christ who strengthens us.

## The Theology of Grace

"For we all with open face beholding as in a glass the glory of the Lord, are transformed into this same image, from glory to glory even as by the Spirit of the Lord" (2 Corinthians 3:18).

We ought to progress from the glory of being created in God's image to the glory of his Spirit residing in us. We move from the glory of God's Spirit working in us to the glory of the Spirit working faith in us. And the glory of faith points us to the substance of things hoped for, and to the evidence of things not seen. Through it all, we have the ministration of righteousness. For behold, the old man is passing away, and all things are becoming new.

It is to the eternal testimony of God's grace that the old schoolmaster is overridden by the cords of love. And the testimony of God's grace is this: "Blessed is he whose transgression is forgiven, whose sin is covered. Blessed is the man unto whom the Lord imputeth not iniquity" (Psalm 32:1-2), and who is covered over by the grace of our Lord Jesus Christ. We are being translated from one degree of glory to another, from the glory of the image of the earthly to the glory of the image of the heavenly. And all is a manifestation of the amazing grace of God.

Concerning the concept of the outer man and the inner man, the outer man is but the overt revelation of the inner. He is the picture of the heart, motives, passions, and inner disposition of the individual. It is in actions or forbearance that the heart of a man is more clearly seen. In all men, as in Jacob, the outward man is controlled by the inner man. The question is this: if the inner man is spiritual, why do we have the dichotomy of living in the spirit in the inner man but living according to the passions of the outward man?

In using the term *outward man* broadly, it is simply that the uncultivated tendency of the natural man tends to control immediate responsive actions. If we have been struck, we wish to strike back instinctively. If we have been injured, we seek vengeance instinctively. If we have been slandered, we seek to return the favor. It is hard to sit still in the face of personal injury, and no man who calls himself a man is born to turn the other cheek.

If the instinctive responses of the natural man are going to be change, it will take nothing short of a drastic revolution of outward characteristic display. This means that the responsive instincts—the senses, passions, desires, hungers, feelings, drives, and even the instinct for self-preservation—will have to be tempered. They will have to be cultivated, blended, and changed. How does this occur?

If the Spirit of God has been shed abroad in our hearts, then Christ has made his abode there. When Christ has made his abode in the temple of clay, then the outward man must surrender to the impulse of the inner spiritual man. But the natural man, the outer man, does not surrender without a fight. And it is usually a long, hard fight. That is why St. Paul said that he had a warring in his members. To make him surrender, the outer man must be wounded in some way. When wounded, he is disabled, and a great deal of his power is gone. One's animation will now come from his inner man, who has been renewed after the image of him who created him. And if the animating, spiritual influence of our Lord now begins to assume control, then the responsive actions will have been tempered, cultivated, and blended. Little by little, the outward man begins to be conformed to the inner man. Then, in some small degree, we move from the image of the earthly to the image of the heavenly.

## The Perseverance of the Saints

Perseverance refers to the continuance in a state of grace until it is succeeded by a state of glory when we depart this life to be with the Lord. We persevere because we have been embraced in the grace of our Lord Jesus Christ. He is able to keep us from falling. Admittedly, we may stumble and fall as did Simon Peter, but the strength of the Christian faith is in its constant and never-failing ability to renew and to restore to a state of grace. In this creative ability of our religion and in the faithfulness of our Lord lies the concept of the perseverance of the saints.

The apostle Paul wrote that no sentence of condemnation fell on those who were in Christ Jesus. Even though we have been redeemed, on occasion we appear as a soul struggling in faith. We still have all our faults and all our sins. He who denies this denies the truth, and the truth is not in him. But we look to him who is our hope in prayer and in confession. And Christ is faithful and just to forgive us our sins and to cleanse us from all unrighteousness. He ministers in the heavenly sanctuary, making intercession on our behalf. Another basis for the perseverance of the saints lies in the efficacy of the atonement of Jesus Christ and on his endless, glorified priesthood. In our mainline Protestant churches, our Lord's ability to preserve us in his grace is known as the doctrine of the Perseverance of the Saints. In the more evangelical expressions of the Protestant faith, the doctrine is known as Eternal Security.

Our Lord said, "That which my father has given me, I will keep for ever" (John 6:27). These words were meant to give us a sense of quiet security. In our human frailty, we tend to forget their eternal significance. We get busy here and there, and the assurance of these words passes out of mind. Then we fret and worry. We become anxious and restless. Then we long once again for a sense of confidence and calm. Quiet security—who does not want that for himself, his family, and his loved ones? Long ago, the prophet Isaiah wrote that in calmly resting our safety lieth, in quietness and confidence shall be our strength.

In the story Death Comes to the Archbishop, the reason why the Acoma Indians of Arizona took to the cliff-dwellings on the high mesas was because they sought security. On the plains below, periodic wars with plunder and death were conducted by the Apaches and the Arapahos. Thy killed the men, took the women and children away, and destroyed the villages. Thus, the Acoma took to the high places for safety and security. We can rest calmly on the promises of God and on our Lord's ability to keep us safe. His spirit will rest with us as a seal of his grace and as a token of our Savior's promise. We must be persuaded that we are in his keeping.

Before the Battle of Trafalgar, Robert Stratford, one of Nelson's commanders, told of the privations and hardships the men had to endure prior to the battle. Then he said that the one thing that kept them going and held them together was that they were with Nelson. Being with Nelson, a strong and victorious leader overcame their fear of failure in spite of the privations they had endured, and they achieved victory. The members of the early church surely must have felt that way. By abiding in Christ and being in his presence, they became triumphant. They conceived of Jesus as being with them in all their sufferings. And with the sense of his presence, they carried out their mission in the face of the world's opposition and mockery. In Christ's keeping, they conquered. And so may you and I here and now.

## The Reality of Adult Conversion

The redemption that we have in Christ Jesus is no fancy or fiction. It is a concrete reality in the lives of men and women who have turned to the Lord Jesus throughout the Christian centuries. And it began in the lives of adult men and women. We will discuss the conversion of Sergius Paulus, a Roman Governor, and Lydia, a business woman. We will conclude the section on the doctrine of salvation with Paul's relating his conversion experience.

### Sergius Paulus, a Roman Governor

This story is found in Acts 13. Barnabas and Saul, being sent forth by the Holy Spirit from the church in Antioch, came down to the harbor of Seleucia. From there they sailed to Cyprus. They made a missionary journey throughout the whole Island of Cyprus. At Paphos, they encountered a magician, a prophet of lies, named Bar-Jesus. The magician was in the company of the proconsul,

## The Theology of Grace

Sergius Paulus, a man of understanding and the Roman governor of the island of Cyprus.

Having heard of these two preachers of the Way, the proconsul summoned Barnabas and Saul into his presence. He sought to hear about the word of God. But there stood forth against them the magician, seeking to divert the proconsul from the faith. But Saul, henceforth called Paul, filled with the Holy Spirit, looked fixedly at him. Paul said, "Oh thou, full of all guile and all villainy, thou son of the devil, thou enemy of all righteousness, wilt thou not cease to pervert the right way of the Lord? And now behold, the hand of the Lord is upon thee, and thou shalt be blind, not seeing the sun for a season." And immediately there fell on him a mist and darkness, and he went about seeking for someone to lead him by the hand. When the Proconsul saw what had been done, he believed, being struck at the heart at the teaching of the Lord.

### Sergius Paulus

The Greek inscription of Soloi on the north cast of the Island of Cyprus is dated "in the Proconsulship of Paulus." One can note the biblical accuracy of the title, *proconsul*, as applied to the Roman Governor of Cyprus. The reality of this adult conversion is seen in that it related to a definite individual who is named, characterized, and identified by title. He was a cultivated and educated man, and was in a position of authority and power. He was man of understanding and, evidently, came from a noble family. He appeared attentive to his duties and kept attuned to the current events and thoughts of his day. He seemed acquainted with the disciplines of economics, civics, philosophy, and ethics.

When the Gospel team of Barnabas and Paul came to the city of Paphos, they did as they usually did in all the cities they sought to evangelize. They began preaching Jesus in the synagogue of Paphos. Knowledge of this new religion and moral philosophy, called "the Teaching of the Lord," and its two teachers appeared to have spread rapidly. Soon they acquired a reputation and appeared to be inspired and were talked about throughout the entire city.

It did not take long for the report about these two itinerant scholars and teachers and their new kind of religious teaching to reach the Roman governor. Being a highly educated man who was interested in current events, philosophy, and morals, his attention was attracted by the news that these two men were giving public teachings on their new religion. Sergius Paulus knew what was going on in his island. Admittedly, traveling teachers of this class were well known through the empire at that time. But this was not what really caught the interest of the Proconsul.

Indeed, it was a new teaching, but it was also a new teaching that claimed to have power to change men's lives for the better. It was proclaimed as a teaching about peace and righteousness and morals. It told about the right way of the Lord. The Word had been made flesh and was full of grace and truth. There was one anointed of God with the Holy Spirit. It was about one who healed diseases and who had power on earth to forgive sins. They spoke of the Crucified One and now the Risen One. The Proconsul was very interested in this Gospel which they proclaimed, a certain apostolic message about a Savior called Jesus.

It came as a message of the Word of God and belief in the name Jesus Christ the Son of God. All came within the Kingdom of Heaven, and it came as good news. It was absolutely breathtaking to a man of understanding such as Sergius Paulus. It seemed as though Sergius Paulus was a man who may have hungered for knowledge of the Kingdom of righteousness and peace and, unknown to him, who also sought for joy in the Holy Spirit. He would hear a specimen of their message. He sought for a demonstration about their subject on the nature of God, this Christ who was called Jesus, and about God's action toward human beings.

### The Attempted Diversion

But there was a magician, a certain Bar-Jesus, who appeared to have had access to the proconsul's court. Regardless of what system of thought or religion he represented, he was an enemy of the Christian faith. He may have been motivated by fear of losing his position of influence with the governor. On the other hand, the magician may have been exactly what St. Paul said he was—an enemy of all righteousness, full of guile and all villainy, and a very son of the devil. He sought to divert the proconsul from knowledge of the faith.

That was enough for Paul. It was more than enough. Henceforth, Barnabas no longer led. It was then Paul who stood forth as the foremost champion of the new faith. In one clear stroke, he exposed the Jewish impostor. We can only imagine that Barnabas and Paul may have been well into their exposition of the new religion. Apparently, the Proconsul had been listening with much interest and pleasure to the Gospel of the grace of the Lord Jesus Christ, when Bar-Jesus, the enemy of the Gospel, intervened and attempted to divert the proconsul from the faith. Instead, for a season, he would be made to cease to pervert the right way of the Lord.

At the word of Paul, the enemy of all righteousness was struck blind. Immediately, Bar-Jesus was in a realm of mist and darkness. He had to go about looking for someone to lead him by the hand. When Paul stepped forth and took the lead in the propagation of the new religion, his words and acts were accompanied by a transport of power. Surely it attested to the grace given to Paul in the ministry of the Gospel. It manifested the divine approval of his mission. And this grace given to St. Paul justified to the world his apostolate in the Gospel of Jesus Christ.

### What the Proconsul Saw

When he saw what had been done, the proconsul believed, and he turned to the Lord Jesus. This was his conversion. He believed because he was struck to the heart at the teaching of the Lord. But what is more, Sergius Paulus believed St. Paul to be the recipient of a direct revelation from God that was guided and controlled by the Holy Spirit. The Roman Governor saw that St. Paul was enabled by the divine power to move the forces of nature in a way that ordinary men could not. It was evident to Sergius Paulus that Paul's word was with power and with the force of the Holy Spirit. He was struck to the heart, and he believed on the teaching of the Lord.

## Adult Conversion

In apostolic times, during the birth and early growth of the church, adult conversion was very much a reality. In the progress of the church, it was an everyday thing. They called this response of men and women to the Gospel *a turning to the Lord Jesus*. And while it may have been true that there were not many wise, not many powerful, and not many proud among the adherents of the new religion, it drew from all classes and conditions of men. Admittedly, all may have been poor in spirit and many more slow of heart. Nevertheless, the new faith drew from all classes because it was the simple Gospel of the grace of our Lord Jesus Christ. The Savior's grace touched the heart and filled the longing of the soul for vision of God. Those who responded were not all slaves, looking for a way out of this life. Nor was it solely the poor that hungered and thirsted for a gospel of righteousness that turned to the faith of the Crucified One. Nor was the early church composed mostly of widows and orphans.

There were, among its many congregations, men of stature, women of beauty, cultivated men of power and influence, and men of understanding like Sergius Paulus. There was Cornelius, the good centurion. All these and many more turned to the Lord Jesus in adult life. The simple Gospel message has lost none of its power to make an impact on human lives, not since the early days when it was first proclaimed. The Holy Spirit is still like the wind, blowing where it will. It ever moves over the face of the waters and ever searches the broad reaches of the land for men, women, and children called of God.

The grace of our Lord Jesus Christ can still be utterly breathtaking to the poor in spirit, to the slow of heart, and to men and women of understanding. The Gospel message and the Holy Spirit have lost none of their power to strike men to the heart with the Word of the Lord. Those who are wise in their own eyes may still be seeking to divert some individuals from the faith. But they shall not stand in the Day of Judgment, or scoffers in the congregation of the righteousness. A mist and darkness have fallen on them, and they shall not be able to pervert the right way of the Lord. Actually, they, with all their sophistication, are like the blind magician, seeking for someone to lead them by the hand.

Sergius Paulus clearly saw that it was only the Word of the Lord, the Gospel of grace, that can strike at the heart and kindle the fire of the Spirit in the human soul. It is solely the Word of the Lord that will cause not only children but also men and women to turn to the Lord Jesus. Though the word of the Lord may come in an hour of quietness in the worship service or at home or even when sorrow has touched your life, in the appointed time it will come. And though it is ever so gentle, and though it is like the still, small voice from the cleft of the rock, its coming to you will be with grace and power. It will come to claim you and to turn you now and forever to the Lord Jesus Christ.

## The Western World: A Woman Named Lydia

It was impossible for the Gospel to be contained within the small boundaries of Judea. Nor could it be restricted to the Roman Province of Asia. It was impossible for the progress of the new religion to be held within national boundaries. It broke every barrier placed before it, for God was not the God and Father of the Jews only but also of the Gentles. God the creator is the

Father of all men. A God of knowledge is the Lord, working out his curious design. From Troas, a harbor city of the province of Asia and a link with the continent of Europe, came the apostolic message—and the evangelization of western civilization began.

It began with a woman, a mother, whose heart the Word of the Lord had deeply penetrated. Lydia was a woman who feared the Lord God. She was a woman of stature and grace and an intelligent businesswoman, and she was strong in spirit. She dealt in fine purple and ran a shop of the highest quality. Yet, in the presence of the Lord, Lydia was humble, and as to his ministers, she was slow in judgment. For the sake of the Kingdom, she was kind, generous, and gracious. Lydia was the mother of the Christian religion for the whole of western civilization.

Led by the Spirit, the missionaries Paul and Silas departed from the city of Troas and came to Philippi. Philippi has a Roman garrison and was a leading city of the province of Macedonia. With the missionaries came the young Greek physician, Luke, who narrated the event. Philippi was founded as a Roman colony, and there seemed to have been no synagogue there. There were scarcely any Jews in the imperial service. Luke wrote, "On the Sabbath day we went forth without the gate (of the city) by the riverside where there was wont to be held a meeting for prayer; and we sat down and spake to the women that came together" (Acts 16:13).

"And a certain woman name Lydia, a seller of purple, of the city of Thyatira, a God fearing, [a person who worshipped God] was a hearer: and the Lord opened up her heart to give heed unto the things spoken by Paul" (Acts 16:14).

The Spirit that directed the work of Paul and Silas also worked in the heart of Lydia. "And when she and her entire household were baptized, she besought us, saying, 'If you have judged me to be faithful, come to my house and abide there.' And she constrained us" (Acts 16:15).

## Lydia: A Business Woman

Lydia was another individual who turned to the Lord Jesus in adult life. She was a native of the Roman province of Asia, from the city of Thyatira. In this city was located one of the churches to whom one of the letters in the Revelation of St. John was addressed. When the missionaries came to Philippi, Lydia appeared to have been settled there for some time. She had established her business. Luke mentioned no husband, and yet she was a householder. In all likelihood, she may have been a widow and the head and support of her family. Lydia was a Gentile—the first convert to Christianity on the European Continent. Lydia chose Jesus Christ for herself and for her entire household.

## A Slow and Gradual Turning

Later, in his book of the Acts, Luke tells of another conversion to Christianity. There was a jailer whose conversion was sudden and dramatic. It was even preceded by an earthquake. But it was not like this with Lydia. Hers was a slow, quiet, and gradual turning to the Lord Jesus. She already revered the Lord God, for she went regularly with the Jewish women to the place of prayer by the riverside. That was where Paul and Silas found the woman. She could not tell you the moment or even the day when the final truing occurred. But there was no doubt in her heart that it had occurred. She, like the good Centurion, Cornelius of the Italian cohort, was of the God-fearing. Even before the coming of Paul, she was not far from the Kingdom of Heaven. Inwardly, she may have been seeking for the Kingdom of righteousness and peace.

We can imagine that when she first heard Paul preach the Word, there had been no outward visible impact of the apostolic message. She said not a word and had withheld judgment on all. But the seed had been planted. Slowly it grew, for she became a regular hearer of the Word. And the roots of the word sank deep, for God had opened up her heart to give heed to the things spoken by Paul.

## Lydia's Response

Lydia heard the message for several weeks. She became a regular hearer of the Gospel preached by Paul. There had been no sudden rending of the veil, no heavenly vision, and no great outpouring to the Spirit as on Pentecost. Still, the slow realization grew in her mind what she had already acknowledged in her heart, the Christ of God as her Savior. It was the gentle, quite, and unseen work of the Holy Spirit, bringing her to grace and leading her gently home. She confessed that she had turned to the Lord Jesus. The certainty of her faith was seen in this; when she realized she had been turned to the Lord Jesus, she took her entire household with her.

But there was more in her response than just them mere turning to the Lord Jesus. Grace never ceased working in her heart. Like the Widow of Zaraphath who undertook to provide for the prophet Elijah, so did the widow Lydia do unto St. Paul and his missionary team. "If you have judged me to be faithful to the Lord, come to my house and abide with me." And Luke added, "And she constrained us" (Acts 16:15).

## If You Have Found Me Faithful

Of all the churches founded by the apostle Paul, the church of Philippi was the most loyal, the most devoted, and the most self-sacrificing for the cause of Christ. It remained loyal and supportive of the apostle in his work of evangelization throughout his life. The church became like its founder, St. Paul, and like Lydia, its first convert. The church of Philippi, which was headed by a woman, went into partnership with Paul in his propagation of the Gospel. It proved a constant source of comfort and support.

The church in Philippi was instrumental in the founding of every church established by Paul during his subsequent ministry. His letter to the Philippians is the most cordial and affectionate written by Paul. "If you have found me faithful," Lydia had said, "come and abide with me." Time and again, Paul must have done so. We will note a few passages from Paul's letter to the Philippian church.

"I am thankful for your partnership with me in the Gospel, from the first day, until now" (Philippians 1:1).

"You yourselves, Philippians, know that in the beginning no other church entered into partnership with me in the Gospel. You sent unto my needs time and time again" (Philippians 4:15).

"I hold you in my heart" (Philippians 1:7).

## Constraining Love

It is ever so that the love of Christ constrains us. Lydia's words ring true. Christ will permit himself to be constrained by those who seek his presence. When the press of the day seems heavy on us and our spiritual life ebbs low, we can turn to the Lord Jesus. We can constrain him to come and abide with us. For those whom he has judged to be faithful, he will allow himself to be constrained. He will come to you with all his love and grace and open up your heart to be receptive to the Word of the Lord.

## Relating the Conversion Experience

We conclude this division of the theology of grace with the apostle Paul relating his conversion experience. There emerged a heartfelt expression in the apostle's lifelong desire to tell others of his conversion experience. Always, he expressed an earnest desire to tell others of the redemption that comes to us by faith in Christ Jesus. When he came to Athens, the Athenians accused the apostle of babbling and preaching strange gods because he preached Jesus and the resurrection. He never failed to mention the resurrected and glorified Lord. But it was not always this way—not until he met Jesus of Nazareth on that lonely road to Damascus and turned to the Lord Jesus with heart, soul, and mind.

He who turned others to the Lord Jesus had in his adult life become the greatest convert of them all. Having turned to Christ, Paul was impelled to make known what had happened to him. He wanted to tell the whole world how the love and grace of Christ had overwhelmed his soul. He had been overwhelmed, indeed, for "straightway he preaches Christ" (Acts 9:20).

## Before the People

On his last visit to Jerusalem, Paul had not begun by preaching. He made his way to the temple to pay a vow and silently worshipped God. But he was seen by those who opposed the way, and they stirred up the crowd against the apostle. They caused a disturbance and Paul was arrested. He asked permission of the arresting Centurion to speak to the people and it was granted. Paul stretched out his hand and began his appeal.

> "Brethren and fathers...hear the defense which I now make before you" (Acts 22:1 and following). I am one of you, a Jew, educated in the strict manner of the law and zealous for God. I even persecuted this way unto death, delivering into prison both men and women. I was making a journey to Damascus to bind and punish more of these people of the Way. But about noon, suddenly, a great light from Heaven shown about me. And I fell to the ground. I fell to the ground and heard a voice saying to me: "Saul, Saul, why do you persecute me?" (Acts 9:4 RSV).
> And I answered: "Who are you, Lord?" (Acts 9:5)
> And he said to me, "I am Jesus whom you are persecuting." And I said, "What shall I do, Lord?" And he said, "Rise, and go; to Damascus, and there you will be told all that is appointed for you to do."...God has appointed you to know his will, to see the Just One, and to hear a voice from his mouth. You will be a witness for him to all men. You will be a witness of what you have seen and heard.
> The Apostle continued to tell his story. And I returned to Jerusalem and prayed in the temple, and I fell into a trance; and I saw him, the Lord Jesus Christ, saying to me, "Make haste and get quickly out of Jerusalem, for they will

not accept your testimony about me." And he said to me, "Depart, for I will send you far away to the Gentiles."

Up to that point, the people heard Paul relate his conversion experience. But the crowd, upon hearing the word *Gentiles* lost their composure. A great disturbance occurred. Paul was arrested, and the tribunal commanded that he be examined by scourging. But it was not lawful to scourge a man who was a Roman and was un-condemned. Nevertheless, once again, the people in Jerusalem would not accept Paul's testimony about the risen Lord Jesus.

## Before King Agrippa

At this hearing, false allegations were made against Paul by his accusers. His enemies defamed Paul as a pestilent fellow, an agitator among the Jews and a ringleader of the Sect of the Nazarenes. Paul now stood before King Agrippa. As a Roman citizen, Paul appealed to Caesar, but it seemed unreasonable to send a prisoner to Caesar, not indicating the charges that had been alleged against him. Looking at Paul, Agrippa said, "You have permission to speak for yourself…Then Paul stretched out his hand and made his defense" (Acts 26:17).

We will paraphrase his appeal.

"King Agrippa, I now stand before you on trial for the hope in the promise made by God to our Fathers. And for this hope I am accused of the Jews. And yet, oh King, why should it be thought by you a thing incredible that God can raise the dead?

"Now, oh King, about this way, this faith in the redemption that we have in Christ Jesus our Lord, at first, I did many things opposing the name of Jesus of Nazareth and his people. All my life, I had been zealous for God. I shut up many of the saints in prison, and when they were put to death, I cast my vote against them. I persecuted them even into foreign cities.

"In this very cause, I was on the road to Damascus. There, oh King, at midday, I and those that journeyed with me saw a light from Heaven that fell around us. It was a thing unbelievable—absolutely startling. I was overwhelmed and fell to the ground. And I heard a voice saying to me, "Saul, Saul, why do you persecute me? It is a hard thing to kick against the goats?" And I said, "Who are you, Lord?"

"And the Lord said, 'I am Jesus of Nazareth whom you are persecuting.' But rise and stand, for I have appeared to you for this purpose that you should serve and bear witness to the things in which I will appear to you, delivering you from this people and from the Gentiles to whom I will send you. To open their eyes, that they may turn from darkness to light, and turn from the power of Satan to God, and that they may receive the forgiveness of their sins that they may find a place among those who are sanctified by faith in me."

"And, oh King Agrippa, I was not disobedient to the heavenly vision as it appeared to me on that lonely road to Damascus. For I declared to all, both Jew and Gentile, that they should repent of their sins and turn to God and perform deeds worthy of repentance.

"Now, may I be permitted to reason a bit, oh King Agrippa? Though I stand before you accused, I have said nothing but what the prophets and Moses said would come to pass—that Christ must suffer, and, being the first to rise from the dead, he would proclaim light both to our people and to the Gentiles.

But then, Festus intervened, and said in a loud voice, "Paul, you are mad. Your great learning is making you mad."

"Not madness, most excellent Festus," answered Paul, "but the sober truth. I am certain that the king knows these things, for they were not done in a corner." Then the apostle turned to the king, saying, "King Agrippa, do you believe the prophets? King Agrippa, I know you believe the prophets."

The king replied, "In such a short time, Paul, you would make me a Christian?" Then the king arose and withdrew. And Agrippa said to Festus, "This man could have been set free if he had not appealed to Caesar" (Acts 26:1-32).

## The Impelling Power of the Holy Spirit

Paul, who had turned others to the Lord Jesus and who proclaimed the way of salvation to all people, always spoke of the incident that had occurred to him on the way to Damascus. He told of the vision from Heaven of the risen and living Savior. And he told of his personal turning to the Lord Jesus. On that lonely road, he had been overwhelmed by the impelling power of the Holy Spirit and by Christ Jesus in his glorified vesture, which had outshone the sun. He had been overwhelmed by the radiance of the glory, which blinded his sight—but a radiance that had set his soul and life afire as a living sacrifice for his newly found Lord. What happened?

Christ, whom Paul had persecuted so vigorously, had enveloped him in compassionate love, forgiven all his trespasses, accepted him into his Kingdom, and elevated Paul to apostleship in his Gospel. Paul could do nothing but to accept the love and grace of our Lord so freely given. And so forceful was the influence of the Spirit on him that "straightway he preached Christ." He would forever remember the day and the hour at midday when Christ entered and took possession of his life forever.

To know Christ and the power of his resurrection, one must believe in a risen and living Savior. To the risen Savior and his Gospel of grace, Paul surrendered his heart, soul, mind, and life. He would only know Christ crucified and raised from the dead for our justification. It was a marvelous grace that was given to this champion of Jesus Christ. He was a recipient of a love that surpassed knowledge. He had thought himself not worthy to be called an apostle because he had once persecuted the Church of God.

Ever after, Paul was amazed at the grace of Jesus the Nazarene. For the apostle Paul, the grace of Christ overflowed and came with no vengeance. He was amazed that where his sin had abounded, the grace and love of Christ did much more abound. What Paul had struggled so hard to achieve through his "works-righteousness" under the law—acceptance and favor with God—he found in Jesus of Nazareth. He found it in Christ through simple faith and trust and acceptance of the Savior's grace.

As an apostle of the Gospel of Christ, an appointed messenger of the Most High God, Paul proclaimed the way of salvation and declared unto men the counsels of God. His turning to the Lord Jesus had been a total religious experience, and he loved to tell it to others. Christ Jesus had placed him at peace and favor with God—and Christ was the Way. The Spirit of Christ entered Paul, cultivated his soul, took total possession of him, and became sovereign in his life. Absolutely nothing ever again would have dominion over him or over those in whom the Spirit of Christ dwelt. Nothing could dislodge them from the grace of our Lord Jesus Christ.

Paul always remembered the occasion of that great transformation that had occurred within him. He would remember that this was the only way—the way of faith and trust in Christ through the acceptance of his grace. And it is still the way, the way which I leave with you today. Do this. Accept our Savior's love and grace, and he will manifest himself to you. He will come to abide with you and to bring you into his Kingdom of peace and righteousness now and forever.

# CHRISTOLOGY: THE DOCTRINE OF CHRIST

Christology deals mainly with the nature and person of Christ. It deals with concepts about his person, which were revealed through the transition of his earthly ministry. These include the incarnation—God and man, two natures, one person forever—his temptation that fitted him for his work, the transfiguration where Peter, James, and John saw his glory, his humiliation and crucifixion, his resurrection where he conquered death and gave us the hope of immortality, his ascension and the sending of the Holy Spirit, his exaltation at the right hand of God, and finally, the promise of his second advent.

The Second Advent includes his earthly rule for a thousand years, his coming as the judge of the quick and the dead, and the beginning of the new Heaven and new earth. These latter concepts, beginning with his second advent, fall under the division of Eschatology, the doctrine of the last things, and we shall discuss them there.

First of all, we are going to deal with two extraneous concepts about the nature and person of Christ. In these two concepts are included most of the adverse doctrines about the incarnation and the person of Christ. Within these two concepts, in various shades, most other distorted concepts are to be found. These concepts are Sabellianism and Arianism. It may well be that these two ideas were an attempt to arrive at a logical conclusion about the nature of Christ through time-orientated limitations. They may have resulted because men find it difficult and even painful to accept the divine revelation about the true nature of Christ.

Nevertheless, Christianity is a supernatural and spiritual religion. Its greatest supernatural event, its greatest miracle, is the incarnation of God in our Lord Jesus Christ. Again, we remind ourselves that the simple reasoning of the human mind leads us to believe that only God can reveal God and his Christ and his purpose of mercy for the human race. When Peter confessed Christ as his Savior-God, "Thou art the Christ, the Son of the living God," our Lord replied: "Blessed art thou Simon Bar-jona, for flesh and blood has not revealed this unto you, but my Father which is in Heaven" (Matthew 16:17).

Christ told Peter that when he confessed him as the Son of the living God, this knowledge about his person came to Simon Peter by revelation. It was a revealed concept—a manifestation of the grace of God. It is the Spirit of God that gives us the ability to see this truth and to accept Christ as our divine Savior and Lord.

Involved in the discussion on the nature of Christ are the distinguishing features of the Christian religion. These distinguishing features are the Trinity—God in three persons, Father, Son, and Holy Spirit. The Holy Spirit, the Incarnation of God in Jesus Christ, and the indwelling presence and outpouring of the Holy Spirit on the church are all supernatural events of God's grace. St. John reminds us that no one can confess that Jesus is Christ unless the Spirit reveals it to him.

Every attempt to resolve the problem of the unity and diversity within the Trinity in human, time-orientated categories has always led to error. One cannot begin by first excluding the basic presuppositions of the Christian religion and then attempt to reconstruct them by human reason unaided by divine revelation. And finally to add the faith principle, when one is unable to fill out his religious concepts in any other way. Following St. Augustine in this, our faith and the intellectual activity of our minds, our reason and our beliefs, are all one, and they are so from the beginning.

## God the Son: The Incarnation

When Christianity had swept like an ever-advancing tide across Asia Minor and crossed from Troas to the continent of Europe, it moved into every corner of the Roman Empire. It also drew the attention of the more astute of the Latin writers. The Latin writers were in their Golden Age. This new religion, together with the devotion and self-sacrifice of its adherents, attracted their attention. They saw it as a new and strange religious movement that was different from all the other religions of the empire.

The Latin writers were endeavoring to seek its heart, its essence. But in seeking to discover its essence, they were compelled to ascertain some knowledge about the founder of the Christian religion, our Lord Jesus Christ. Tacitus, a Roman historian wrote:

"This was a certain Christ, who lived in…the Roman province of Judea in the reign of Tiberius; and had been brought to capital punishment by the procurator, Pontius Pilate." (cf. Tacitus, Annals xv 44)

Pliny, in his report to the emperor Trajan, wrote, "This Christ was worshipped by Christians as their God" (Pliny Epistles xcvi-xcvii). The Latin writers were looking at the Christian religion from outside of the movement. Tacitus identified him, and Pliny characterized Christ as being worshipped by the Christians as their God.

The belief in Christ as the eternal Son of God, who left his glory and became man and who continues to be God and man in two distinct natures, has been the belief of the Christian Church universal for over two thousand years. Christ is God and man in two distinct natures, yet is one person, forever.

In all branches—Protestant, Roman Catholic, and Greek Orthodox—the church has held to this high belief concerning the nature and person of Christ. The Incarnation of God in Jesus Christ—both God and man, two natures, one person forever—is the greatest miracle and supernatural incident of the Christian religion.

# The Background of Sabellianism and Arianism

In Paul's letter to the Colossians, he wrote, "He is the image of the invisible God...In him were all things created. He is the head of the body, the church...The first-born from the dead...For in him all the fullness of God was pleased to dwell" (Colossians 1:15-19). The church and the individual believer must be aware in whom we abide. Our belief in God the Son is the most energy-infusing belief our faith possesses. If the church is to be kept from dying a slow and lingering death, it must once again renew its faith. It must resound once again in the glory and grandeur of its great beliefs. A great faith with great beliefs, alive with the power of God and the enlightenment of the Holy Spirit, is what the world most needs today.

As to Sabellianism and Arianism, we must remember that they were intellectual attempts to arrive at some logical conclusion about the person of Christ apart from divine revelation. From the multiplicity of a hundred and one gods, the dignity and reality of the Christian movement was gaining wide recognition. It found acceptance throughout the length and breadth of the empire and even within Caesar's own household.

The idea of one God for all the nations and peoples of the world was a new, strange, and exciting teaching. This concept came with the tidal wave of the new faith—Christianity. The new religion also had to contend for recognition against the many pagan religions of the empire. The early Christian apologists stood in the foreground of the battle for recognition. Some of the early Christian writers held up the multiplicity of a hundred and one pagan gods to scorn and ridicule. They reduced the concept of the multiplicity of gods to absurdity. The human mind was reacting from polytheism. In perceptive reaction, the intellectual activity of the human mind was attracted to the new religion, but it was puzzled by the concept of the Trinity.

The question arose of how the Christians could say that they worshipped the one true God when they worshipped their God as Father, Son, and Holy Spirit. Were they not talking about three Gods? For minds limited to a dialectic expression, the three persons of the Godhead posed a basic question in epistemology. This was the problem of the unity and diversity in knowledge. What occurred is that in attempting to come to a solution by human reasoning alone, they moved from one extreme to the other.

## Sabellianism

Sabellianism stressed the unity of God at the expense of the personal distinctions within the Trinity. Sabellianism refused to acknowledge God as a Trinity of three persons. The basic assumption of Sabellianism was that there was only one God but with three manifestations.

They alleged that God made himself known as Father, then as Son, and now as the Holy Spirit. In attempting to hold what they conceived a necessary unity, Sabellianism substituted manifestation for persons. Hence, they excluded all personal distinctions within the Godhead. They claimed some new learning and to be an intellectual movement. Yet the Trinity is so frequently delineated and implied in the New Testament that the average layman or woman could search out the concept. The church rejected Sabellianism as contrary to the revealed teachings of Scripture.

## Arianism

Arianism has been around in one form or another for a very long time. The Arians thought themselves clever and astute. They used double meanings for their words and appeared polished and sophisticated. They presented themselves as theological sophists and made a pretense of being an intellectual movement. They attempted to make a sophisticated presentation of their views, but they fooled no one.

Moreover, they used guile, deceit, and distortions. And when all else failed, they used political power to forward their views. Four emperors and hundreds of bishops were involved in the struggle. But what did the Arians do? They swung the pendulum directly in the opposite direction from Sabellianism.

The Arians so stressed the personality of the Son that they got him out of the Trinity—out of the Godhead. They stressed diversity at the expense of unity. Had they gained the ascendancy, the logical result would have been that they saved the unity of God by the sacrifice of the divinity of Christ. The victory of Arianism would have been the demise of our faith in Christ Jesus as our Savior-God and the end of the Christian religion as portrayed in the New Testament.

## The Arian Jesus

The Arians told us that they held a high view of Jesus. They would acknowledge that the Son was infinitely high; nevertheless, he was still lower than the Father and not quite equal with God. Actually, the Son, because he was so high, was the great intermediary—the mediator between God and man. Do not these words sound pious? Furthermore, the Arians claimed not to be dogmatic. However, for the sake of grace, they paid extreme compliments to Jesus because he was of supreme religious value to us. (Hence, we have the heresy of the "value judgments.") They acknowledge not only Christ's human nature but stress that it was a very good human nature. And although Jesus was only a creature, he displayed that winsomeness and purity of life that made him gracious. Every true Christian, they asserted, ought to make his way of life their own way of life.

Even though Jesus was not of the same substance of God in the incarnation, "somehow" he had the "value" of God for us. Therefore, we may worship him and accept his message. The human Christ served to reveal God the Father to us and, in fact, he pointed the way. The Arians wrote that there was a time when God was not the Father. They asserted that the Son is a creature and a work; neither is he like in essence with the Father nor is he the true natural Word of the Father. Moreover, the Arians alleged that the Son was subject to change and variation.

To the average layman then, as well as to the average layman today, their anti-Trinitarian construction and implication were obvious. If the Arians were to win, it had to be by guile, deception, and by a show of intellectualism. They had to show that the Trinitarian concept of the church was based on sheer credulity. They failed.

## By an Open Statement of the Truth

The Arians and their cunning and their ruse were exposed by Athanasius. He did so by plain and simple words and an open statement of the truth. Athanasius, Bishop of Alexandria, rested his all on the Lord God, possessed a quiet, calm soul, and was clear-eyed and single minded. He used simple and direct thinking and was a man of God. Like the prophet Isaiah and like St. John, his voice was like the sound of many waters because it rang with the sense and presence of the Almighty. Christianity possessed him and became a possessing reality in his heart, mind, and soul. It pervaded and dominated his thinking, his feelings, and his actions.

Athanasius knew, as you and I must surely know, that to keep Christianity living and filled with life, it had to keep thinking. It must be kept vital and strong. It does make a difference how we conceive Christ's nature. He must ever remain the Incarnation— our Savior-God. Athanasius felt this, sensed this, and knew it in his heart, soul, and mind. He was absolutely committed to keeping the church doctrines in line with accurate, honest, and correct theological thinking.

## For Us Today

Our church and our people must be aroused by way of remembrance, aroused to a new interest in doctrine, and aroused to a new interest in the great teachings of the church. For the very life of the church, there must be a revival of strong doctrinal preaching. Let us be simple and honest with ourselves. Let us acknowledged this truism—a half-hearted Gospel is not going to redeem anyone or preserve the church. We are not for one instant talking about a cold and lifeless formula, or even about creeds. We are talking about the great doctrines and teachings of the church. We would want to feel that it is the very life of our church that its cardinal doctrines contain. We must open up our lives to them and be immersed in their faith, life, vitality, and warmth. We want a living Church with a living doctrine.

Involved in all of this is the efficacy of the atonement of Jesus Christ and our justification by faith in him. This is the essence of the redemption that we have in Christ our Lord. We must be persuaded that nothing less than God Incarnate can meet the needs of sinful man. He is God the Son, both God and man, two natures, and one person for ever—the very Incarnation of God—He is our Lord and Savior. We dare not depend on the most exalted creature no matter how much value he may have for us.

If the church is to be robust and vital, then Christology must be lifted out of the nebulous haze characterizing most of our modern thinking and preaching. It does make a difference who Christ was, what he did, and how he did it. If we are true to the church then we ought not to settle simply for a pious agnosticism about the person and nature of Christ. If we cannot be sure that our Lord is no more than a creature, then our faith is vacated of all significance.

We feel that we cannot say this strongly enough; the theology of reverent ignorance about the person of Christ ought not to be named among us. We believe that just a cursory reading of the New Testament, church history, the Apostolic Fathers, the great reformers, and the creeds of the church will prove us right.

"[Christ] is the image of the invisible God…In him were all things created…He is the head of the body, the church; and the first born from the dead…For in him all the fullness of God was pleased to dwell" (Colossians 1:15-19).

Who does not know that the belief of the Church Militant for over two thousand years has been that Christ is conceived as divine, the very God, and the eternal Son of the Father? With all his tender sympathy and humanity, with all the deep humiliation of his life and death on the cross, he is still God. And is not our hope this, that the eternally-existing Son of God who was equal with God emptied himself and entered upon a mission of humiliation and mercy for us? That he for us and our salvation became man, suffered death on the cross, and so wrought our salvation? This concept, this great teaching of the church and of God the Son, the Incarnation of God in Jesus Christ, is what makes our faith grand and glorious. It gives the human race a faith triumphant—a faith that alone can translate us from mortality to immortality. It brings us from life to life eternal and from the image of the earthly to the image of the heavenly. It alone is the power of God unto eternal salvation.

It is the past promise realized in the gift of God's only begotten Son that brings to light the grandeur, glory, and immensity of the grace of God. Justin Martyr wrote,

> In the book of the prophets, we find Jesus, our Christ, foretold as coming, born of a Virgin; growing up to man's estate, healing every disease and every sickness, raising the dead, being hated, unrecognized, crucified, and dying and rising again; and ascending to Heaven; being and being called the Son of God. For our God, through the prophetic Spirit, announced beforehand the things that would come to pass.
>
> *First Apology*—Justin Martyr

The things that would come to pass were the purposes of God's mercy and grace for man to be realized on the very earth on which man lived, walked, and had his being. It was about the coming of the only righteous one in the fullness of time. In the book of the prophet Jeremiah, it is written, "For I have loved thee with an everlasting love: therefore with lovingkindness have I drawn thee to me" (Jeremiah 31:3). We have this love displayed in the fulfillment of the promise. In the Incarnation, we see the majesty and immensity of God's love. And we still look to the first but now past advent when Christ came born of a virgin. He grew up to man's estate, healed diseases and sickness, and raised the dead. He was hated, unrecognized, and crucified. He died, rose again, and ascended to Heaven, being and being called the Son of God.

## The Temptation

In our brief introduction to the division of Christology, we said that Christ's success in overcoming the temptation in the wilderness fitted him for his redemptive work. What we ought to bear in mind is Satan's purpose in this deceptive endeavor. That purpose had only one objective. It was an effort to destroy Christ as the Savior of man and to destroy his effectiveness as the Redeemer of mankind. We would also note that some of the words used by Satan came from Scripture. His was a distorted and deceptive allusion of Scripture's real intent and meaning.

There is a marked difference between a test and a temptation. A test of one's character seeks only to reveal the nature of the individual or to make his character more spiritual. On the other hand, temptation deludes in order to destroy. Even though God may test our faith and character as he did with Abraham on Mount Moriah, it is Satan and the forces of evil that tempt. Unlike the Lord Jesus, there are times when each one of us may yield to the seduction of temptation, and the seduction of temptation is generally a seduction to do wrong. If we are to overcome, it must be through faith, trust, prayer, and most especially by the inward grace of the Holy Spirit.

Our salvation is that Christ is able to keep us from falling utterly. He can cleanse and restore by his grace that what sin has blighted. And is this not why we have come to love our Lord? He gave himself for us, won our hearts, and redeemed our souls from destruction. Is it any wonder, then, that Mary loved him, worshipped him, and served him? Since with Mary Magdalene Christ had forgiven much, she loved him all the more.

In the epistle to the Hebrews, we read, "It behooved him in all things to be like his brethren. And so to be in all things tempted as they" (Hebrews 4:14-17). There are two lines from Shakespeare's play *Measure for Measure* which read, "Tis one thing to be tempted, Escalus; but 'tis another thing to fall."

The story of the temptation of Jesus is narrated in the Gospel of Matthew 4:1-11. But we pause to ask, "Could Jesus be tempted?" Absolutely! As to his human nature, yes, Jesus could be tempted. "He was in all things tempted as they." Our Lord lived out his human nature as we all do, and he did it in complete dependence on God. In Matthew's narration about our Lord's temptation, the Spirit led the Lord Jesus out into the wilderness far from the throngs and press of the city. In the solitude of the wilderness, spiritual forces engaged in warfare. They clashed and contended. The powers and principalities engaged each other over the destiny of our Savior's commitment to his mission and over the spiritual destiny of the human soul.

Even though our Lord was anointed with the Holy Spirit and with power from on high, with him as also with us, the cross must come before the crown. And though at times he may have appeared as a meek Redeemer of men, our Savior's grace and presence are the most powerful spiritual forces that have affected human hearts. To the disciples and the early Church, Jesus was an object of worship. He was a Lord of reverence and of love to all who came to him in believing faith. His presence alone can evoke in us a response as it did with Simon Peter, and it can lead to penitence, to the cross, and to a changed life.

Christ's love and grace still give hope to the wanderer. His spirit gives strength to all who are morally weak, and he has always been a source of inspiration to those in despair. Through his cross and triumph over death, the Lord Jesus has given to all the hope of immortality. But first, even he, as laid out in the counsel of God, was fitted for his task through his temptation. And he also learned obedience through the things he suffered.

"Then Jesus was led up by the Spirit into the wilderness to be tempted by the devil" (Matthew 4:1, RSV).

This was to be a spiritual engagement—warfare—a battle not of flesh and blood but a battle of powers and principalities fought in and around the strong Son of God. Sunset and sunrise, night and day, eternal light and eternal darkness, fought their struggle around Christ's soul. All the while, the stars in their course and the angelic host of Heaven kept their watch. After forty days, the battle drew to a close, and for a time, all was peace and quiet. Darkness was unable to abide the light. The darkness was broken, dispersed, and driven from the field of battle. Jesus had brought forth light and immortality, and the power of Satan was broken. And God the Son, Jesus, emerged to be victorious.

## The First Temptation

How did it all begin? It began by an insinuation of doubt. We note the dialogue, "If…If…If thou art the Son of God." *If* is an insinuation of doubt. "Really, are you the Son of God? Of course, you don't mind if a poor creature like me doubts just a little. Now, you may be or you may not be the Son of God. Really, I cannot tell. A little lower than the angels? You, the Son of the Most High?

"But me, I am only a lowly creature, and I can be persuaded. So persuade me. Command these stones to be made into bread. Israel ate manna in the wilderness. I hear tell it fell from Heaven.

There—stones are at your feet. You, the Son of God? Supernatural power? Show me, if thou be the Son of God."

In this struggle, the real issues are hidden. In the beginning, they were concealed and would not come out into the open until near the end. One point should be clear: for whatever reason that Satan may have wanted the Lord Jesus to do his bidding, it was wrong, just plain wrong. If Satan wanted it done, it had to be wrong. Jesus would not use the divine nature to rescue the human in himself. If he had served himself and saved himself, then he could not have saved others. He would live as we all must live, in complete dependence on God.

"But he answered and said, 'It is written, man shall not live by bread alone, but by every word that proceedeth out of the mouth of God'" (Matthew 4:4).

The stones would remain stones. In his physically weakened condition, caused by fasting, the fast continued. And this was just the opening of the contest.

We ask once more. What is temptation? In essence, it is a seduction to evil and a solicitation to do wrong. Temptation is different altogether from any trial that we may undergo. Hardship, suffering, or trial only seeks to unfold the moral qualities of character. They refine and bring out hidden qualities of the soul and spirit. But not so temptation; it persuades to lead to evil. It always deceives, and it deludes in order to ruin. We may say that trial, when permitted by God, aims at man's good. Afflicted in bondage, the children of Israel were molded into a nation. By being sold into slavery and cast into prison by the captain of the guard for a wrong that he did not do, Joseph's faith and moral character grew strong. And like our Lord, he learned obedience to faith through the things that he endured. Trial leads to the tempering of a man for his own good, making him and those who know him conscious of his true, moral self. But temptation always leads directly to wrong. God may try. Satan tempts.

When Abraham ascended Mount Mariah, he believed it was to sacrifice his only son. Nothing of sorrow or pain was spared him. He was to take his only son whom he loved. His faith was to be proven and purified, and by his trial, he was fitted to be called the "father of the faithful." Is it not true that the trial of Job was instigated by Satan solely because Job served God? Here, too, Satan was unable to make Job lose his faith in God for one brief second. This was true even though Satan demanded successively heavier afflictions. With Christ, the first encounter was just the beginning.

## The Second Temptation

Our Lord's response was that man should not live by bread alone but by every word that proceeded from the Lord God. This settled nothing as far as Satan was concerned. The devil would persist. Besides, Satan is a very poor loser. He wanted much more than to see a simple miracle. The bread from stones, the guardian angels, the kingdoms of the world—all these offers had concealed the main issue. Satan wanted to destroy Christ.

Then Satan took Christ up in to the holy city and settled him onto pinnacle of the temple and said, "If thou be the Son of God, cast thyself down, for it is written, 'He shall give his angels charge concerning thee: and in their hands they shall bear thee up, lest at any time thou dash thy foot against a stone'" (Matthew 4:4-5).

Satan again raised the issue of doubt and quoted scripture to achieve his purpose. "If thou be the Son of God…It is written." And does not Satan do the same thing to us? He raises the issue of doubt about faith, about God's ability to hear and answer prayer, about our trust in a loved one, or about a friend. As with the Savior during his period of fasting, Satan does it when we have been weakened by some personal calamity. Doubt, you see, is the chief weapon of the Evil One.

Again we note that if Satan wanted Jesus to do it, it was wrong. And again, the issue was concealed. The devil wanted Jesus to act at his bidding. The ultimate goal was to destroy Jesus as the Savior of men. Undaunted, "Jesus said unto him, 'It is written, thou shall not tempt the Lord thy God'" (Matthew 4:7).

## The Third Temptation

> Again, the devil taketh him up into an exceedingly high mountain, and sheweth him all the kingdoms of the world, and the glory of them. And said to him, 'All these things I will give thee, if thou will fall down and worship me'" (Matthew 4:8-9).

This time, Satan did not say, "If thou be the Son of God," and the issue was out in the open at last. The whole world, all of it, you can gain the whole world and its glory. They are yours if you fall down and worship me. I want no Messiah and no Savior for mankind. You want a kingdom? You can have all the kingdoms of the world. Just worship me and let me be your god. There we have it. This is the ultimate issue of all temptation, and it is ultimately Satan who tempts.

It is just a little thing. Just do it once. That is how it begins. Fall down and worship me, and all the kingdoms of the world are yours. To one of even the slightest discernment, it was eminently gross. It was far too gross not to be rejected immediately out of hand. Our Savior replied as it is written, "Thou shalt worship the Lord thy God, and him only shalt thou serve" (Matthew 4:10).

Having assumed our nature and having been found in fashion as a man, in our stead, Jesus stood, fought, and conquered. He preserved for us the Kingdom of Heaven and the Kingdom of righteousness, peace, and joy in the Holy Spirit. He loved us. His heart and soul strained in the struggle. And through his anguish and pain, the victory he won, he won for us. It behooved him in all things to be like unto his brethren, and so to be in all things tempted as they. Christ can be moved by the feelings of our infirmities. And we can come to him in our sin and weakness, and we can draw near in joy or sorrow.

We can come to Christ with the assurance, knowing that as "he suffered, being tempted, he is able to succor them that are also tempted" (Hebrews 2:18). This was the Son of God who learned obedience to the Father's will through the things he suffered. In overcoming his hour of temptation, Christ revealed that we have a Savior to whom we can come to find grace in time of need. What is our need? An uncontrolled passion, pride, resentment, or doubt? Is it an uncontrolled temper or wounded spirit? What ever it may be, we can bring it to our Lord and trust him to deal with it. This gentle, meek, and winsome Galilean will surely deal with it and with us.

Like the coming of a new day, our Savior will help us conquer our faults, failures, and even our sins. His conquest can overwhelm your soul and fill you with his love and peace. Ultimately, it is not really the fierce fire that refines; it is the hand of God. His love never fails, however immense, intense, or prolonged the strain. Confronted with the grace of our Lord Jesus Christ, whatever means Satan may employ, they will prove impotent. God will hold them in derision. No weapon that is formed against thee shall have success—none at all. We know that his mercies are new every morning. And the whole world is unable to compete against this because thou art, indeed, the Son of God and Savior of mankind.

## The Transfiguration: A View of His Glory

As the Lord Jesus moved among the people ministering to their needs, the four Gospels characterized him as full of grace and truth. In his redemptive mission, the four Gospels bring out his sympathetic understanding and concern for all classes and conditions of men. He dealt with all who confessed need of him with a love that seemed unending. Among the lame and blind, and among the poor in spirit, he did many mighty works. For all who have become aware of spiritual realities, these incidents in Christ's ministry were signs of God's presence, power, and Spirit

## The Theology of Grace

in him. They were also signs of the Kingdom of Heaven. All the incidents of our Lord's earthly ministry were also revelations of the grace of God, for in Christ Jesus the grace of God appeared, bringing salvation to all men.

To grasp the significance of our Lord's ministry, we need to catch a glimpse of his divine presence—a flash of his power and Spirit working in human lives. We can see him redeeming their souls, being mindful of their humanity, and reconciling them to God the Father. Our Lord ever works his redemption in human hearts. His Spirit comes with a healing presence for every human situation. During his ministry, he brought love and grace to him who lay on a bed of pain—the paralytic. In the wonder of his grace, he who had lost all power of sensation was restored to wholeness of life. But there was more, for our Lord not only said, "Arise, and take up thy bed, and walk," but also, "Thy sins are forgiven thee" (Mark 2:9).

Christ never failed to touch those who lingered in the sorrow of bereavement when death had left them destitute. He brought comfort to their hearts, and he brought the hope of immortality to the human race when he proclaimed, "I am the resurrection and the life… He that believeth me shall never die" (John 11:24-25). His grace always restores the soul. And he whose coming can be like the gentle rains that fall from Heaven can give us grace for every human situation—each according to his need. Through these acts of mercy, and through the Lord's dealing in our own lives, we catch a glimpse of his presence, power, and Spirit work in human lives.

Is this not also true with us? If we are mindful of him in our own past experience, we can remember when he spoke to our souls in whispers of his grace. We can remember when we were given a sense of his presence and power. This is what occurred on the Mount of Glory, in the Transfiguration of Christ. There, Peter, James, and John went with Jesus up the high mountain. There they received a view of our Lord's glory, power, and divinity.

Have you ever held a prism in your hand? In your hand, it looks like an ordinary piece of crystal. But hold it up to the sunlight and let the light strike it fully. Immediately, a radiant spectrum of colors is displayed. The sunlight is transformed into a glorious splendor of its radiant hues. This is like what occurred during the Transfiguration of Christ. The incident is told in the Gospel of Luke.

"And as he prayed, the fashion of his countenance was altered, and his raiment was white and glistening: they saw his glory" (Luke 9:29).

## Close Friends

The Master of Galilee had sustained a hard and difficult day and a busy week. He felt spent, and his spirit weary. It was time to get away for a short while, a time to watch, pray, and rest. It was time for a quiet retreat for refreshment and renewal. He felt a need to be in communion with the Father, for his soul and spirit to feel the strong hand of God at his side once more.

And don't you and I also feel the need on occasion to get a way for a short while? We sense the need to be away from the noise of the busy day. We need a time to see God's grandeur in a high mountain or to watch the immensity of the ocean. We wish to feel the peace—the depth and strength of creation's splendor. We sense the need to mediate, to watch and pray, and to be renewed in body, soul, and spirit.

From among his disciples, our Savior had three close friends. Often they are called the *inner circle*: Peter, James, and John. When the need arose, Jesus would take these three close friends with him to a garden or to John's home for a time of prayer and meditation. On this occasion, "He took Peter, James, and John. And went up into the mountain to pray" (Luke 9:28). These were Christ's close friends, those among the first Jesus called to him for the work of the kingdom. They were to share his labors, failures, and successes. Friends first called and first loved: Peter, James, and John.

## The Theology of Grace

A friend believes in you always regardless of what the whole world may say. Turning to him as our Lord and Savior, Jesus becomes our Savior-Friend. He is a friend who stands closer than a brother. And what has our Savior said to us? I will no longer call you servants, "But I have called you friends" (John 15:15) if you do the will of my Father. In Christ, we have a Friend who cares and who walks with us in a fellowship of grace. This applies to you and me. In Christ, you have a friend who never doubts you and who will walk in when the rest of the world walks out. You may be sure of this: there are no disappointments in turning to the Lord Jesus. It is true that at times we may fail him and, like Peter, fail him shamefully. But he knows our hearts, and that is enough. There is forgiveness, restoration, and renewal with the Lord Jesus.

With three close friends, Peter, James, and John, Jesus went up to the high mountain to watch and pray. He ascended up high where the air was purer and where the soul could soar into the bosom of the Father on the wings of prayer. Up high the Heavens were nearer, and the mountains pointed to God the Father. Christ ascended with three friends who were close to him because they needed to catch a glimpse of his divine presence and power.

They needed to see and to know that the Spirit of God worked in and round the Lord Jesus and in and around them. Peter, James, and John needed a vision of his glory to remember when he would be gone to be with the Father. They were to carry on his work of faith and labor of love. Peter, James, and John would need that vision of his glory— the afterglow—to strengthen them later on in the work of the Kingdom. Soon they reached that place in the mountain where they could rest, watch, and pray.

## The Transfiguration in Glory

As Jesus began to pray, the three friends began to drift off to sleep one by one. As always, the spirit was willing, but the flesh proved weak, and after the long climb, the flesh was even weaker. The three friends were overcome by sleep. Jesus now prayed alone.

"And as he prayed, the fashion of his countenance was altered, and his raiment was white and glistening" (Luke 9:29).

As the Savior prayed to the Father, the Father responded in power and Spirit. This was the well-beloved Son. And God's splendor and glory shone through the Son's countenance. Even his garments were affected as the hues of the glory burst through. The narrative depicts the garments as "white and glistening." Even the heavenly glow about Moses, when he descended Sinai with the tablets of stone, paled in comparison. And all the while, the three close friends were heavy with sleep.

"And behold, there talked with him two men, which were Moses and Elias, who also appeared in glory, and spake of his decease which he should accomplish at Jerusalem" (Luke 9:30-31).

Peter, James, and John slept while Moses, Elias, and Jesus all in glory shone. The very splendor of the ages was being revealed, and those for whose benefit the splendor of the Most High had been revealed were fast asleep. And is it not also this way with us on occasion?

Surely there were times when God in Jesus Christ sought to speak to us, reassure us in our faith, and quicken our spirits. But we were unable to be still and listen. Perhaps it may have been through a friend, through a word fitly spoken, or perhaps through the smile on a loved one's face. And even though the nearness of God came through the warm touch of a caring hand, we were unaware of it. The Father may have sought to touch our hearts to remind of his caring love, but like they on the mountaintop, our eyes were heavy with sleep.

But then they on the mountaintop were awakened. Still, they had not been just asleep but heavy with sleep in deep, sound slumber. But God's glory could not be denied. The grace, even for those heavy with sleep, was impossible to resist. The sheer splendor of the moment broke through their sleep. They were startled. When awake, they saw. "And when they were awake, they saw his glory; and the two men that stood with him" (Luke 9:32). This they were to remember. They remembered that moment when they had seen the divine presence, power, and Spirit of God in their Lord. They had seen his glory and had basked in its splendor.

When Jesus had gone to be with the Father, they would remember that they had been on that holy mountain with their Lord. With their own eyes, they had seen the Lord's glory, and they later heard the voice. Simon Peter wrote in his second epistle.

> For we have not followed cunningly devised fables, when we made known unto you the power and coming of our Lord Jesus Christ, but were eyewitnesses of his majesty. For he received from God the Father honor and glory, when there came such a voice to him from the excellent glory...And this voice which came from Heaven we heard, when we were with him in the holy mount.
>
> 2 Peter 1:16-18

When their work for the Kingdom took them to lonely places, when all alone they faced trying situations or had suffered for the name, they would remember that hour of spiritual height in their lives. They would remember when they had been with the Lord Jesus and had awakened to see his glory. This experience became for them a source of spiritual strength and growth.

And so it may be with us, with you and me. When we have lost a mother, father, brother, spouse, or son, we can remember. When the tide will appear to have run out on us, or when we contemplate the moments of awful loneliness in our lives, we can remember when God in Jesus Christ spoke to our souls—even the moment when Christ entered and took possession of our hearts. And then in that moment, faith, heart, and soul awaken in us once again. Praise the Lord, oh my soul, and praise the glory of his grace!

# The Afterglow of Glory

"As they departed from him, Peter said unto Jesus: 'Master, it is good for us to be here. Let us make three tabernacles,' not knowing what he said" (Luke 9:33).

Impetuous, rash at times, strong and weak, loveable Simon Peter—he alone of the three responded to the occasion. He was struck to the heart by the revealed glory of our Lord. In the boat with the multitude of fish, when he fell on his knees before Christ, Peter responded to his majesty. At the Last Supper, though boasting, Peter replied that even if all the world would deny Christ, he, Peter, would not. Here again, on the holy mount, Simon Peter responded to the occasion though he did not know what he said. And do we not love Simon Peter for just that reason?

Simon Peter always responded to Christ. It may not always have been what Jesus wanted to hear, but Peter was affected by his Lord, and the Lord Jesus loved Simon Peter for that. The Lord loved him and prayed for Simon that his faith not fail. Our Lord loves us, too, when we respond to his Word, grace, and Spirit. And I imagine he would love us especially when we do the work of the Kingdom however little or much we have to offer. And Christ has prayed for us also—that our faith may not fail.

Where was Simon Peter as they were leaving the holy mount? Peter was basking in the afterglow of the glory of the Transfiguration. It was still with him, and he wanted to preserve it. He always wanted to retain the heights of grace—the high moments of his spiritual life. In those moments, in his heart, Simon had soared on the wings of grace, and to him that was real glory. The Lord Jesus understood. It was the heart that counted—not the words. It really mattered not at all that Peter failed to understand what he had said. Jesus understood, and that was enough. For those who have known him, has this not always been the moment? We have sensed his glory and caught the afterglow of his presence, and on that occasion we felt the silent, deep stirring of the Spirit.

"While he thus spoke, there came a cloud and overshadowed them. And there came a voice out of the cloud saying, 'This is my beloved Son; hear him'" (Luke 9:36).

Then the cloud was gone and the voice faded away. Moses and Elias were no longer visible. They looked and saw Jesus only, standing in the serenity of his glory. They would indeed hear him. But the view of our Savior's glory, the heavenly cloud, and the voice speak to us also. And the words that come to us are also the same. "This is my beloved Son; hear him." And Jesus says, "Come you that labor and are heavy laden. Come and find rest for your souls. My yoke is easy, and my burden is light…Come you blessed of my Father into the kingdom prepared for you from the foundations of the world…Come with me unto the Father; and we may come in any quiet hour of prayer or meditation."

When moving through his earthly ministry, every now and then Jesus had to leave the milling of the multitude and go off to be alone with God—not because he sought to escape the burden of his ministry, but so he might be better prepared to carry it out. For this reason, he often retired for prayer. In these moments, we can discover that faith in Christ brings peace, calm, and fortitude of the soul. Prayer and contemplation and worship can do this. Prayer unburdens the soul and clears the mind of anxiety because we are resting in God. Is this not what our Savior did when he retreated to the holy mount of glory? He rested in God.

From this experience in the life of our Lord, we come to understand that any life, my life or your life, can deepen with a richer concept of faith and trust. In these quiet, secluded moments, we sense a sharing of our burdens. A sorrow shared is always a sorrow halved. In these moments of spirit and truth, our souls blend with the Lord Jesus in mystic, sweet communion. We realize we are not alone in the struggles of life, for we sense him near. We have caught a glimpse of his divine presence and Spirit working in our lives. And while God is mindful of our humanity, he redeems our soul, reconciling us to himself through Jesus Christ our Lord. The view of his glory is also for you.

## The Humiliation: The Golden Passional

In St. Paul's letter to the Philippian church, we read,

> Let this mind be in you which was also in Christ Jesus: Who being in the form of God, thought it not robbery to be equal with God; but made himself of no reputation, and took upon him the form of a servant; and he was made in the likeness of men: and he humbled himself, and became obedient unto death, even the death of the cross.
>
> Philippians 2:5-8

In the passage above, St. Paul depicted the humiliation of Christ. Humiliation means to be removed from a position of honor. It means to come to a lower rank or status and to become lower in dignity. It also means to hurt another's feelings and sense of pride by causing him to seem contemptible, despised of men, and rejected as an outcast. The end of our Lord's humiliation was found in his passion—his suffering and crucifixion. When we speak of the love that surpasses knowledge, we have many things in mind about the love of our Redeemer. In his humiliation, Jesus undertook becoming the Suffering Servant. It was a voluntary act because he loved us and gave himself for us. He humbled himself, and became obedient unto death—even the death of the cross.

No one likes to see suffering or pain in another individual, nor do we ourselves like to suffer. The very word brings memories of pain and anguish we have experienced. Our hearts go out to children and infants, who must, from birth, carry the stigma of a crippling and painful disease throughout their lives. But who would voluntarily surrender an exalted state? Who would denude himself of unlimited power and assume the form of a servant and the restrictions of human flesh? And who would undergo the torment of anguish and suffering for others? No one would voluntarily do such a thing except our Savior, the Lord of glory. He did so with a love that surpasses knowledge.

Christ's humiliation began. In his pre-mundane existence, the Son dwelt with the Father rich in glory, honor, dignity, and reverence. The Son's grace and grandeur were vested in the worlds of the universe created by him and for his glory. He was God the Son, Prince of the Godhead, crowned in splendor. And yet, "You know the grace of our Lord Jesus Christ, that, though he were rich, yet for your sakes became he poor; that you through his poverty [and humiliation] might be rich" (2 Corinthians 8:9).

The nativity story laid the Savior's birth in a manger in the humblest of circumstances. The world turned him away from the inn at birth and denied him the fruit of his creation. His earthly father, Joseph, was a village carpenter. And as he grew into man's estate, Jesus earned his way through life by daily toil. Like his brethren, he came to know the weariness of labor and the contentment of rest. Even during the height of his ministry, poverty was his constant companion. "The foxes have their holes and the birds of the air their nest, but the son of man hath not where to lay his head" (Luke 9:58). Yet to this end he was born to be a man of sorrows and acquainted with grief. Christ not only lived in poverty during his earthly walk but was touched in all points in the flesh as you and I were. The good of this is that when we have a need or want and express these in prayer, Christ will be sympathetic to our petitions.

Still, his humiliation must go ever deeper into the valley of degradation if God were to see the travail of his soul and be satisfied. A jealous and offended priesthood thrust him out of the temple. He came unto his own, and they refused to hear his message or heed his ministry. When he claimed to be the Son of God, they were incensed and inflamed with anger. "This man ought to die," they insisted, and would have stoned him. From that moment on, Jesus became a man of sorrows and was acquainted with grief. The cross drew ever nearer, and he was watched and spied upon. His every word and act of grace or healing was reported in detail—that his enemies might have the wherewithal to accuse him. Their intent was to bring the Lord Jesus to perverse judgment followed by condemnation and death.

In his humiliation, Jesus was hated by the established priesthood for no justifiable reason. According to the common people, he only went about doing good—and God was with him. Justin Martyr, an apologist of the second century, wrote, "Though we say things like the Greeks say…about God and goodness…We alone are hated for the name of Christ: though we do no wrong… And we are accused and put to death by sinners" (*First Apology*, Justin Martyr).

The allegations against the Lord Jesus were these. He befriended publicans (tax collectors) and sinners and sat at their table. He made and drank wine at the common people's wedding banquets. He befriended a harlot, ate grain without washing his hands, and broke the Sabbath by daring to heal the sick on such a day. These could have been overlooked, for he was simply a "rustic prophet," claiming to have come from Nazareth. Besides, as the supreme interpreters of the law, the Pharisees knew that out of Nazareth had come no prophet. But when Christ accused them of having made his Father's house a den of thieves and threw out the money changers, his doom was sealed, and the cross was certain.

Though weak morally, Pilate had asked, "Why? What evil hath he done?" Christ's distinction, which they took for wrong, was that he refused to behave and think as they did. "Away with such a man. To the cross he must go. Thrust him up between the thieves up with the malefactors. A King? We will not have this man to rule over us. We have no king but Caesar." But Pontius Pilate, though a weak man, was no fool. He knew that for envy they had delivered him up. Pilate knew the cross came from intense hatred, emerging from a stunted and limited mentality—and from an unbelief that was simply perverse and blind.

## The Theology of Grace

In his theological work entitled *Cur Deus Homo?* Anselm asked, "For what necessity and for what reason did God take upon himself the humiliation and weakness of human nature?" He was pondering the question of why the eternal creator of the universe became subject to human limitations in the Incarnation. Why did God become man, and why did he undertake to die the shameful and accursed death on the cross? What brought on the passion, humiliation, and suffering of our Lord? The church has given its answer in the doctrine of the atonement of Jesus Christ. Ages ago, the prophet Isaiah, in a clear and precise prophetic vision, gave us the reason in his Golden Passional. The concept of the humiliation of Christ is a valid doctrine.

We are living in a day when doctrine appears to be avoided. But a doctrine is simply a teaching of our faith, an item of all our believing. It is a focus of intellectual activity. Here, with heart, soul, and mind, one may look upon the wonders of God's grace and then worship in spirit and in truth. In his prophecy, Isaiah foretold the humiliation of Christ as follows.

> He is despised and rejected of men; a man of sorrows and acquainted with grief. We hid our faces from him; He was despised and we esteemed him not. Surely he hath born; our grief and carried our sorrows. He was stricken, smitten of God and afflicted. But he was wounded for our transgressions, He was bruised for our iniquities; and the chastisement of our peace was upon him: and with his stripes we are healed. And the Lord laid on him the iniquity of us all. Yet he opened not his mouth: he is brought as a lamb to the slaughter. He was cut off from the land of the living and made his grave with the rich in his death; because he had done no violence, neither was any deceit found in his mouth. Yet it pleased God to make his soul an offering for sin...God shall see the travail of his soul and be satisfied.
>
> Isaiah 53:3-11

Putting the doctrine in the words of the church, in his humiliation, Jesus Christ, the Lord of glory and your Savior and mine, and in all his sinlessness and innocence, came and dwelt among us. He identified himself with us through the Incarnation. Having been found in fashion as a man, he carried our sins, condemnation, and death to the cross. There he suffered the agony of death. God saw the travail of his soul and was satisfied. All those things that once stood as a barrier between God and us are gone forever. In brief, this is the doctrine of the atonement of Jesus Christ—the reason for his humiliation. Why did God the Son become God the suffering Redeemer in the valley of his humiliation? In answer to Anselm's question, the reason given in Isaiah's Golden Passional was to make atonement for sin.

To express God's purpose of mercy to us, Isaiah wrote,

> Fear not for thy maker, the Lord of host is thy redeemer. The God of the whole earth shall he be called. For a small moment have I forsaken thee; but with great mercy will I gather thee... "Arise and shine: for the Lord is risen upon thee."
>
> Isaiah 60:1

Touched by his grace, may our souls bow in humility and gratitude to a love so grand that it passes all knowledge.

## The Crucifixion: The Cross and the Crown

St. Augustine wrote, "How hast thou loved us, O good Father, who sparedest not thine only Son: How hast thou loved us, that he should become obedient unto the death of the cross...How hast thou loved us that he should be both the victim and the victor" (*Confessions,* Augustine).

> In the days of his flesh, Jesus offered up prayers and supplications to God who was able to save him from death.

## The Theology of Grace

> And although he was a Son, he learned obedience through what he suffered; and being made perfect, he became the source of eternal life to all that obey him, being designated by God a high priest after the order of Melchizedek.
>
> Hebrews 5:8-10 (RSV)

The church must once again become aware that it through faith in Christ and through faith in his passion that we obtain the reward of righteousness in this life and peace with God. Through his passion, Christ made the cross the primary symbol of our faith. In the days of the Roman Empire, the cross was a cruel instrument of death. Death on the cross was one of infamy and disdain whose chief end was oblivion. But this was changed forever by Christ our Lord.

The crucifixion was the climax of our Savior's passion. In his passion, we see Jesus in his priestly function. May we say again in historical form but in simple fashion, the church has always presented Christ in the function of his three offices: as prophet, priest, and king. In his office as a prophet, he brought his Gospel of grace and redemption, and through his Spirit, he leads us into fellowship with the Father. As a priest, Christ calls us through his Spirit and leads us into his Kingdom of righteousness and peace.

As king, through the Incarnation of God in Jesus Christ, he came and dwelt among us. He left the vastness and glory that he had with the Father to come to earth and found his Kingdom. Our Lord's Kingdom is one of spirit and truth and of grace and glory for those who inquire. Its hallmarks are peace and righteousness. Through his Spirit, he reigns in our hearts, for God shed abroad his love in our hearts through the Holy Spirit, which was given us.

In his priestly office, Christ took upon himself the travail and suffering of the human race, and he became a priest after the power of an endless life. In an immutable decree, God the Father ordained the Lord Jesus a priest after the order of Melchizedek, but with much greater glory. As our priest, he is the one Mediator between God and his people. He makes intercession for his people, offering sacrifices and prayers and supplications on their behalf. He leads his people in worship. In the climax of his priestly office, Christ endured the agony of the cross. Through his resurrection, death was overcome by the power of his endless life and now glorified priesthood. As a priest, he also transformed the meaning of the cross. The cross stands over the graves of our loved ones as a symbol of hope and immortality.

From the beginning of his ministry, Christ proclaimed to all who would listen that he came to serve the Father and to serve those who would believe on him. His birth, life, and cross were given in service and self-sacrifice. They were given with faith, hope, and love unfeigned. Next to the resurrection, Good Friday and the crucifixion are the most significant redemptive factors of the Lenten season. In the Lenten season, the greatest contrast is between the cross and the crown. The cross always looms in foreground. At times it is hovering in the background, while through it all the crown seems completely hidden. Yet the crown at the right hand of God was given to our Lord as the reward for his obedience. Even in our own lives, the cross must always come before the crown.

Has this not always been true in our own personal experience? There is the cross of agony and toil and of struggle and suffering before one obtains the crown of achievement. There is no new birth without the birth pangs and the travail of labor. No life matures without the trials and sufferings of growth. Even a lovely rose endures both the sun and the rain to fully emerge in all its beauty. The words of our Lord are familiar to all of us. "If any man will come after me, let him deny himself, and take up his cross, and follow me" (Matthew 16:24). It is also true that a cross in our lives can lead to a crown. This has been true of many individuals within the fellowship of our faith.

## The Theology of Grace

# The Cross, the Crown, and You

Our religion is grounded in Christ our Lord and on what occurred on the cross—the atonement of Jesus Christ. Our religious belief and expression involve knowledge of who Christ was, what he did, and how he did it. His crucifixion is but one aspect of our Lord's redemptive mission. Our High Priest, after the power of an endless life, gave us righteousness, peace, and acceptance with God. When all is said and done, when all the scholars have written their books, when all the sermons have been preached, and when every voice is silent, our standing with our heavenly Father rests upon our faith in Jesus Christ as Lord and Savior. We bear his name, his sign, his seal, and however lightly, we bear his cross.

The sense of our Lord's presence causes hope to spring eternal in the human heart. When we come to worship, we come with expectancy. We come to sense our Lord's presence. to sense the Spirit gently awakening our souls to his glory and grace. And the exceptional grace of it all is that we can come to the cross just as we are. We can come to his cross, the fountain of all grace, with all our faults, failures, and sins. We can plunge them all beneath the cleansing flow, and we can take our stand under our Lord's cross as under a great rock. The giving of ourselves that we do lovingly for our family, friends, and loved ones, and the occasional emotional suffering we may endure through the grace of our Lord Jesus Christ, can bring his power and spiritual force into our lives.

Are there a cross and the crown in our own lives? Yes, absolutely! It is to the eternal testimony of our religion that one's character can be endowed with strength which becomes gentleness. There will come sympathy, understanding, and compassion. All fear, doubt, and anxiety can vanish away like a vapor on the soft, summer air. All this comes to one end, that we might experience the reality of our faith in Christ Jesus. As we love him and seek to follow him, we till take up our cross. On Good Friday, when the cross was lifted up, all was hushed in silence and darkness covered the land.

# The Resurrection

The resurrection, along with the Incarnation of God in Jesus Christ, is one of the greatest supernatural events of our religion. Its impact on all other facets of our faith can never be overestimated. It is something that we must sense in our minds, feel in our souls, and embrace in our hearts. St. Paul stated the matter in one brief sentence. "And if Christ be not raisen, then is our preaching vain, and your faith is also vain" (1 Corinthians 15:14).

In the belief that Jesus could not be held of the grave and saw no corruption, the early church was endowed with the energy of our faith's supernatural power. They knew they served and worshipped a living, victorious Lord. "But now is Christ risen from the dead, and become the first fruits of them that slept" (1 Corinthians 15:20). We will look at the resurrection from three different perspectives: On The First Day of The Week; Sunset-Sunrise; and Alleluia, He is Risen.

## On The First Day of the Week

> But on the first day of the week, they went to the tomb. And they found the stone rolled away, and they did not find the body. And behold, two men stood by them in dazzling apparel, and said unto them: 'Why do you seek the living among the dead? Remember how he told you, while he was still in Galilee, that the Son of man must be delivered into the hands of sinful men, and be crucified, and on the third day rise.' And returning from the tomb the women told all this to the disciples; but the disciples thought it was an idle tale, and they did not believe them.
>
> Luke 42:1-12

At the early dawn, before the breaking of the day, in the stillness of the morning, that is when the whole wide world is awakening. That is the time when amazing things and even miracles can occur. That was the time when Mary

> Magdalene, and Joanna, and Mary, the mother of Jesus, went to the tomb. And what an amazing story they had to tell the disciples. They went to see Jesus. They did not find his body. They saw visions of angels. They saw the Angel of the Resurrection, who said that Jesus was alive, that he had risen even as he had said. This was the early dawn of the New Testament Faith: "Concerning Jesus of Nazareth, who was a prophet mighty in deed and word before God and all the people. Whom the rulers crucified, but whom God raised up.
>
> Luke 24:19-20

The resurrection was proclaimed first not to the disciples or even to the inner circle of Peter, James, and John. But it was proclaimed to the women who had attended Jesus, who had cared for his needs and washed his feet and anointed him for his burial. It was to Mary Magdalene, Joanna, and Mary, the mother of our Lord Jesus to whom the glad tidings were first given. And today, throughout the length and breadth of the land at the early dawn, millions gather in his name in sunrise services to worship Jesus of Nazareth, Lord of the resurrection morning. They wait with hope and expectancy for the coming of this day and for the message of the three women that they gave to the disciples. "He is not here, but he is risen, even as he had said."

I would imagine that the first thing that struck the women as amazing was that the stone had been rolled away. From the narrative story, we know that the stone had been paced there to seal up the tomb. It had been meant to close up the grave site. But the stone that the builders rejected had already become the chief corner stone of the kingdom. In the early dawn, before the breaking of the day, the seal had been broken. And quite clearly, all three women could see that the stone had been rolled away. We hear as a foreshadowing of a new day the words from the Revelation of St. John; worthy is the Lamb that was slain to open up the seals and to declare unto men the counsels of God.

The two Mary's and Joanna were also worthy to open up the seals and to declare unto the disciples what had occurred, but not so the disciples. As Jesus said, they were still too slow of heart to believe all that the prophets had written. Like foolish ones, they thought that the good news brought to them by the women was only an idle tale. So at first, the disciples did not believe Mary Magdalene, Joanna, and Mary, the mother of Jesus. However, a few things still perplexed them: they knew that the body was gone, that the stone had been rolled away, and that Jesus had said that on the third day he would rise. And this was the first day of the week—the third day since the crucifixion. On the first day of the week at the early dawn, the stone had been rolled away and the women claimed to have seen visions of angels.

## Why Do You Seek The Living Among The Dead?

The angel of the resurrection had said to the two Mary's and to Joanna, "Why do you seek the living among the dead? He is not here but is risen even as he said." You seek Christ, the crucified one. He is not here. He is risen. He is now the risen and living Savior. He is Christ whom God declared to be his Son by the power of the Spirit of holiness in the resurrection. You will not find the living among the dead." In the words of Justin Martyr, we have the following.

"He became man by a virgin, according to the Father's design, for the salvation of those who believe in him. And he endured both to be set at naught and to suffer; that by dying and rising again, he might conquer death" (*First Apology*, Justin Martyr).

We do not look for the living among the dead. We do not base our faith on an empty tomb or on an open grave but upon a resurrected and ascended Lord. Ours is a Savior whom death could not hold, who opened up the seals and who rose victoriously from the grave and did so by the power of the eternal Spirit. He ascended to glory at the right hand of God exalted. For

## The Theology of Grace

it was necessary that he should suffer all these things to enter into his glory.

Yet for three days the disciples were fearful, perplexed, and confused—and perhaps for more than three days. "We had hoped," they said to each other, "we had dreamed, and we believed that it should have been he that would redeem Israel." But with the crucifixion, their hopes came to an end. They were too slow of heart to believe all that the prophets had written. The good news brought to them by the women could not break through the darkness and despair that lingered in their hearts from Holy Saturday.

These three women remembered the things which the angel of the resurrection spoke to them. And all the while, the disciples still thought their Lord made his bed with the dead. The risen Savior had to draw near to two disciples on their way to Emmaus and sup with them and make himself known to them in the breaking of the bread. Then, they told the others how Jesus had made himself known to them in the breaking of the bread. And as they were saying these things, suddenly Jesus stood among them. They were startled, thinking they saw only a spirit. Thoughts turned in their heads. Slowly, they were beginning to understand.

Gently, with grace and compassion, the Teacher come from God and opened up the eyes of their understanding. With love, with patience, and with grace—for that is ever the way one must deal with the slow of heart—Jesus enlightened them.

"Why are you troubled, and why do questionings rise in your hearts: See my hands and feet, that it is I myself; handle me and see; for a spirit has not flesh and bones as you see that I have" (Luke 24:36-40).

And he opened up their minds to understand the Scriptures; "Thus it is written, that Christ should suffer and on the third day rise from the dead, and that repentance and forgiveness of sins should be preached in his name to all the nations" (Luke

24:45-47). And when the disciples departed from their risen and living Lord, they returned to Jerusalem with great joy. At last, the disciples of the Lord had joined the company of their woman. No longer would they seek the living among the dead. They remembered that their hearts had burned within them, and their spirits quickened when he had walked with them along the way. That had been the third day when the risen Lord drew near to them on the way and later when he appeared to all his disciples.

## On The First Day of the Week

"We hold our common assembly on the day of the sun, because it is the first day of the week on which God, having transformed darkness and matter, created the world: and on the same day, Jesus Christ our Savior rose from the dead" (*First Apology*, Justin Martyr).

On the first day of the week at the early dawn, the stone had been rolled away, and Jesus Christ, the Lord of glory, rose from the dead. On this day, the power and fear of death were broken, and Christ was declared to be the Son of God through the power of the Spirit of holiness. At the early dawn before the breaking of the day on the first day of the week, Christ had changed the sunset of Good Friday to the sunrise of Easter Morning. What a morning! What a morning, indeed.

It was changed. The entire concept of the cross was changed. Now since the first day of the week, the cross is the primary symbol of the Christian religion. It is a symbol of hope, faith, love, and redemption. It is a symbol of life everlasting and of immediate access to God the Father. On the first day of the week, on the day of the sun, the Holy Spirit manifested abroad the reality of an endless life for all who would embrace the risen Christ as Savior and Lord.

It was at the early dawn before the breaking of the day when the stone had been rolled away and the angel spoke to the women and they remembered. They remembered all that had been written by the prophets concerning Jesus of Nazareth. Ever since that grand resurrection morning, the faithful in Christ Jesus have gathered to worship in his name on the first day of the week. They have gathered in churches in this land and in churches throughout the entire world—and repentance and forgiveness are preached to all nations even as the Lord Jesus commanded.

It was not by chance that the first day of the week was set aside as a day of Christian worship. On the day of the sun, Sunday, that was the day when darkness and death were vanquished, and the strong Son of God rose victoriously from the grave. Our Savior said to his disciples (and his words apply to us), "Why do questionings rise in your hearts, for thus it is written that Christ should suffer and on the third day rise from the dead...offering repentance and forgiveness to all nations." And by believing in his name, ours can be a life everlasting.

## Sunset-Sunrise

> Now on the first day of the week, Mary Magdalene came to the tomb, at the early dawn while it was still dark, and she saw that the stone had been rolled away. And Mary stood weeping, because they had taken away her Lord, and she knew not where they had laid him. Then she saw the two angels. They said to her, "Woman, why are you weeping?"
>
> John 20:13 (RSV)

She answered that she wept because they had taken away her Lord and she knew not where to find him. But Jesus was standing there. He had been there all the time, but she did not know him because she thought him to be the gardener.

Jesus said to her, "Whom do you seek?" And she asked him if he knew where they had taken her Lord? Then Jesus called her by name, Mary. And by the inflection of his voice, she knew him. "Master," she replied. Mary Magdalene had found her risen and living Lord. St. Paul wrote in his first letter to the Corinthians:

Now is Christ risen from the dead; and become the first fruits of them that slept. For since by man came death, by man came also the resurrection of the dead…For this corruptible must put on incorruption, and this mortal must put on immortality. Where, O Death is thy sting? Where, O Grave is thy victory.

1 Corinthians 15:20-21, 53, 55

A risen and living Lord is the triumphant hallmark of the Christian religion and glory of the church. It is the resurrection that makes the church triumphant. Though it may be our primary symbol, we do not pay homage to a cross. We worship a risen and living Lord. We acknowledge that by man came death, but we also acknowledge that by man came also the resurrection of the dead—by the man Christ Jesus. If we believe that one day this mortal shall have put on immortality, it is because the Lord Christ Jesus became the first fruits of them that slept. What happened on Easter Morning when Mary Magdalene came to the tomb shattered the sting of death forever. It destroyed all hope of victory for the grave.

It is true that one day there shall be a sunset for our lives. But it is also true that those who are in Christ Jesus shall awaken to a beautiful sunrise. All through the first Lenten season, Mary's love carried within it the hope of the sunrise of the resurrection morning. While the disciples' minds were still on the cross and the tomb, Mary Magdalene had seen and conversed with her risen Lord. His form, when first Mary saw him, was not recognized by her. She supposed him to be someone else. She appealed to this supposed stranger for assistance in finding the one whom she sought with many tears. Yet in the mystery of God's providence, Jesus was very close to her all along. But for a time, the spiritual sensitivity of her soul had not awakened to her Savior's presence.

## The Theology of Grace

Then Jesus called her, speaking her name. And the voice she had heard many times before, that voice with the inflection of love and sympathetic understanding, she knew to be that of her Master. Our Savior's voice stirred and awakened her soul. And while his presence overwhelmed her, it also called out her heart. With one simple word, she responded, "Master." Her response, one word, came as a response of faith and trust. And with Mary Magdalene, there was not a trace or even a thought of a doubt. From the entire band of our Lord's disciples, she stood alone with her Lord as when she had anointed him and accepted his death. For those few moments, she stood alone with her Savior as her resurrected and living Lord. And this was true even though at first she did not recognize him until he called her by name.

In the weakness of our flesh, we too can fail to recognize the Lord Jesus when he may come to us in some other form or through other means than we may have known him. And yet, such is the nature of Christ's love and grace that, like Mary, when he speaks our name or we sense his presence, we will know him.

But for the disciples, it was still sunset in their hearts. Their thoughts were still on the cross and on Christ's death. And those who were walking on the way to Emmaus permitted their voices to give expression to their thoughts. The conversation they held with each other was about Jesus of Nazareth—a mighty prophet in word and deed who had been condemned to death by the religious authorities. Night had fallen, and while gloom lay in their souls, they faith and hopes were fading into the sunset. "We had hoped that it were he that should have redeemed Israel." They were disillusioned. But a God of knowledge is the Lord—a God working out his curious design. They were explaining these things to the risen Lord who had drawn near to them as they walked on the way. Like Mary Magdalene, at first their eyes were holden, and they did not recognize the Lord Jesus. Still, as they talked with him, it was as though their hearts burned within them.

Unknown to them, they sensed the divine presence of the Lord Jesus. They sensed it as when spirit to spirit speak. And as though hope refused to die with Jesus so near, the narrative adds, "And this was the third day since these things happened." As night was falling, not wanting to part from this supposed stranger, they bade him to come and sup with them. The Lord Jesus will never turn away from any that seek him, nor will he do so even if our faith is weak and imperfect. He consented to stay and broke bread with them. As if awakening from a dream, immediately in the breaking of the bread, they knew him. Though night outside had not completely fallen, Jesus Christ had changed sunset in their hearts to sunrise in their souls. Faith, hope, and love soared again on the wings of the Spirit in the sure and certain hope of the resurrection unto eternal life. They were no longer disillusioned.

## Sunrise-Heroic Optimism

When the realization of what had occurred on that first Easter Morning finally came home to the disciples, it released within them a heroic optimism in the Lord Jesus, in them, and in their faith. The resurrection of Christ raised a hope for the human race that was nevermore to die.

> Into a dark tremendous Sea of Cloud,
> It is but for a time: I press God's lamp
> Close to my breast: its splendor soon or late
> Will pierce the Gloom: I shall emerge one day.
>
> Robert Browning

Robert Browning also wrote, "Sun-Trader, I believe in God and trust." Browning was a man for whom disillusion was impossible. No defeat could overwhelm the poet who wrote for the entire world to take note that "I was ever a fighter." His faith and trust in God gave him a heroic optimism that never once failed. He knew, as you and I must surely know, that we live and must proceed on the belief that life is worth living even from one day to the next. The game of life, despite its unfortunate turns, pains, and set-backs, is ultimately worth while. Without faith, blind though it may seem at times, life would cease. To faith and trust in God, to faith in the goodness of life, Robert Browning gave poetic and heroic expression.

With heart and soul, we must believe in the redemption of man, in the grace of our Lord Jesus Christ, and in the love of God our Father who shed abroad his love in our hearts through the Holy Spirit, which was given to us. Even though our faults, failures, and sins may reveal our imperfection and humanity, God's grace gives us a foretaste of glory. Through the sunrise of Easter morning, mortal life holds the promise of immortality. "I was ever a fighter," wrote Browning. So did St. Paul. "I have fought the good fight." So said the heroes and martyrs of our faith, and so said the Protestant reformers when darkness overshadowed the whole earth. Then, once again, the light of the simple Gospel of grace with all its power and redemptive spirit and with all the power of the resurrection burst through the gloom and darkness of the long night. And the night shall be as day, for Jesus Christ, the risen Lord of glory, has changed sunset to sunrise.

## Alleluia He Is Risen: Jesus Christ Is Lord

"Therefore, let all the house of Israel know assuredly that God hath made that same Jesus, whom you have crucified, both Lord and Christ" (Acts 2:36).

Acknowledging the words of Simon Peter, the Protestant Church has always affirmed the Lordship of Jesus Christ. He is the one Savior and head of the church that bears his name. He alone has the words of eternal life. The love of God the Father was fully revealed in him. From Heaven, he came and founded his church. And with his own blood he bought her, and for her life he died. There was no question in the minds of the disciples as to who was Lord of the church. To his disciples, Christ was the very life of the church. And to the apostolic fathers, no other name, no other power, and no other love could substitute for that of their Redeemer. They were persuaded beyond any trace of a doubt that God had made Jesus both Christ and Lord.

We can almost imagine the hopelessness and sense of futility that possessed the disciples as they approached the tomb; and then, to find Jesus not there. Their women claimed to have seen the angel of the resurrection who chided them lightly with these words, "Why do you seek the living among the dead: he is not here. He is risen, even as he hath said." The good news seemed incredible and too good to believe. "Christ the Lord is risen today." But such was the voice of men and angels. Still, it took time for the truth of the message to enter into the hearts and minds of the disciples. It was not confirmed to them until they actually saw their risen and living Lord.

But we should not chide them unduly. We of this present age are also slow of heart to believe all that the prophets have written concerning Jesus of Nazareth. It seems as though an angel's voice is needed to rouse us out of our sleep, to quicken our perception, and to quicken our minds and hearts to grasp this wonderful truth; alleluia, he is risen. Jesus Christ is Lord.

## Ours is a Living, Vital, Active Faith

Our hopes and expectations of God's love do not lie in the past, entombed in an ancient grace. Nor did they go down into the dust. They were not trampled underfoot by death. All were gathered together in our Redeemer, Jesus Christ. Our heroic religion is like a heavenly flame that shall never die because Christ is risen and has taken our hopes to Heaven with him. Ours is a vital, active faith alive with the Spirit and power that brought again the Lord Jesus from the grave. Against the majesty of his person, the powers of darkness are helpless. The grave was incapable of holding fast the strong Son of God. And in the struggle against the redemption that we have in Christ Jesus, death broke itself and lost its terror over the children of men.

This was what finally came home to the disciples of our Lord. The faith that they professed in Christ Jesus was alive with the power and Spirit of the Most High God.

They took this power and Spirit with them and spread it through the vast Roman Empire, and the fire of their faith was not consumed. In the name of the Lord Jesus, the early Christians outlived, outthought, and out died all the pagan religions. The way of the Galilean was shown to be the triumph and power of God. Julian the Apostate confessed it centuries ago. "Galilean, Thou hast conquered." This is what the resurrection proclaims; "The Lord God is a living God." The Lord of Heaven and earth has power and dominion over all. His eternal Son, Jesus Christ, the risen Lord of glory, has assured both the life and growth of the Christian faith.

This lesson must come home to every generation as it did to the disciples; ours is a living, active faith, and vibrant with power. Our religion has proven itself victorious over the most difficult of obstacles. Lives again our glorious King and lives forever the faith that reposes in him. This knowledge is meant to give us confidence in our religious expression, to value our religion, its goodness, and to lay hold of its promises. We must not allow the Spirit, life, and loveliness of our faith to die out. We dare not pass on a dead religion or a dying faith to our children. We must preserve for them a faith that is alive, vital, active, and vibrant with the Spirit of our risen, living, and ascended Lord.

## We Shall Live

Our faith is more specific as it applies to us. Because Christ lives, we too shall live. Death had no power over our Lord, and we all died in him. Dying once, he saved all. We who have turned to the

Lord Jesus will follow to where he has led. We are not composed solely of skin and bones. We are more than a mere blotch of flesh that shall rot in the ground, taking with it also our spirit. Man was created to be immortal and to enjoy the fellowship of God forever. We believe that our soul will live on and return to God. But this is not the entire promise of our faith; this not the half of it. It is voiced over and over again in the Scriptures; the body of God's people shall be resurrected. I believe in the resurrection of the body and in the life everlasting. This is the confession of the Christian.

Following our exalted Lord, made like him, like him we shall rise. It was to restore us to fellowship with God that our Lord assumed our flesh and identified himself with us. Raised with him, we shall follow after him. He is the first fruits, we the fruits to follow. "But now is Christ risen from the dead, and become the first fruits of them that slept" (1 Corinthians 15:10). Because he lives in a new and glorious body, so shall we. This is the promise of God's Word and of our religion. Our faith is still the substance of things hoped for—the evidence of things not seen. We believe in things that we have not seen as yet, but which God has affirmed in his holy Word.

To have a vital, living faith, we must believe in things unseen. For the things that are seen are temporal of earth, but the things that are not seen are eternal. They are of faith and of the spirit. What all this means is that we must trust to the truth of God's Word, incline our hearts to him, believe in his Son, and accept through faith the glorious good news of Christ's resurrection. Only those who believe in the great teachings of the church will have a faith that burns life a flame of fire, like the consuming fire of the Almighty.

Let us remind ourselves that the things of God speak not so much to our minds or to the wisdom of this world, but to our hearts and souls. They speak to that innermost part of our souls that we keep from the eyes of the world. But it is precisely there that the Word and Spirit of God would touch us. God sends us his Spirit—that same Holy Spirit in whose power he wrought the resurrection of our Redeemer, Jesus Christ. And we shall live because we have the Spirit of life, the Spirit of God's love, and of God's grace. Ours is the cross, the grave, but ours also the height of the skies. Christ lives in us, and our faith lives with us.

## The Triumphant Faith

In our risen Lord, the success of the Christian religion is assured. Through the centuries, Christianity has demonstrated its power in the lives of men and women the world over. I have seen in my lifetime how easily God can overcome obstacles and remove barriers that stand in our way. As of old, it was said to his people, "Stand still and see the salvation of the Lord." As sovereign of Heaven and earth, he is the foundation of all our believing. He accomplishes what he proposes and proposes what he shall accomplish. The whole thought of our triumphant faith is this: we attribute ultimate power to God and to our Lord Jesus Christ only. There is not a power apart from God that can withhold the blessings he would give or that can hinder the working of his will. It is God, in the grace of our Lord Jesus Christ, who works in us both to do and to will his good pleasure.

Our Redeemer is the Lord and head of the church, and the victory he achieved, both in life and in death, is promised to us. The church will not be consumed by the world. We shall grow, multiply, and prosper. When the time shall come for us to lay down the mantle of this earthly life and enter into the region that lies beyond, we will do so without fear. As long as we are Christ's and Christ is ours, death can hold no terror for us, nor can the universe in any part of it. Our passing from this life will merely indicate that our days of walking upon this earth are over. And we will have moved into that state of a glorified existence with our Lord.

While we live, the wonder of the resurrection remains. Its message does not die out but grows brighter and brighter with each passing year. It is like the promise of the sun after the rains. It says we live again, we love again, and there is time to build, to plant, and to dream and work. There is room enough and time enough, for Jesus is both Lord and Christ. This is our hope and strength; we do not seek the living among the dead. We serve a risen, living, and ascended Lord. May God in his grace make our expression of faith strong and vital in the church once more. May he touch our souls with the life of his Spirit. May he cause us to grow in the love and grace of our Lord Jesus Christ. And as our faith lives in us, may we always be responsive to God—the Father of our spirits.

## The Ascension of Christ

In Glacier National Park, Montana, there is a mountain called "Going to the Sun Mountain." It has the look of immense majesty, power, and strength. But its most peculiar facet is that its sheer, massive inclination causes you to look up—all the way to the sun. As you stand there craning your neck, looking at the mountain ascending, you find yourself gazing up at the Heavens. Of course, the mountain does not move; it does not actually, physically ascend. But it gives the appearance of ascending. We will discuss the doctrine of the Ascension of the Lord Jesus Christ.

There is a painting by Raphael, entitled, "Noli Me Tangere" or "Touch Me Not." The scene depicts Jesus immediately after his resurrection. He is standing outside the empty tomb in the garden. Mary Magdalene sees him, but as St. Luke wrote, she supposes him to be the gardener. She pleads with him, "Sir, if you have carried him away, tell me where you laid him, and I will come and take him away."

Then Jesus spoke her name, "Mary," and by the inflection in his voice, Mary recognized him immediately.

She reached forth her hand to touch Jesus, saying, "Master."

### The Theology of Grace

But Jesus replied, "Touch me not, for I have not yet ascended unto the Father: but go to my brethren and say to them, I ascend unto my Father and your Father, to my God and your God" (John 20:17).

"Verily, verily, I say unto you: He that believeth on me, the works that I do, shall he do also; and greater works than these shall he do; Because I go to the Father, to my God and your God" (John 14:12-13).

## Because Christ Ascended to the Father, We Worship in Spirit and Truth

During our Lord's earthly ministry, he could not always tell his full mind to his disciples. At times, what he did tell them was imperfectly understood by them. They were not able to bear it. Having so soon left their boats and fish; they were too rude and limited in their spiritual perspective to take it all in at first. Our Lord had to carry some of the mysteries of the kingdom with him to the cross. He would trust the Holy Spirit, whom the Father would send in his name, to lead the church to grasp them in the course of her subsequent development.

With pernicious tenacity, from the beginning of their walk with the Lord Jesus, the disciples held to a temporal, physical kingdom. They hoped he would redeem Israel and drive out the hated Romans. They dreamed of an Israel restored to the physical grandeur of King Solomon's time. And they held to this concept in spite of our Savior's repeated characterization of his realm; "My Kingdom is not of this world." When the disciples first began to walk with the Master, spiritual realities were difficult for them to grasp.

But the disciples were not alone in their obduracy. When an eager and inquiring Nicodemus came to Jesus by night, it had been the attraction of spirit upon spirit that drew him to Christ. Learned and sophisticated though he may have been, Nicodemus was moved by the ministry of the Lord Jesus and all his good works. "Miracles," Nicodemus had called them. He sensed the presence of God in and around the Lord Jesus. And he sensed also the power of our Lord's grace and glory. Moved with compassion for this leader of the people, Jesus gave an answer to his earnest inquiry.

Quietly, gently, in that obscure upper room, our Redeemer lifted the veil, revealing the advent of the Kingdom of Heaven. Here, one was born of the water and the Spirit. With patience and sympathetic understanding, the Teacher come from God revealed the mystery of the ages. Now had come the fullness of time for Nicodemus.

> Except one be born of the water and spirit, he cannot enter the Kingdom of God…That which is born of the flesh is flesh; and that which is born of the Spirit is spirit…God is a spirit; and they that worship him must worship in spirit and truth.
>
> John 3:5-6, 4:24

"Our Lord had said to his disciples, 'And, behold, when I ascend to my Father, I will sent the promise of my Father: the Comforter. The Holy Spirit will come upon you with power from on high'" (Luke 24:29). The Holy Spirit speaks to our spirits, seeking the pure in heart—the children of the Kingdom of Heaven. In these moments, if we are attentive, we can sense his presence. The promised coming of the Spirit stills the trouble soul and removes doubt and anxiety. He replaces these with the love of God. And all the while spirit worships upon Spirit, revealing the spiritual nature of the kingdom of God. We will know because the Lord, ascending to the Father, has sent us the Comforter.

## Because I Go to My Father, My Gospel Is for All Nations

"Go," said Jesus to his disciples prior to his ascension, "and preach my Gospel to all nations." From the beginning, the Savior's Gospel

## The Theology of Grace

was meant for all the people of the world. But the disciples, as before, were still too limited to take it in. They were hemmed in by the narrow walls of parochialism and exclusiveness. Limited in range and scope, the disciples had restricted themselves to the area around the Sea of Galilee. I remember seeing a beautiful home surrounded by a wall. And I thought that a wall was to keep things out, and then I realized that a wall can also keep things in.

Here were the disciples, their instruction and training completed, and that by the Teacher come from God. The Master has given them his Gospel of grace, placing into their hands the care and development of his Kingdom. In doing this, Christ has also given his disciples the Grand Commission. But they were like men surrounded by a wall. They kept it in—localized to Jerusalem and Palestine.

It was not until after Jesus had ascended to the Father that enlightenment came to them. It was not until after those of many nations had gathered in a certain place that the dawn of a new age came. At last the disciples began to understand the power of our Lord's resurrection and the power of the Holy Spirit that had been sent from on high.

"And when the day of Pentecost was fully come…suddenly, there came a sound from Heaven as a rushing of a mighty wind; and it filled all the house where they were sitting…And they were filled with the Holy Spirit" (Acts 2:1-2, 4).

It is narrated by St. Luke that those from all nations heard the Gospel in their own tongue. *How can this be?* they wondered, each hearing the Gospel in his own tongue. Others supposed the disciples to be mad or drunk with new wine. "They are not drunk as you suppose," said Simon Peter, being filled with the Spirit. "This is what was promised by God before through his prophets. The Lord Jesus, having received from the Father the promise of the Holy Spirit, has shed forth the Holy Spirit upon these that you now see and hear."

With the ascension of Christ to the Father, a new epoch began for the church with the dispensation of the Holy Spirit. For the church of Jesus Christ the fullness of time had also come. That which had been promised in times past at the birth of the church, the promise of the Father came to fulfillment.

> And it shall come to pass, that I will pour out my Spirit upon all flesh; and your sons and daughters shall prophesy, and your old men shall dream dreams, and your young men shall see visions. And also upon your servants and upon your handmaids, in those days will I pour out my Spirit.
>
> Joel 2:28-29

The high, narrow wall of partition was rent asunder with the coming of the Holy Spirit in power. The beautiful, saving Gospel of Jesus Christ would henceforth go to all the nations of the world. Though they had to be prodded by persecution, the disciples had been transformed into a team of untiring apostolic messengers of the Gospel. Their mission eventually led to the uttermost parts of the world. After Pentecost, the disciples could do their work with a true understanding of their Great Commission.

"What," one may ask, "was the content of their Gospel message?" They proclaimed it so urgently that they were accused of having turned the world upside down. Their Gospel message was simply this:

That God, according to his gracious promise, broke into the stream of history when God the Son emptied himself, descended to earth, born in fashion as a man, born of a virgin to begin his mission of mercy and redemption; that God the Son as Jesus Christ revealed the Father's love and offered men forgiveness and absolution to all who believed on his name; that God the Son, as our Redeemer, took our faults, blame, sin, and condemnation to the cross and there made an end of them; that he suffered death under Pontius Pilate, rose victorious from the dead, and promised his people his power and presence; that he ascended to his exaltation at the right hand of God from whence he shall return in wondrous glory at a time appointed by the Father.

This, in brief, was the Gospel preached by the disciples of Christ and by the early church. And it remains to this day the Historical, Protestant, and Evangelical Gospel of Jesus Christ.

## The Holy Spirit Will Sustain You with Power from on High

"It is expedient for you that I go away; for if I go not away, the Comforter will not come unto you: But because I ascend to my Father, I will send him to you" (John 16:7).

"Tarry, until you be endued with power from on high," (Luke 24:29). Power is the energy to do and to achieve all things. All the stars in the Heavens have at their center a vast nuclear furnace of tremendous energy. They can send out their rays of light through space for hundreds of light years. As far as man is concerned, this power of the stars is almost unending. The early church had need of a power like this—a power that was unending. As the ascended Lord, Christ had the power of his universal domain. Even more, he received all power, and he sent his power to the church in his Holy Spirit.

The church is endued with power from on high. Our Savior's presence is power, and his presence and power the Lord Jesus gives to all who claim him as Savior and Lord. The Lord Jesus tells us that the church received this power because he ascended to the Father. His Spirit and power touch those who believe on him. And from the shores of that small lake in Galilee to the uttermost parts of the world, the Gospel of Christ continues to touch human lives.

# The Exaltation of Christ

"When I look at the Heavens... the moon and the stars, which thou hast ordained: What is man that thou art mindful of him: and the son of man that thou visitest him?" (Psalm 8:3-4).

The writer of Psalm 8 felt overwhelmed by the majesty of God revealed in creation. He was awed that God was both mindful of man and cared about him. With the advent of the radio telescope, there has opened up to the astronomer a vast new expanse of the universe. It is one of immensity and grandeur. The marvels of the expanding universe are almost incomprehensible to the human mind. How majestic and powerful must be the God of all creation. And we are once again reminded of the Psalm's words, "What is man that thou art mindful of him; and the son of man that thou visitest him?"

At first, the problem seems as immense as the universe itself. How can God, who holds a billion galaxies and their stars in their course, be mindful of our little planet Earth and of me? Out of the trillions of stars in the universe and out of the billions of people on earth, how could God have time for me? How can he hear my prayers through the vast splendor of the expanding universe? How can he answer the prayers of my child? How can God know what is in my heart, or the periodic anguish of my soul when I feel estranged from him? And how can he reach out his hand to me when I need him or touch my soul to remind me of his love and grace? Viewed from a purely rational perspective, the difficulties seem overwhelming and almost insurmountable.

In his first chapter of his letter to the Colossians, St. Paul wrote,

> Christ is the image of the invisible God, the firstborn of every creature: For by him were all things created, that are in Heaven, and that are in earth; visible and invisible, whether they be thrones, or dominions, or principalities, or powers: all things were created by him and for him: and he is before all things, and by him all things consist.
>
> Colossians 1:15-17

And there is more. "That in the dispensation of the fullness of time, he might gather in one all things in Christ, both which are in Heaven, and which are on earth, even in him" (Ephesians 1:10).

This was Paul's theme—Christ above all. This is Christ exalted, Christ of the cosmos, who upholds all things by the word of his power. He is Lord and head of the church that bears his name. Paul was making known to the church in Colosse the greatness and prominence of our Savior's majestic sovereignty. With all his majestic sovereignty, the Savior promised to abide in us. While he abides in us, we also abide in him. Paul said that we sit with him in heavenly places. And although he ministers in the heavenly sanctuary, his is a living, active, operative presence throughout the universe. The overwhelming, insurmountable obstacles of space and time, the vast reaches of the expanding universe, and the eternity behind and the eternity before are nothing in the sight of God. They are but mere instants in time and space.

## All in All

The greatness and prominence of our Savior's majestic exaltation is his because all is his. He is Lord of creation, Lord of redemption, and the exalted Lord of Heaven and earth. Space, time, and the universe, the billions of galaxies and trillions of stars, were created by him. They consist in him and are summed up in Christ of the cosmos. It is little wonder that Paul took time in leading his readers to this grand truth.

The expanding universe of our Lord's glory is eternally in the process of creation. In his immanence, our Lord is everywhere and everywhere active. All occurs within his sovereign domain. "That in the dispensation of the fullness of time, he might gather together in one all things in Christ, both which are in Heaven and which are in earth, even in him." To sum up all things in Christ, this is the sovereign, majestic, exaltation of Christ our Lord.

## All in Him, and For You, Grace and Glory

What does all this mean for me, for you? Of what significance is Christ's sovereign, majestic exaltation? It means that those who are in Christ are destined to share in the glory and grace of our exalted Lord. He has made us to sit with him in heavenly places…for I abide in you, and you abide in me that where I am, there you may be also. This our Savior has promised, and with him a promise is as good as done. We are bidden not to stagger at the promises, not to be appalled at the immensity or vastness of the riches in grace, which we have in Christ Jesus our Lord. We are to believe them, embrace them in our hearts, and give thanks to God. There is revelation, the giving of knowledge, in all of this.

"That you might know…the exceeding greatness of his power…which he wrought when he raised him from the dead; and set at his own right hand in heavenly places" (Ephesians 1:19-20).

As vast as the unexplored universe may be, the love and grace of our Lord are far greater. Though our exalted Lord is far above in the Heavens, his love is still near to us. It is in the exalted Lord of the cosmos that we live and move and have our being. While he may manage the most distant galaxy in harmonious order, yet is he nearer than hands and feet that we may reach out and touch him. In so doing, we become aware of his abiding presence. As God's avowed purpose is to sum up all things in Christ, the apostle Paul would have us know that in the greatness and majesty of our Savior's Lordship, we have confidence to approach him in the knowledge of his love and the nearness of his presence.

You and I with our troubled thoughts, anxious hearts, hidden sorrows, and seeming impoverishment are immensely rich. We are rich in the spiritual powers that continually intervene on our behalf. Our daily companion, he who walks with us in the fellowship of the Spirit, is none other than the Lord of the universe. Though the church is often silent on this matter, she has always believed in the exaltation of Christ.

## As We Are in Christ, He Can Be Reached

Since we abide in Christ, living and having our being in him, he can be reached. And even though he upholds the worlds by the word of his power, he is able to hear our prayers. And even though he holds the entire universe in harmonious order, he still hears the prayers of my child. And though Christ has set the day course in its place, and though he is the Father of the rain drops, and has begotten the drops of dew, he can be reached and touched by the feelings of our infirmities. He will extend his hand to us when we are in need of him. He promised to do this. And we must believe in his promises as much as we believe in him. Should we not believe in him, then we would have nothing but despair and darkness. But as we do believe in him, knowing our Savior's majestic sovereignty, ours can be an assurance unimagined in our common hours.

Finally, if I am in him, and Christ abides in me and has created me, then he can know my heart. He can know my secret thoughts, my hopes, and my aspirations. My dreams and loves are all open to him.

> Thou understandest my thoughts afar off. Thou compassest my path and my lying down, and art acquainted with all my ways. For there is not a word in my tongue, but lo, O Lord, thou knowest it altogether. Thou hast beset me behind and before, and thou hast laid thy hand on me. Such knowledge is too wonderful for me, it is high and I cannot attain unto it. For whither shall I go from thy Spirit? Or whither shall I flee from thy presence? If I ascend unto Heaven, thou art there…if I take the wings of the morning and dwell in the uttermost parts of the sea: even there shall thy hand lead me, and thy right hand shall uphold me. For thou hast possessed my reins: thou hast covered me in my mother's womb…My substance was not hid from thee…I am fearfully and wonderfully made…thine eyes did see my substance, yet being unperfected; and in thy book all

my members were written...when as yet there were none of them... When I awake, I am still, still with thee.

Psalm 139:1-18

If God can know my heart, my thoughts, and my words before they are spoken, surely he can answer my prayers. And since he knows me better than I know myself, he can touch my soul to remind me of his grace. He can touch your soul also to remind you of his grace and love for you. And he can give us an assurance of his watchful care for us. He will hear our prayers, respond when we have need of him, and lead us in the way everlasting.

## The Second Advent of Our Lord

The Second Advent of our Lord, also known as the second coming, has been an essential eschatological concept of the church from the beginning of the Christian religion. From the committal for the funeral service we read:

> [In Jesus Christ our Lord] At whose coming in glorious majesty to judge the world, the earth and the sea shall give up their dead; and the corruptible bodies of those who sleep in him, shall be changed, and be made like unto his own glorious body; according to the mighty workings whereby he is able to subdue all things unto himself.
>
> (*Committal*—Common Book of Prayer)

Certain events will occur at or near the time of the second advent of our Lord. Immortality will have become a reality. There will be the resurrection of all who sleep in Christ. Their bodies will be changed and made like unto his glorious body. There will be the final judgment, the final period of trial for the church, the final judgment on Satan, and the creation of the new Heaven and new earth. These are eschatological concepts. They involve the doctrine of the last things, and we will discuss them under the division of eschatology. We only mention them here to note that the Second Advent has always been a cardinal doctrine of the Gospel of Christ Jesus. It is stated in Scripture as surely and as clearly as the promise of the first advent of our Lord.

The apostle Paul wrote:

> Behold, I shew you a mystery: We shall not all sleep, but we shall all be changed. In a moment, in the twinkling of an eye, at the last trump: for the trumpet shall sound, and the dead shall be raised incorruptible, and we shall be changed. For this corruptible must put on incorruption, and this mortal must put on immortality…then shall be brought to pass the saying that is written, Death is swallowed up in victory. O Death, where is thy sting? O Grave, where is thy victory? The sting of death is sin; and the strength of sin is the law. But thanks be to God which giveth us the victory through our Lord Jesus Christ. Therefore my beloved brethren be you steadfast, unmovable, always abounding in the work of the Lord, forasmuch as you know that your labor is not in vain in the Lord?
>
> 1 Corinthians 15:51-56

## Prayer

Eternal and loving Savior, we come to thee as thou has bid us come, to find rest for our souls. We embrace thy redemption in our hearts and thy Spirit in our souls. Forgive us, we pray, for not living fully up to thy grace and glory. We are mindful that thou dost remember us, our frame, that it is dust. But do thou now continue to abide with us that we, beholding as in a glass thy glory, may be transformed unto that same image even as by thy grace and Spirit. Amen.

# Pneumatology: The Doctrine of the Holy Spirit

As God's redemptive dealings with men unfolded in the course of human history, he also made a new covenant with man. This new covenant involved the indwelling and outpouring of the Holy Spirit upon the church of Jesus Christ. The promise is narrated in Ezekiel and in Jeremiah. As God brings to light the mystery of his redemptive counsel, the incidents, factors, and agency involved in man's redemption gradually unfold. As the history of the nations unfolds and is played out amidst all its changing fortune, so also does the redemptive aspect of revelation unfold in its historical development. At each stage in its progress, more light, new light, is added as man is able to bear it.

The covenant written on the tablets of stone was done away with. God's people were no longer able, if they ever were, to walk before God as required by the tablets of stone. These stones made no provision for the weakness of the flesh. They became a slave master and a coffin of stone. In the book of the prophet Jeremiah, the promise of the indwelling Spirit is narrated as follows.

> Behold, I will make a new covenant: not like the covenant which I made with their fathers when I took them by the hand to bring them out of the land of Egypt: My covenant which they broke, though I was their husband, saith the Lord. But this is the covenant which I shall make with the house of Israel: I will put my law within them and I will be their God and they shall be my people. And they shall know me: for I will forgive their iniquity, and their sins I will remember no more.
>
> Jeremiah 31:31-43

In the book of the prophet Ezekiel, it is written as follows.

> A new heart will I give you, and a new Spirit I will put within you; and I will take out of your flesh the heart of stone and give you a heart of flesh. And I will put my Spirit within you and cause you to walk in my statutes and to be careful to observe my ordinances.
>
> Ezekiel 63:26-27

God proposed a new covenant with man and a new way of dealing with him, not like the one which God had made with his people after he had led them out of the land of Egypt. The old covenant was embodied in the tablets of stone, but the meaning of the new covenant was more extensive than this. Here, the tablets of stone referred symbolically to the whole body of minute ritualistic procedure, which St. Peter acknowledged that even our fathers were unable to bear. It had become too oppressive. The narrative stated that the old covenant would be done away with because it was broken. It was broken because men found it impossible to keep. They were unable to walk before God with the tablets of stone.

Even though the law had a spiritual foundation and meaning, it had become a "weight of stone," sinking men down and making them despair of their ability to be what God had intended them to be. It also made them despair of their own ability to approach God in worship in the proper manner. They were never able to overcome their failure to adhere to its incidents of holiness and worship. What the old law really brought home to them was that any concept of redemption that would be of spiritual benefit to man would have to be wholly of God and a pure manifestation of his grace.

It would be a manifestation of God's grace that would permit both the saint and sinner to worship God. It would include within it a means of grace that would enable those who knew that they were ritualistically unclean in themselves through the beauty of divine compassion and forgiveness to approach God in worship.

They were to appropriate and accept this divine compassion through the exercise of their faith in God.

If the old law was done away with, where would men then find the law of the Spirit and the essential knowledge of God? God would send his Spirit to dwell within them. Through God's Spirit dwelling within them, they would have knowledge of God in their hearts, souls, and minds. Impelled by the Spirit, men's hearts and minds would turn to God. The rule of the Spirit is clear; when the heart turns to God, the mental assent is sure to follow.

The battle marked by the Stone of Ebenezer foreshadowed the promise that God would manifest his Spirit in the hearts of the people. To ensure victory, the prophet Samuel urged the people to turn and rededicate themselves to God. They were to turn to God with their whole heart. The people did so, and the victory they won over their enemies was enabled by the Spirit of God present with his people.

In Old Testament times, generally only the outward influence of the Spirit was experienced, not his permanent, indwelling presence. The law written in our hearts refers to the law of the Spirit. We are to understand the abiding and sanctifying power of the Holy Spirit dwelling in the heart as dwelling in a temple. This is true even though it is a temple of clay. Through the proceeding of the Holy Spirit, Christ is in our hearts and also at the right hand of God exalted. He makes intercession above in the presence of the Father, and he covers us over with the righteousness of his grace. He warms our hearts in our inner being by the grace of the Paraclete. And the Spirit is also our advocate with the Father; the Paraclete is an intercessor for the temple in which he dwells.

The moral effect of the Spirit's working on the individual is direct and primary. Even though it may not always appear to be so, the moral effect of the Spirit's working on the heart is a many-splendored thing—the working of right conduct, urging one to be honest, upright, virtuous, and honorable, and working in the redemption of the soul and turning the heart to God. The moral effect of the working of the Spirit also gives enlightenment and acceptance of the things of God. When the Spirit applies these principles, the outcome is spiritual gifts and understanding.

We confess with St. Paul and St. Augustine that we still have a warring in our members. Even though the Spirit abides with us and we have been given understanding of the things of God, no one achieves the fullness of Christ in this lifetime. Nevertheless, our inclination is toward God and the spiritual life. The warring in our members is between the natural man and the spiritual man. What occurs is this; it is the grace of God that prevents those morally estranged from God from acting consistently in a perverse and evil way. So also the old man, the natural man in us, prevents us from consistently manifesting the spiritual life.

Nevertheless, where sin does abound, the grace of God does much more abound. Even though on some occasions evil may wholly surround us, the morally wrong does not dominate us; it is not the predominant or controlling influence in our lives. None of this detracts from the promise and reality of the indwelling presence of the Holy Spirit in those who confess Jesus Christ as Savior and Lord. What it does prove is that, alas, the Spirit resides in temples made of clay.

Besides the promise of the indwelling presence, there is also the promise of the outpouring of the Spirit. The indwelling presence refers to the Holy Spirit residing and dwelling with the individual believer. The promise in the book of the prophet Joel is that of the outpouring of the Holy Spirit on the body of believers as the church of Jesus Christ. It is a special gift of God to the church.

> And it shall come to pass, that I will pour out my Spirit on all flesh; and your sons and your daughters shall prophesy, and your old men shall dream dreams, and your young men shall see visions. Even upon the menservants and upon the maidservants, in those days I will pour out my Spirit.
>
> Joel 2:28-29

# The Promise of the Father

It is the outpouring of the Holy Spirit that gives the church growth, guides and protects the church, and keeps the church vital and overflowing life. The prophet Ezekiel wrote about the time that God caught him up in a vision.

> And he brought me out by the Spirit of the Lord, and set me down in the midst of the valley and it was filled with dry bones, and lo, they were very dry…And he said to me: Son of Man, can these bones live? And I answered, O Lord God, thou knowest…Behold, I will cause breath to enter you and you shall live: and you shall know the Lord.
>
> Ezekiel 37:1-7

When Jesus ascended to the Father, he left behind his confused and bewildered disciples to carry on his mission. But they did not have all that which they needed to stand up to a world bent on self-destruction. They knew that Christ's personal, physical leadership was no longer with them. Yet, he had said to them that it was to their advantage that he go away. And then he told them of the promise of the Father. And, "He charged them to wait for the promise of the Father…You heard from me that John baptized you with water, but you shall be baptized with the Holy Spirit" (Acts 1:4-5).

A promise is an agreement to do something, and it is a basis of expectation for the recipient of the promise. God's promises carry with them blessings and gifts of spiritual significance. This particular promise was about the gift of the Holy Spirit. To the prophets, the promise of the permanent presence of the Holy Spirit was the one promise that gave them hope through the long years of darkness.

You shall live, and you shall know that I am the Lord. These two aspects—one of the spiritual life and the other of knowledge—have always come from the presence of the Holy Spirit. And they come whether there be only the outward manifestation of the Spirit's influence or the permanent indwelling presence of the Spirit. Inwardly, the life principle of the Spirit affects the thinking, feeling, and motivating part of man. It is a divine animating influence that is distinct from flesh and blood. And life is what makes one take in food and get energy from it. The Holy Spirit brings spiritual life with its presence. We are told in the Nicean Creed that "the Holy Spirit is to be worshipped as the Lord and Giver of life, who proceedeth from the Father and the Son; who with the Father and the Son, together is worshipped and glorified, and who spake by the prophets."

## Waiting for the Promise

The church is charged by its Lord, Christ Jesus, to wait for the promise of the Father. We must believe in this promise in order to wait for it, and we must make our believing a basis of hope and expectation. It is always time to wait, watch, pray, and remain in anticipation of the Spirit. We, like the disciples, are aware that the personal, physical presence of the Lord is no longer with us as the Master of Galilee. But because our Lord trod the way that led through Gethsemane and the cross and ascended to the Father, the Comforter has come. He is one who stands alongside us to help. Before the coming of the Holy Spirit, the disciples turned to Jesus as a physical presence for help and direction. But now they were to turn to the Holy Spirit for counsel and leadership.

It is the Holy Spirit who leads the church, who convicts the heart and conscience of right and wrong and of sin, and who brings us to the cross. It is the Spirit that calls us to service. He comes to us also as the Spirit of grace, glory, and divine love. He is promised to us by God the Father, and our Lord Jesus bids us to wait on the promise. And if we wait in anticipation for the Spirit, we may sense his presence.

There is a story in the Gospel of Luke about the blind beggar of Jericho (Luke 18:35-43). He sat by the side of the road, waiting for people to pass by. He was blind, so he could not see those of whom he might ask something. We do not know how long he may have been blind or how long he may have sat by the road waiting. But one day, he heard and sensed an unusually large crowd gathering. The noise of the multitude indicated that they were drawing nearer. He asked what it might be and was told that Jesus of Nazareth was passing by. Even though he was blind, he was aware of who Jesus might be. He had heard men speak of his grace and truth, of the Gospel he proclaimed, and something about his Kingdom. He also heard that the Master of Galilee had a wonderful, healing spirit, and that God was with this strange and wonderful prophet. All his life, he had waited in the darkness, for what, he knew not. Perhaps he may have waited for such a moment as this. As Jesus drew near, he resolved that he would cry out to him for healing.

"Jesus, thou son of David, have mercy on me." Those about the Savior bade him hold his peace. But he cried out so much the more. "Jesus, thou son of David, have mercy on me." From among all that mass of milling humanity, Jesus heard the once voice that cried out to him for mercy. "What will thou?" "Lord, that I might receive my sight."

Jesus said, "So be it unto you. Receive your sight, for your faith has made you whole." And he received his sight, and the long, dark night of waiting was over. When Jesus was passing by, though blind, the beggar cried out to him because he had sensed the near presence of the Lord's Spirit.

Even today, our Savior passes by no matter what the time or season. When we have turned to the Lord Jesus, we can sense his nearness in the quickening of our spirit and in the remembrance of the promise of the Father. We can wait in anticipation as he draws near, for he comes in Spirit to touch his own. Christ comes with healing in his wings and with the gentle grace of the Comforter. He comes to baptize us with the fire of the Spirit and to leave his presence as a permanent indwelling abode—and as a guarantee of his love and care. The Lord Jesus comes to fulfill the promise of the Father—the fulfillment for which we have been waiting.

At home in the stillness of the morning or in the quietness of the evening or in the worship service partaking of Holy Communion, he comes to us as of old. In the fellowship of prayer, Jesus passes by, ready to fulfill the promise of the Father. Like the blind beggar of Jericho, we need only acknowledge his presence and ask for his mercy and grace. As we wait for the promise, we must believe it, embrace it in our hearts, and look to it in expectation. And Jesus of Nazareth who passes by will baptize you with fire and with the Holy Spirit.

## When the Day of Pentecost Had Come

"And when the day of Pentecost had come: like the rush of a mighty wind...as with cloven tongues of fire, all were filled with the Holy Spirit" (Acts 2:1-2).

How the disciples had needed this gift of grace. What a tremendous difference we see in them after the day of Pentecost when the promise of the Father had come for them like the rush of a mighty wind. Before the coming of the Spirit, even after the resurrection, they seemed confused and bewildered. Not much is heard of them. And then like the rush of a mighty wind, it came upon them. It was as though they were suddenly endowed with wisdom, understanding, and power from on high. They became bold, fearless preachers of the Gospel and were transformed by the power of the Holy Spirit. The words of their Lord and of the prophets burned in their hearts and were expressed in their preaching. Simon Peter stood in the middle of the mocking multitude and, on fire with the Holy Spirit, boldly proclaimed:

> Men of Israel, hear these words: Jesus of Nazareth, a man attested to you by God with mighty works and wonders and signs which God did through him in your midst, as you yourselves know, this Jesus, delivered up according to

the definite plan and foreknowledge of God, you crucified and killed by the hands of lawless men. But God raised him up, having loosed the pangs of death, because it was not possible for death to hold him. This Jesus, God raised up and of this we are all witnesses. Being therefore exalted at the right hand of God, and having received from the Father the promise of the Holy Spirit, he has poured out this which you see and hear. Let all the house of Israel therefore know assuredly, that God has made him both Lord and Christ, this Jesus whom you crucified.

Acts 2:22-26 (RSV)

The darkness lasts only for the night, but joy cometh with the morning. It came with the bright morning of Pentecost. The Holy Spirit, coming upon them, enabled Peter and all the disciples to speak with authority and knowledge, having been led unto all the truth. The power of the Holy Spirit came to drive away the darkness of mockery, unbelief, confusion, doubt, and despair. But only as we claim the performance of the promise will the Spirit of truth and grace come upon us. And it will enable us to see the glory shining through the shadow of the cross.

Perhaps we may never speak with the tongues of men and angels. Much less are we likely to speak as with cloven tongues of fire. But the coming of the Holy Spirit will confirm the knowledge that God has made Jesus both Lord and Christ. This is the final fulfillment of the promise that of the Redeemer come from the heart of God together with the gift of the Holy Spirit that we might confess that Jesus is both Lord and Christ.

Christ is Lord because it was not possible for death to hold him, he is Lord whom God raised up and Lord at the right hand of God exalted. We accept him as Christ—the Crucified One who took all our faults, failures, and sins and nailed them to the cross. And he is Christ who suffered all these things that he should enter into his glory, according to all that the prophets had written. The promise of the Father can be yours, and you may make it your own. You need only believe it, embrace it in your heart, and claim it for your own. And as surely as day follows night, it will come to you in your own appointed time.

When the men heard all that Peter had to say, they were cut to the heart. "What shall we do?" they asked. Peter did not pussyfoot the Gospel. "Repent and be baptized every one of you in the name of Jesus Christ, for the forgiveness of your sins; and you shall receive the gift of the Holy Spirit…For the promise is to you and to your children…And those who received his words were baptized" (Acts 2:37-41 [RSV]).

And all were filled with the Holy Spirit.

## The Power Pentecost

The most powerful things in the universe are invisible: honor, character, and fortitude. Even the power to visualize and make dreams come true is invisible. We have also learned that faith is both the substance of things hoped for and the evidence of things not seen. Because we do not see this power, it does not mean that it does not exist. We know the power of the Spirit to be real because we have seen it work in the lives of countless numbers of people. And we have seen people with no power at all. Before the day of Pentecost, there appears to be in the disciples of our Lord a strong tendency toward vacillation. They seem to have lacked the power to stand firm. And when Jesus died, they fled their separate ways.

Then came the resurrection, and with it a transformation occurred among the followers of Christ. To men who had been confused, disappointed, and bewildered, a new morning had dawned. He on whom they had set their hopes was not dead but alive. The full impact and meaning of this grand event, however, remained obscure to them. Something was lacking. This lack was met on Pentecost fifty days after the resurrection of our Lord. A stirring deep in their hearts brought the disciples together. It was on the day of Pentecost that the Holy Spirit fell upon them.

The Spirit possessed them and overwhelmed them, having been given to them in full measure. And what a difference the Holy Spirit made in their lives and upon the apostolic message that they proclaimed.

What occurred that it made such a vast difference in these men? What exactly happened to them? They underwent a radical transformation. The hearts, minds, and lives of the disciples were changed. Willpower seldom changes men. Nor does time really change them. But the Holy Spirit can and often does change the lives of men and women. Admittedly, the Holy Spirit may not always act with such prominence as he did on the day of Pentecost. Generally, he comes like a still, small voice, effecting an inner transformation that eludes the eyes and defies description.

The change that occurred in the disciples in one day was dramatic. We don't wonder that some of the onlookers said, "These men are filled with new wine" (Acts 2:13). But Peter, standing up said, "These are not drunken, as you suppose, seeing it is but the third hour of the day" (Acts 2:15). They were filled with the Holy Spirit. This spiritual energy included within it the power to witness, work signs and wonders, and the power to heal the sick. Whereas the disciples had been previously destitute of this ability, the coming of the Holy Spirit on Pentecost endued them with power.

How was this change manifested in their lives and outlook? How did the Spirit of power make such a difference? To begin with, their entire outlook changed from one of confusion and despair to one of hope and expectation. What had been strange events obscured in darkness now turned into windows, streaming with light and glory. There is nothing so dejecting as to lack completely the expectation of obtaining anything in life or of not knowing how and where one is going. This had occurred with the disciples; how would they ever accomplish the task which the Lord had set them to do? Where would they acquire even half of the needed energy and ability to carry the Gospel to all the nations of the world? Who were they, anyway, even to attempt such an undertaking? The very immensity of their mission staggers the imagination.

With God, all things are possible. As the prophet Isaiah wrote, "Nothing, O God, is too great for thee." After Pentecost, it seemed as though the disciples had been endowed with supernatural power from on high. They were impelled from uncertainty to understanding of the meaning of the resurrection for their lives and its significance for the Gospel message. The realization slowly awakened in them that, "Surely this is the Christ, the Son of the living God." The Holy Spirit with all his creative wisdom and power brought these things home to them. In his sermon, Peter, when he stood with the eleven, referred to the teaching of the Scriptures where they told that Jesus was the Christ who was to suffer these things. The story was coming together, the Old Testament prophesy was being fulfilled, and there were the wonderful works of the Lord Jesus crowned by his resurrection.

Peter and the early church saw in the victory of the Lord Jesus over death irrefutable proof that he was the promised Redeemer. Confirmation came with the outpouring of the Spirit on Pentecost that Jesus was the Son of the living God. It filled their thoughts, overwhelmed their minds, and added power to their preaching. No longer would they be a fearful handful of men hiding together in some dark, obscure upper room. But from henceforth, they were a brave band of Gospel preachers that made the world take notice of the grace of our Lord Jesus Christ. Luke, in his narration of the growth of the church in his book of Acts, expressed the opinion that it was the Holy Spirit that directed their work and prepared their way.

## The Holy Spirit in Power Founded the Church

The group of people that had gathered together at the time of Pentecost came from every walk of life. They had followed Jesus for different reasons. Most of them were fishermen, one was a tax collector, and another was a scribe. Who would have expected that from this group of poverty-stricken men would raise the leaders of a movement that, in time, would circle the world? The Holy Spirit, working in the lives of the disciples, sent them and the early followers of Jesus out to be untiring messengers of the grace that redeems and restores.

When the wider expansion of the movement came, it was the Holy Spirit that directed the church in Antioch to this endeavor. "The Holy Ghost said, 'Separate unto me Barnabas and Saul for the work where unto I have called them'" (Acts 13: 2). From then on, it became a ministry of the Spirit—the Spirit seeking, calling, warming hearts, and sending the messengers out with the words of life. And ahead of them, in the grace of God, moved the Holy Spirit, preparing the way and the people and calling out the children of the Kingdom of Heaven.

As though by an unseen hand, the disciples became fitted for the arduous work that lay ahead of them. Their way was beset with hardship and difficulties. Ahead lay privation, suffering, and even death. As opposition from the religious authorities grew, it made their task even more difficult. In time they were to need all the encouragement, strength, and support Heaven could send them. And yet, everywhere the early church went, it triumphed. It never knew the meaning of defeat. At times, it slowed but only for a moment. It always pushed ahead. As it moved, it gathered power and new converts who in turn became preacher, teachers, and missionaries.

If the early church had one thing that the present day church appears to lack, it is the Holy Spirit in power. This gave the church the ability to act in all manner of circumstances. It possessed the capability of reproducing itself many times over. It gained controlling influence over the lives of millions. Over the first three hundred years of its existence, in the face of the most extreme and unjustifiable opposition, it exerted a tremendous amount of energy and spiritual force. It was "power packed." The church reached into every part of the Roman Empire. This was so even though the empire that opposed the church was massive and full of strength. It was the power of the Spirit that enabled the disciples to answer, "We must obey God rather than men." Wherever and whenever men of God take this stand, the result is always bound to bring blessings.

With persecutions taking their leaders and false teachers causing disturbance, the miracle is that the church did grow so abundantly. But then, this is what the Holy Spirit always seems to do in the lives of individuals and in the life of the church. He works miracles.

As a growing religious movement, the church was oblivious to its dangers. It was oblivious to all its dangers because the men of the church knew they served a risen and living Lord. The church knew very few apostates. They learned to give their Lord the love of their hearts and the service of their lives. Being a Christian was not a part-time affair with them. It was the biggest thing in their lives. With the Holy Spirit stirring them to new understanding and new undertakings, they surmounted every obstacle that confronted them. Nothing seemed impossible. So daring and courageous were they that they were accused of courting death. "Who knew that but die were gain." Their concept of achievement was, "I can do all things through Christ Jesus who strengthens me."

Moreover, the early church knew how to suffer for the cause. They rejoiced that they were considered worthy to suffer for the Name. Yet in all these things, they considered themselves as more than conquerors through Jesus Christ who loved them. The spiritual energy the early church received on Pentecost was beyond doubt the power that laid the foundation of the Christian church.

## Only the Spirit Gives Life

While we may intellectually analyze the church, let no one doubt that we love it and give it the devotion of our hearts. What an amazing contrast the early church is to that of the modern era. It had no central office or board of missions, no system of literature, no prescribed educational requirements for its preachers, no printed programs, and no community allocation. What it did possess was Jesus Christ and the presence of his Spirit. With these alone it conquered an empire.

As a whole, and we say this with deep concern, the twenty-first century church lacks the spiritual depth and vitality of the early church. It wavers in its beliefs and moral standard. It lacks strong and positive convictions on Jesus Christ, especially as to how his death is related to the forgiveness of sins. And more often than not, it is vague in its presentation of the atonement of Jesus Christ. We seem to have lost the meaning and power of the name *Redeemer*. And we must confess our greatest sin: we are not a generation prepared to suffer for the Name. We like our religion free and easy, attended with as little difficulty or discomfort as possible. In short, we lack the power and deep influence of the Holy Spirit as a permanent, indwelling presence.

We say this with all sincerity and conviction of heart and mind. More than ever, we need the power of Pentecost in our churches today. We need it because it is the one source of energy that brings life for the individual believers and energy for the existence of the church. In gratitude and humility, we thank the Lord God for his saving grace of forgiveness. And we confess that without the redeeming power of the Spirit, we are all lost and yet in our sins. Without the Spirit, it is impossible to distinguish between life and death. Oh, Lord God, "Thou turnest thy face, they are troubled: thou takest away their breath, they die…But when thou sendest forth thy spirit they are created" (Psalm 104:29-30). Only the Holy Spirit, the Lord and Giver of life, gives life to every living thing. To live means to grow, to bud, to bring fruit, and to increase manifold. The Spirit is the animating life principle in the church of Jesus Christ.

## THE THEOLOGY OF GRACE

# Thou Hast Stricken My Heart

> You are manifestly declared to be epistles of Christ, ministered by us. Written not with ink, but with the Spirit of the living God: not in the tablets of stone, but in the fleshy tablets of the heart...not of the letter, but of the Spirit: for the letter killeth, but the Spirit giveth life.
>
> 2 Corinthians 3:3-6

The letter without the grace and Spirit of the Lord Jesus always kills. But when God, in his grace, shed abroad his love in our hearts through the Holy Spirit which was given us, the Spirit gave us life. Even though some individuals in the past and present question the deity of God the Son, no one has seriously denied the deity of the Holy Spirit. We are talking about God the Holy Spirit that proceeded as a divine being. His presence is the life principle in the spiritual part of our being. The Spirit works as a divine, animating influence in human lives. We describe this principle best by how it works and by what it does. We know that in the beginning the Holy Spirit was active in creation, and the church conceives him as the Lord and Giver of life.

In Old Testament times, the Spirit of God was felt as a power and as an outward influence. At times, for a specific purpose, its power and influence possessed and motivated individuals. Holy men of old spoke as moved by the Spirit. King David came under the Spirit's influence in his rule over God's people. From David's Psalms, we see that the Spirit filled his soul with a holy desire—a longing for God and a sense of his presence.

In the dispensation of the church of Jesus Christ, the Holy Spirit is a special gift of God's grace, and it comes as a permanent, abiding presence. The Holy Spirit works in many ways in human lives and gives different gifts to different individuals. The Holy Spirit is always active in the process of redemption. When the Spirit touches the soul, we confess the reality of the living God because the Spirit comes as a guiding power and as an enabling light. Then again, he is manifested as the Spirit of all comfort who comes with ineffable consolation.

We also know him as the Holy Spirit, the Lord God who heals. When he comes as the Spirit of grace, he works miracles of transformation in human lives and opens up the eyes of our understanding. As an animating, divine influence, the Holy Spirit fills our souls with a longing for God and a sense of his presence. We also note the marvel of his grace; in God's mercy, the humble of heart, the poor in spirit, and those who hunger for a kingdom of peace and righteousness are the dwelling places of his Spirit. This is a wonder of grace—the spirit residing in the lives of believers. The indwelling of the Spirit leads to this; while the outward man is perishing, the inner man is being renewed day by day. Thus, the Holy Spirit, in bringing the love of God into our hearts, manifestly declares us to be epistles of Christ.

"Written not with ink, but with the Spirit of the living God: Not in tablets of stone, but in the fleshy tablets of the heart. Not of the letter, but of the Spirit: For the letter killeth, but the Spirit giveth life" (2 Corinthians 3:3-6).

## Thou Hast Made Me Love Thee

"Thou hast stricken my heart with thy word, O Lord my God; and I love thee" (*Confessions*—St. Augustine).

The Holy Spirit also overshadows the work of the church, its members, and the Gospel message. He convicts the soul of right and wrong, of sin, and leads us to repentance and grace and glory. It is the Spirit of the living God that cultivates the soul, making the heart receptive to the word of the Lord. "Thou hast stricken my heart with thy word, O Lord my God;" thou hast made me love thee and given me the desires of my heart. What is desire but volition of consent to the things we wish? When consent takes the form of seeking to posses the things we wish, that is desire.

If we surrender to the influence of the Spirit that dwells in us, the Spirit will control our desires. The difficulty lies in complete surrender, which is never an easy thing to do. Still, the Spirit can give us a holy desire to know and want spiritual things. He gives us the desire to serve God with a willing mind and with a perfect heart. Moreover, in order to protect us, the Holy Spirit has the power to make us insensitive to those things that are harmful to the spiritual life.

The Holy Spirit is also called the finger of God. Augustine wrote that on the tablets of stone, the finger of God did operate. Conversely, the finger of God as the law of the Spirit also operates on the hearts of men. One was written without and served only to condemn men. But the law of the Spirit was written on the heart by the Spirit of him who justifies the ungodly. And rather than condemnation, the Spirit gives life. He awakens the soul toward God. In the Old Testament, the grace of God was hidden behind the veil, but the veil was removed in Christ, and in him the grace of God is given. The apostle Paul wrote that the grace of God was revealed in Christ Jesus, bringing salvation to all men.

## The Spiritual Life

"With a wounded heart, I have felt thy brightness, O Lord" (*Confessions*—St. Augustine). For what is man that God should be mindful of him? And yet man has been crowned with the glory and honor of God's presence. One thing is most certainly true; we need not struggle to attain the spiritual life. But many individuals make this mistake when seeking a more meaningful spiritual life. The reality is simplicity itself, for has not God chosen the simple things to confound the wise? All one needs do is to willingly surrender to the influence of the Holy Spirit. Surprised? That is it. Don't resist its desire to assimilate your life. Let the Holy Spirit have his way with you, and then your spiritual life moves into the mysterious working of him who works all things after the counsel of his own good will.

Stephen said it simply: "You do always resist the Holy Spirit" (Acts 7:51). Don't resist the Holy Spirit. Let your desire be a willing submission to the Spirit's gentle grace, and seek to cultivate the Spirit, welcoming his coming and influence. It is just possible that something wonderful may happen to you, and you will behold wondrous things out of his law. You will rejoice in the glory of God's grace, and you will have obtained the certitude of your faith in Christ Jesus. You will find that God has not written on your heart the spirit of fear but of power, love, and a sound mind. And though the outward man may be perishing day by day, you will discover that the inner man is being renewed day by day even as by the Spirit of the Lord.

God the Holy Spirit was active in creation, and God the Holy Spirit is active in the new creation. He will not leave that which he has begun in you, and though he has stricken your heart with his word, he has loved you. By his grace, through which he who is weak is made strong, he will sustain you. He will complete that which he has begun in you through the grace of our Lord Jesus Christ.

## The Holy Spirit Working in Human Lives

"And to him that overcometh and keepeth all my works, I will give him the Morning Star" (Revelations 2:26-28).

"The Morning Star," is it not beautiful? Have you ever seen it? It is the star that ushers in the dawn of a new day. There is a painting from the ancient classical period entitled, "Aurora, Goddess of the Dawn." In this painting, far to the west, there is nothing but darkness. But far to the east, there appears the chariot of the Goddess Aurora, driving away the darkness and issuing in the dawn of a new morning. This is mythology. But the Morning Star is real, and you can see it in the Heavens early in the morning. Admittedly, one needs to arise early to get in touch with the spirit of the morning. All is quiet and serene. There is the stillness—the utter immensity of the vast, expanding universe. And if you

## The Theology of Grace

do arise early, you can see the Morning Star for yourself—the harbinger of the new day. If you continue looking, you can see the first streaks of new light far to the east.

Like the chariot of the Goddess Aurora, the Holy Spirit moves over the length and breadth of the land, driving back the darkness. He is looking for a heart, a soul, and a life that he can make ready for the Master's work. The Spirit is looking for men and women of the Morning Star. It is written that when the fullness of time was come, God sent forth his Son. That is when the men and women of the Kingdom appear. That is when the Holy Spirit separates them out for the work to which he has appointed them—in the fullness of time, God sends forth a man or women of the Kingdom.

Like the Morning Star, the Holy Spirit molds men, makes them, and uses them to usher in the dawn of a new spiritual awakening. They drive away the darkness. And like the Bright and Morning Star, they do so with the light of the Gospel of grace. With soul-quickening faith, they proclaim once again that Jesus Christ is Lord. They are Spirit-chosen, Spirit-led men and women of the Morning Star. "I am Alpha and Omega," said our Lord. "The First and the Last" (Revelation 1:11)—the Bright and Morning Star.

The church needs men and women of fortitude who have the flame of the Spirit in their blood and in their character. Men possessed of the simple manliness to do the will of God are needed by the church in every age and in every generation. More than ever, the church needs men with energy and brains—resolute men who, like St. Paul, will not be disobedient to the heavenly vision whenever and wherever it may appear to them.

When the heavenly vision does appear, it seems as though it is always on some lonely road to Damascus. More often than not, it may be in a desert place with not a soul or voice around for miles. It generally comes away from the haunts of learning and away from the milling of the multitude. There is just Heaven and earth, soul and spirit, and the heavenly vision that appear on that lonely road. The love of Christ constrains these men to follow the heavenly vision. We can sense the Spirit working in their lives. And by God's grace, we may yet be able to emulate them.

Were these men of the Morning Star? Yes. It was the Master Workman of the race, working in and through them. They were the harbingers of an expanding and conquering Christianity. It is Christ of the abiding presence who is the same yesterday and today and forever. These are men who walk hand in hand with the Lamb of God. We must understand the character of these men. There is the unseen hand behind what we see—the Holy Spirit building men, raising them up, and setting them afire with the Gospel light. Blessed are the overcomers in the work that the Holy Spirit has appointed for them to do, for they will inherit the Kingdom in this world and the next. These men, like Stephen, resist not the Holy Spirit and his desire to mold, shape, and forge their lives into instruments for his use. The Holy Spirit enables them to conquer themselves, their passions, their hates, and their ignorance. They are empowered to march out like heroes of their faith, building up the work of the kingdom of God.

## The Morning Star in Their Work

Rise up, O man of God. The Church for you doth wait.
Her strength unequal to the task;
Rise up and make her great.

Lift high the Cross of Christ;
Tred where his feet have trod,
As brothers of the Son of God,
Rise up, O men of God.

(William Merrill)

All harbingers of the morning, whether they were named John, William, or Martin, were God-chosen men who rose up. They were men whom the Holy Spirit enabled to gather up the various forces of their time and weld them into a flowing river of light and glory. In their time, they rose up on the wings of the Spirit and made the church equal to her task. They shattered the powers of darkness and were accused of turning the world upside down. They gave the church a new day, infused her with a new spiritual impulse, and filled with redemptive possibilities. They have held high the cross of Christ. They have trod where his feet have trod. And they have redeemed their faith from cold, formless strictures. And they have caused the church to seek further horizons. How greatly does the church rely on these men that are called out by the Holy Spirit at each forward movement of its rebirth.

There can be no greater work for the church than this—to drive away the darkness over center city and to bring the weary and poor in spirit the Gospel of the Lord Jesus Christ. Through its ministry, the church must give hope, inspiration, and desire to each individual to strive again for an exalted and noble manhood in Christ Jesus. We must remind ourselves that this is none other than the house of God and none other than the gate of Heaven.

There is instruction in the history of the church, examples of devotion and self-sacrifice. We learn from the path that holy men trod from their spiritual brilliance, clear insight, and absolute strength of conviction. We would note how determined they were, holding to their course in resolute will. With sincerity of heart and religious fervor, we see them deeply committed to the Gospel. We would seek to emulate their open-mindedness and sympathy for all classes and conditions of men.

## The Star of Christ May Come to You

From the Lord Jesus Christ, we have this promise: to him "that overcometh and keepeth all my works…I will give the morning star" (Revelation 3:26-28). To become men and women so endowed, we must have a willing surrender to the Holy Spirit and submission to the hand of God. Through the dark and lonely nights, we must cling to our hope in Christ and the knowledge of his presence. And when the fullness of time will have come for us, we will know it.

Every believer can be touched by the greatness of the work as spirit answers to spirit. Every believer can be one of our Savior's overcomers who "keepeth all my works" and receives the Bright and Morning Star. You may not think you can't be great, but you can be; you can have some greatness. You can help build the Kingdom. You, too, can love courage, moral strength, truth, beauty, and a high purpose in life. With God, all things are possible, and Christ can surely work in you as he has in other times and in other men and women. The Lord Jesus can do that. Because he did it with Simon Peter, he can do it with every one of us. When all is said and done, we really do not conquer ourselves. But Christ can surely do that.

It is really this gentle Savior whose presence is like the coming of the soft dawn of the new day that overcomes in us. Quietly, slowly, gently, he conquers our passions, our temper, and our selfishness and sins. Knowing the reality of the Savior's living presence, you can become men and women of the Morning Star. Ours can become a church quickened with the divine words of grace. And we would be concerned with kindness and sympathy for all classes and conditions of men, women, and children.

Know that these men of the Morning Star who drove away the darkness were just ordinary men. Just about all were physically weak. One was blind. They were not really very much to begin with. They were just like you and me. Christ can fill us, take possession of us, and use us to usher in a new day for his church. This is the Savior I would leave with you: he who is Alpha and Omega, the Bright and Morning Star. I would want you to give him an invitation into your homes, families, and hearts. He has promised to come again in wondrous glory, and I would like you to know the wonders of his coming to you now.

## THE THEOLOGY OF GRACE

# The Ebb and Flow of the Spiritual Life

When Mary Magdalene poured the precious ointment on our Lord, she was reproached by the disciples. But Jesus silenced them. "Let her alone; why do you trouble her?.She hath done a beautiful thing to me...For you will not always have me with you" (Mark 14:6-7).

From what the Christian religion has achieved in the lives of men and women and in the society where its influence has been felt, it has demonstrated its redemptive and heroic nature. When entrenched evil and darkness threatened to enslave humanity, these powers of darkness were shattered by a great outpouring of the Holy Spirit. Yet there were times, even decades, when the strength of the church appeared to recede and when its influence seemed to wane and grow ineffective. There seems to be an ebb and flow to the progress of the church. Our individual spiritual life also appears to be on a tide. It ebbs and flows.

Still, our religion is heroic; it has those moments of the strong manifestation of the Spirit. Those high moments of the Spirit offer great adventure and opportunity. But like the disciples on occasion, we may not see too clearly; we may think that the precious ointment poured on Christ to be a great waste. Actually, we may suffer from an illusion. We seem to think that the strength and power of "Christ in us" is not always constant. But this is only an illusion and a deception brought on by the father of lies. While it is true that there is an ebb and flow, a tidal characteristic to our faith and spiritual life, and while it is also true that it was meant to be this way, we do have a constant source of appeal. We have a great unfailing Lord; Jesus Christ, your Savior, and mine. He is the same yesterday, and today, and forever.

There have been days, even weeks, when we felt under the complete domination of God's Spirit and the sense of his presence was a living vital reality with us. Isaiah wrote, "Seek you the Lord while he may be found; and call upon him when he is near" (Isaiah 55:6). Those high moments of the Spirit, those moments of great adventure and opportunity must be taken at the flood when we sense our Lord near. There are other times when they may not be taken so readily. Our Lord said to his disciples, "You will not always have me with you."

There are times when our spiritual life and minds are at low ebb. Who has never felt low? Who has never had those moments when he felt weak and helpless? How do we get out of it? What can we do to overcome those times when we feel down? After the cross, with the two disciples on the way to Emmaus—before Christ drew near—disillusion began to set in. For them, the tide was going far out to sea, taking with it all their hopes and dreams.

Then as the Savior drew near to them, their hearts began to burn within them. Faith and hope began to flow rich, strong, and vibrant once more. Though unknown to them at first, our Savior's presence awakened their spiritual life and revived their hopes. And it is ever so; Christ's presence will work the same in us, for he alone is the source of our spiritual life. As he renewed the spiritual life of those who knew him not on the way to Emmaus, he can do as much with every one of us. In the ebb and flow of our faith and spiritual life, and at any time of our lives, our Lord can draw near to us whatever the occasion. Time does not hold him. Space is unable to contain him, and he will come and draw near like he who walks on the wings of the wind.

## We Have a Constant

We should know that amidst all the ebb and flow of life and the constantly changing circumstances, in the high tide and in the low tide, and in the strong and weak moments of our spirits, we have one great constant. We have an unfailing, unchanging Lord. Even though there is an ebb and flow to our spiritual life, our Lord can hold us steady. In all of life's constantly changing circumstances, it is comforting to know that we have a faithful and unfailing Lord. Our Lord is reliable, dependable, honest, and true. With him as our Redeemer-God, hope becomes an anchor of our souls, and by hope we are saved. Our faith in him is still the substance of things hoped for—the evidence of things not seen.

But then we have known all along that life will not always seem to be at the flood tide—when all goes our way, when all is progress, and when the heart is constantly warmed by his presence. There will be times when faith will ebb. We have a feeling of mild estrangement, a spiritual diminishing, and an emotional fading away. The cross appears hazy, and its meaning seems far distant from us and from the present incidents in our lives. Then, the mind, if we let it, will try to expand the concept. We endeavor to give intellectual reasoning to such feelings. It is as though our emotional letdowns were drawing the mind away from the cross, letting all its saving grace flow out with the tide. If we remember anything at all, we must realize that now will be a time of waiting on the Lord and of hoping on his Word, for our souls will have become disquieted within us.

## When He Is Near

But our Lord is faithful. His spirit reminds us that with all diligence we must guard our hearts and minds. We will look to him. We will turn our eyes upon Jesus, and the fading away begins to cease. The feelings and emotions are controlled. Thus far and no further ebbs the tide. Then the tide turns. And once again, the mind, heart, and soul will acknowledge his grace and love. Slowly, like it went out, the tide returns. And with heart, mind, and soul, we will have been restored, and it is Christ Jesus who strengthens us. We sense again that he is near. It is the uplifting power of his presence that we feel that we have acknowledged and that we have awakened.

Even though we may not always sense our Lord's presence, he is ever near. We have a Savior-Friend who is closer than a brother. Constantly abiding, the reality of his presence can be a true spiritual experience for each of us. When Christ is near, all is peaceful and at rest. All seems constant and sure. The promise of our Lord is that he abides with us. We must hold to this truth and hold our minds fast to it even when our feelings may seem otherwise. We will look to his presence even though our emotions ebb and flow. We turn our hearts, minds, and souls to him, for we are known of him, and he will awaken us to the reality of his presence now, tomorrow, and forever.

## The Healing Presence

While the Holy Spirit is the Lord and Giver of life, scripture also characterized him as the Lord God that healeth thee. In our Lord Jesus Christ, all the fullness of God is pleased to dwell, and this is especially true about the Holy Spirit. There is a healing—physical, emotional, and spiritual—in the very presence of our Lord. The following story is found in the Gospel of Luke.

> And as he went, the people pressed round about him, and a woman who had a flow of blood for twelve years, and could not be healed by any one. And she came up behind him and touched the fringe of his garment; and immediately her flow of blood ceased. And Jesus said, "Who touched me?" And when all had denied it, Peter said, "Master, the entire multitude surrounds you and presses upon you." But Jesus said, "Someone has touched me..." And when the woman saw that she was not hidden, she came trembling, and falling down before him declared in the presence of all the people why she had touched him; and how she had touched him, and how she had been immediately healed. And he said to her, "Daughter, your faith had made you whole: go in peace."
>
> Luke 8:43-48 (RSV)

### Jesus Is Touched in Faith

There are thousands and even millions of people who crowd the Christian churches every Sunday. And so it was with our Lord as he ministered to the throngs that pressed about him during his earthly pilgrimage. The Spirit of grace with which he was anointed drew them to him. While he talked to the multitude along the banks of the Jordan or by the shores of the Galilee, people generally surrounded him. But on one particular day, only one humble woman availed herself of his presence, and she touched him. She had need of the Lord Jesus, and in simple faith she reached out and touched him. And Jesus healed her and made her whole. The door to a richer and fuller life was opened wide before her by the grace of our Lord Jesus Christ. This door also stood open before the entire multitude, but only one individual had the faith to enter in.

Ever the Teacher come from God, our Lord wanted to make his disciples aware of what had occurred. "Who touched me?" Jesus asked. His disciples could hardly believe the question. Their Master was being pushed and elbowed on all sides by an inquiring group of people. Those of the inner circle thought the question out of place. And loveable Simon Peter, who always responded to the Lord, answered simply, "Master, the multitude throngs thee and presses upon thee, and sayest thou, who touched me?" What Simon Peter meant was that the question was superficial because everyone near Jesus had touched him.

Yet our Lord knew that from this milling mass of lost humanity, one single soul had made contact with him and had become the recipient of his grace and healing power. He said again, "Someone hath touched me." What our Lord meant was that someone had reached out and touched him in believing faith. The woman, receiving our Lord's grace and Spirit, felt the flow of his healing power enter her body. She was conscious that her healing had been complete. She fell down before him and told him all the truth. The Lord God that heals had worked his miracle of grace. And to open the door to a new and fuller life, Christ said, "Daughter, thy faith hath made thee whole; go in peace" (Luke 8:48). We have indeed a beautiful Savior.

## Our Savior's Response

Christ always responded to any individual who reached out to him in believing faith. And he was glad this had occurred. He was ever willing to give of himself and of his grace. His entire mission was one of service for others and of self-sacrifice. Yet as a man of sorrows, our Lord suffered from a broken heart. While he was ever so willing to give of himself, those about him were so reluctant to receive. And is this not always true? He is ever so ready to do so much for us, and we permit him to do so little. We know that his coming was an invitation to us, for he came in love and not in judgment. He would win by persuasion of his Spirit and grace and not by compulsion. He will always come to us if we give him an invitation.

The great Shepherd of our souls would come to fill the emptiness that we feel on occasion, but many are reluctant to receive the love and grace that make us whole. Still, he does come as the Lord God that heals, and the Father does send the Spirit in his name. For the many ills that trouble the human race, we need this healing. And while our Lord may rejoice over the few that really touch him, he cannot but be heavy with sorrow over the many that are content to merely crowd and throng around him.

## His Touch and You

Despite the hundreds of years that separate us from this incident, we have much in common with the multitude that crowded around Jesus on that day. We have tasks to perform. Occasionally we are confronted with difficulties too heavy for our own strength alone. Like the humble woman with the flow of blood, we need to receive our Lord's power, his fullness, and his healing. The prophet Isaiah characterized his healing ability, saying that he heals the brokenhearted and every stroke of your wound. He heals every sickness of your heart, and every desire gone wrong. He heals every disease of your soul. He heals those that are oppressed and those in sorrow. He comes with healing in his wings to those that languish in loneliness and to them that are distressed because they have lost the vision of God's mercy. Why then will you refuse to be healed? Was there no balm in Gilead? Was there no physician there? Why then has the health of my people not been restored?

Some of us have lives that need to be held up to his fullness. Others have fears that make us look with foreboding for the morrow. There are those who have need of the comfort of him who has promised to be with us always. We have all come with our hungers and thirsts with our burdens and fears and with our sins even as did that multitude of long ago. The same Christ, who was thronged by that ancient multitude, moves among us today with healing in his wings. We have two choices. We can throng him, or we can touch him.

The simple fact remains, like the woman in the Gospel story, we must reach out and touch the Lord Jesus. When we do this, he gives us the grace to enlarge our lives to contain the joy and healing that he brings. This is my Savior of whom I am writing—the Lord God that healeth thee. By her simple touch, the woman appealed to the grace of our Lord Jesus Christ. Her act distinguished between those who merely throng Jesus and those who really touch him. Indeed, we must touch him or be touched by him. Touch him once, and life is changed. Healing flows on the grace of his Spirit, and Jesus Christ will have come into your life. You will have been touched by his healing presence, and you will have been touched by the Lord God that healeth thee.

## The Lord and Giver of Life

Even though the Holy Spirit moved over the face of the waters at the beginning of creation, our immediate concern is his ministry in the "new creation." We have in mind his work of love and grace in awakening a once dormant heart to a new spiritual life. In the Gospel of John, there is the story of the Samaritan woman who came to the well to fetch water while Jesus was there. She came to fetch water in the common duty of a housewife in every day life. In this encounter with Christ, our Lord would transform that simple water into a symbol of spiritual life.

Our Savior had the gift of taking the ordinary things of life, using them, and pointing people to Heaven and to the grace and glory of God. To this woman at Jacob's well, to us, and to all people of the world, Christ revealed the new life that he brings. It is new life that comes from the heart of God. From a single encounter with Christ, things are viewed from a different perspective.

To the woman at the well, the Savior told her of the true worship of the Father. It is worship in spirit and in truth because God is a Spirit and the one true God. From the Father's throne of grace flows a stream of living water, and he who drinks of this living water becomes heir to eternal life.

When she left the Lord Jesus to return to her home, the woman spread the word of the new prophet. She told of the perception Jesus had made of her heart and life. And we are inclined to think that she believed in him. How long the effect of her having met and talked with the Lord Jesus may have lingered with her, we do not know. We who have turned to the Lord Jesus may not remember the exact day or the moment, but we do remember the encounter. We remember the feeling of his love and grace shed abroad in our hearts when we first turned to the Lord Jesus.

With some individuals, the effect of having met the Lord Jesus may last only a day or so because they have not permitted the experience to sink deeply within. Others may be careless and through neglect, over the passage of time, permit the glory of the moment to fade away. But with others, those who hunger for a kingdom of peace and righteousness, the afterglow of our Lord's glory remains. It remains within like a slow, eternal flame. It pervades the soul and overwhelms the heart. In his gentle way, the Lord and Giver of life is at work in the inner man. And this occurs from one encounter with Jesus of Nazareth.

## THE THEOLOGY OF GRACE

### The Lord and Giver of Spiritual Life

An encounter with the Lord and Giver of spiritual life can be a transforming experience. It is the beginning of a work of love and grace. As the Giver of spiritual life, the Holy Spirit has power to work in us the wonders of his grace. But we must reach out and touch him or invite his presence. Truly, to know the Lord Jesus as he is, we must have our own personal experience with him. We must feel his love and grace sounding the depths of our soul. And we must open up our lives and hearts to the indwelling of his Spirit. His words echo in our minds. "I abide in you, and you abide in me" now and forever. If we meet him, call upon him, and believe in him, he will come and abide with us. This is the power of our Christian religion, the Holy Spirit, as the Lord and Giver of spiritual life, residing in the hearts of his people.

We who have turned to the Lord Jesus believe that he is, and that he rewards those who diligently seek his presence. And so we wait for the coming of the promise of the Father for the Spirit to touch our lives, and we wait with hope and expectation.

# Responding to the Presence

> I love the Lord because he has heard my voice and my supplication. Because he has inclined his ear to me, therefore I will call on him as long as I live…Gracious is the Lord, and righteous: our God is merciful. The Lord preserves the simple; when I was brought low, he saved me. Return, O my soul, to your rest; for the Lord has dealt bountifully with you.
>
> Psalm 16:1-7

The Spirit of Christ ever seeks to awaken a response in us. God desires our devotion, prayers, gratitude, and worship. While our redemption is still an unfinished product, it is also an ongoing process. Though redeemed, our journey in the spiritual life has just begun, and until we respond, we can never be made whole. We may still suffer from internal discord of mind, soul, and spirit. But as we learn to respond to our Lord's love and grace, we can be made whole. Our lives can be harmonized and be in tune with God and spiritual realities.

Our response is that which we do in answer to our Savior's love and grace. It is a type of spiritual behavior. We respond with faith and trust, with praise and thanksgiving, and with worship. Thus did David pray in his Psalm, "I will love the Lord because he has heard my voice and my supplication; because he has inclined his ear to me, I will call upon him as long as I live." We assent to the truth of David's works. "Return, O my soul, to your rest; for the Lord God has dealt bountifully with you."

## The Presence Encountered

In *Confessions*, St. Augustine wrote,

> How shall I find rest in thee, O Lord my God; and who shall send thee into my heart? Tell me of thy compassion, O Lord my God, what thou art to me. Say unto my soul, I am thy salvation. So speak that I may hear. Behold, Lord, the ears of my heart are before thee; open thou them, and say unto my soul, I am thy salvation.

Augustine, Bishop of Hippo, expressed the universal desire of every human heart: how shall one's soul find rest in God? We would like to know how the certitude of our faith may be a reality for us. Can we reach out to touch the hand of God? In our daily life with all the details it embodies, can we truly encounter the presence of the Eternal?

Yes, we can. I do not know all the ways one may sense the presence of God, of Jesus Christ, or of the Holy Spirit, but I know of the Lord's Supper, the Eucharist, and the sacrament of Holy Communion. In instituting the sacrament of Holy Communion, Christ assured his disciples and his people that this was so.

## The Theology of Grace

The Lord Jesus said that although little as two or three are gathered in his name, there he would be present also. He assured us that we would know him in the breaking of the bread. And as often as we eat of this sacramental bread and drink of this sacramental cup, we give witness to the Lord's death till he comes. We keep his memory alive, and we display our faith and worship. We show our loyalty to the church for which he died and rose again.

Our Savior has promised us his power and his presence, and at the sacramental table, we worship in his presence as a fellowship of believers. This is our response to his love and grace, which becomes for us a spiritual experience of strength and renewal. This experience at the sacramental table is for us that moment of personal encounter with him in whom we live, move, and have our being. As we take the elements of bread and wine into our bodies, Christ comes to each of us as our own personal Redeemer. He comes to us to restore our soul and strengthen our faith in him.

Here too, in the celebration of this holy sacrament, we are cleansed from all unrighteousness. We may come just as we are even though we may reach out to him with lame hands of faith. And as we sense the presence of the Eternal, we will find rest for our souls. And we will feel after him until we find ourselves safe in the arms of Jesus. With him, we find the words of eternal life—the words of comfort and rest; "Let not your heart be troubled, you believe in God, believe also in me." When you eat this bread and drink this cup, believe in me. And as we come, we come with knowledge of his reception. This is the bread of his presence.

For we have come to Mount Zion and to the city of the living God, to the heavenly Jerusalem, and to innumerable angels in festal gatherings, and to the assembly of the first-born who are enrolled in Heaven, and to a judge who is God of all, and to the spirits of just men made perfect, and to Jesus the Mediator of the new covenant: your loyal and faithful high priest. Amen.

# Ecclesiology: The Doctrine of the Church

Ecclesiology concerns itself with the study of the church, its nature, its composition, and its structure. Included also are the discussions of its mission, ministry, and the sacraments. We will preface this division with a discussion of the concept known as the Kingdom of Heaven, which is also known as the Kingdom of God. They are one idea. We give the Kingdom of God the widest possible sweep. It includes, in a broad view, all the bodies of believers—past, present, and future—the church of Jesus Christ.

The term *Kingdom of God* is also used to refer to the rule of God's Spirit within the heart and soul of the individual believer. In essence, in viewing the promise of the indwelling presence of the Holy Spirit, the Kingdom of God is within. "For the love of God is shed abroad in our hearts through the Holy Spirit which was given us" (Romans 5:5). Once again, let us remind ourselves that we are dealing conceptually with these matters, and we will not go into minute details.

## The Church: Its Nature

We are interested in the church's nature, composition, and structure. Nature refers to the quality and essential character of the church. Composition refers to its makeup and the combination of its elements. Structure refers to its type of organization, which is either a sacerdotal hierarchy or an evangelical form.

In looking at its nature, we are seeking its life principle as did the historian Tacitus and the proconsul Pliny. What is the church's heart and driving force? And what is the essential germ of its existence? Why was it created by its Lord and head Christ Jesus? Quite simply, as is the King, so is his kingdom, and as is the head, so is the body. Peace and righteousness are the essential elements of the Kingdom of Heaven, and in his rule as sovereignty, the Lord Jesus Christ is King of peace and righteousness. Through his mission in the saving way of God's forgiveness, the Lord Jesus brings peace to the soul of the believer. And through his atonement on the cross, the imputation of righteousness is bestowed on all who believe in his name. God is a Spirit, and all who worship him must do so in Spirit and in truth.

The essential nature of the church of Jesus Christ is spiritual. Her life principle and driving force is Jesus Christ her Lord. The hymn "The Church's One Foundation" declares, "From Heaven he came and sought her; and for her life he died." The church's life, outreach, and growth rest solely on his grace and upon the love of Christ, which constrains us to her mission. At his ascension, our Lord promised the church his presence and the power of the Holy Spirit. This spiritual realization is the essence of her life, its vitality, and the pulsating beat of her heart. This alone is what makes the Christian religion and the church different from all other religions of the world—the presence of Christ in the Spirit with his people. This is also the ultimate reality of our religion. In the success and growth of the church, the presence of the Holy Spirit has always made the significant difference.

## The Significant Difference

In the early days of the church, when the Roman Empire was at the peak of civilization, the pagan world looked upon the Christian movement in utter amazement. They were compelled to exclaim, "Behold how these Christians love one another!" Lucian, an ancient literary critic of Christianity, thought Christians to be held captive by *the crucified enchanter*. The early Christians lived and walked in a manner that was in marked contrast to the general concepts of the society in which our faith was born. There was a deep conviction in the citizens of the empire that the Christian church was entirely different from any other institution they had known. This difference, and its growth, was so outstanding that it attracted their attention, and at times that attention was hostile.

In making a simple and frank appraisal, we are compelled to acknowledge that today modern men and women are not much impressed with any significant difference in the church as it compares with other institutions in our society. It is seen as merely one among the many institutions of our civilization. But if the church is really different from all other institutions of our society—and we hold that it is—and if it does have a special mission to perform, then that difference should be apparent to everyone who comes into contact with it. If the church is to be outstanding, it must avoid conformity to the secular at all cost. In the twelfth chapter of his letter to the Romans, the apostle Paul instructed his readers not to be conformed to this world but to be transformed by the renewing of their minds. Let us, for a moment, look at the early church.

## How Was the Early Church Different?

If the apostolic fellowship was much more than simply a communion of people who followed Christ, we are bound to ask what made them more than a mere fellowship. What made the early church, the body of Christ, stand out so much from that ancient culture? Why was their appearance and conduct such a startling contrast to that affluent and powerful society?

First and foremost, they were a communion of people whose souls were enlightened through a personal encounter with Jesus Christ. The Savior had awakened their souls and kindled them with the flame of his Spirit. They looked to Christ as their Savior-God. The hopes and promises made by God to the fathers were given realization in Christ Jesus. To the church, Christ was the ultimate revelation of those promises as the Lamb of God who takes away the sins of the world. All it took for most of the disciples was one encounter with Jesus of Nazareth, and they forsook all to follow him. When they stood in his presence, strode in his path, heard him speak, and watched him work, they could only exclaim, "Thou art the Christ, the Son of the Living God." In this glorious adventure, their hearts were transported to Heaven.

They were different not only because they had met the great Galilean but because their personal meeting with the Lord Jesus became a transforming experience. They were changed. They were not the same, and they knew it. The old things, old motives, old dispositions, old hearts, and old minds all passed away. The Holy Spirit had worked in them a new creation. They renounced the past and looked forward to the Kingdom of Heaven. Christ had shown them the Father, revealing the fullness of God. They saw in the Lord Jesus the expressed image of God's glory—full of grace and truth—and it only takes one such vision to transform the heart of any man or woman.

When Christ was taken from them abruptly by the crucifixion and then restored to life by the resurrection, they were assured beyond all doubt that God had visited his people. They were renewed in heart, soul, and mind. Henceforth, they would live not unto themselves but unto him who died for them and rose for them to Heaven's height.

Turning to the Lord Jesus brought on a thoroughgoing transformation, and this transformation brought on an unswerving faith. The early church believed. What did it believe? They believed that God for Christ's sake had forgiven them their sins. They believed that in and through their Savior they were restored to fellowship and favor with God the Father. Their trust in God and their faith in Christ gave them release from anxiety and guilt. They were comforted, strengthened, and renewed. This enabled them to overcome temptation, suffering, and the opposition of the entire world. Because the early Christians believed, fear vanished away. Because the church believed, it challenged the pagan world with the Gospel of Christ. And because the church challenged that ancient society, it compelled men to heed its voice.

The early church had an unswerving faith in God. They knew Christ in their hearts, and the message they proclaimed moved from continent to continent and from city to city until it spread the length and breadth of the empire. They believed the message of love and forgiveness which the Savior had brought to them, and they took this good news out into the world. This is what made them different, and this is what made them more than a mere fellowship. They became the militant church of Jesus Christ.

## Is the Present Day Church Different?

We ask, "Is the modern Church different from other institutions in our society?" Is the impact it has on society so startling and evident that men see its significance at once? Is it that one particular fellowship so blessed with the love and grace of our Savior that is stands out as the agent of God for the salvation of human souls and the preservation of our civilization? It takes a little self-searching when we endeavor to examine the modern church intellectually, for we are a part of it. Again, let no one think that because we analyze the church in the modern world that we do not love it.

One of the issues clawing most deeply into the souls of men and women is the lack of certainty and sense of futility they find within themselves. The modern church, through lack of certainty, does not speak out with a commanding voice to the multitudes that are perishing. Because of this, it has lost its moving influence over the lives of millions of men and women. The high moral values of the church (the issues of right and wrong and holy living) do not weigh as heavily in our society as they once did. Men simply are not impressed with much that the modern church has to offer. True religion is not an essential part of their daily lives. They can take it or leave it. And it ought not to be this way.

Why has the church lost its commanding influence? Why is the modern man not impressed with much that the church has to offer? They are not impressed because the church has temporized its message. The church has lowered its standard; and because in thinking that to redeem the world it had to appeal to the wisdom of the world the church became conformed to the ways of world. The average man is no fool, and neither is the average woman. *They do not want a church that conforms and temporizes, nor does our society need such an expression of religion.* There are fools enough in the world as it is.

On occasion, it seems that the church has grown less redemptive, less outstanding, and less appealing than it should be. And the reason is that it gives the impression that it has lost the certainty of its great beliefs. So much water has been poured into the new wine that is no longer appears to be wine. The incarnation, the atonement of Jesus Christ, justification by faith, sanctification, the resurrection, the ascension, and the glorification of the Lord Jesus Christ are conspicuous in our modern pulpits by their absence.

I know and you know that if you are aware of your heart and its silent yearnings, men and women do not go to church to learn about science, philosophy, art, or sociology, as useful as these subjects may be. Men and women come to church because they are sorely needing and seeking something else. We come to church longing to hear a voice out of Heaven telling them of things eye hath not seen nor ear heard. We come seeking, as of old, the healing touch, the forgiving word, the hand put forth in the darkness which makes us know that we are not alone in our struggles. We seek assurance and wish to hear it again that there is a God in Heaven that cares for us and that he has sent his beloved Son to be our Savior. This is the application to the heart of the believer of the great beliefs of the church and of its strong doctrines. And these great beliefs, the modern church is in danger of losing, of losing them by neglect.

The result is this: to lose its influence because it has lost the force of its great beliefs means that the modern church has lost much of its power. You know, I know, and the man outside the church knows that to pay mortgages, to build new parish houses, to put over a financial drive, and to hold bazaars, lunches, dinners, and even bake sales is not true religion. These are not the reasons why the church of Jesus Christ exists. The eternal claim of the Christian religion is that God in Jesus Christ has given to the church the redemptive power and message of the Gospel of grace. The church possesses the Gospel of Jesus Christ to effect the reconciliation of men and women to God and for the preservation of the society of which it is a part of. She has also received the power of the Holy Spirit to enable her to discharge her mission. But the average man is not at all impressed by this claim of power. And if what we see taking place in our churches today is a sample of how the church exercises its saving power, one can hardly blame him if he fails to be moved.

We have to admit that the modern church tends to merge into society. Instead of standing out clear and distinct as the saving agency of God in this world, it has suffered, like every other phase in our life has suffered, from conformity. One is inclined to conclude that when compared to other institutions of our society, the difference is fast disappearing. Our one saving grace is this: it is still the church of Jesus Christ, and he shall not suffer his church to be lost.

## What Can Make the Modern Church Different?

We ask ourselves, "What can make the modern church stand out as the unique and distinct redemptive agency of God once again? How can it regain the full certainty, power, and convictions of its great beliefs?" First of all, we must have developed a personal relationship with Jesus Christ as Savior and Lord. We must know him as the disciples knew him, believe in him as they did, and acknowledge him as our Redeemer-God. When the experience of the disciples becomes our own experience as it truly can, then a significant religious impulse will have been born in the church.

## The Theology of Grace

Until this occurs, nothing of any religious impact will have taken place.

Religion is a real and personal thing, and a personal relationship between Christ and us is absolutely essential. The master and the disciple must come to a meeting of heart, soul, and mind, or the fire can never be struck. The issue is simplicity itself. Unless one meets Christ and knows him and believes in him, how then can he become a Christian?

Perhaps a little review is in order. Prior to his own personal encounter with the Lord Jesus Christ, Paul, who was then called Saul, knew about Christ, his church, and his claim as the Son of God. It was precisely because he knew them so well that he set out to destroy the church. Then on his way to Damascus, he ran squarely into the resurrected and glorified Christ. He was compelled to acknowledge that Jesus was both Lord and Christ. And Saul of Tarsus became the champion of the new faith.

Let us not stop here. Something happened to Paul during his meeting with Christ that transformed his entire life. He became a life-long devoted servant of Jesus Christ. What had happened to him? Christ revealed himself to Paul as his Savior-God, and through his revelation, Christ gave him the content of the Gospel of the Kingdom of Heaven. Paul's acceptance of the saving way of God's forgiveness and of the love of Christ made him a new creation of the Holy Spirit. He went forth from that revelation to preach Jesus Christ as crucified and risen from the dead and ascended to glory. He formed a deep spiritual relationship with the Lord Jesus. In his work in the evangelization of an empire and the opposition he overcame, he wrote to the church in Rome, "And be not conformed to this world; but you transformed by the renewing of your mind." In every age, the church must ever seek to be transformed into a true servant of Jesus Christ.

To have an unswerving faith, power, and influence of the early church, we must acknowledge that Christ is not only Savior of the church but also its Lord. We must affirm and hold to the concept that the origin of the church is different from the origins of all the secular institutions of our civilization. We must hold that its mission is unique and distinct. It is only a saving and atoning Christ that makes the difference. He is her life principle—the vine without which the branches cannot exist.

Your new moons, your Sabbaths, your incense, your appointed feasts, my soul hateth, saith the Lord (paraphrased from Isaiah 1:13-14). "But wash you, make you clean. Draw nigh with your heart, and I will restore you to the joy of my salvation. You shall be my people, and I shall be your God," saith the Lord that hath mercy. What is the revelation? An encounter with Christ, a new religious impulse, and unswerving faith can make the difference in the life of any man or woman and in the life of the church.

### Prayer

Oh, Lord our God, thou art very great. Thou art clothed with glory, honor, and majesty. Thou coverest thyself with light as with a garment. Thy people would worship and honor thy name. Receive us, oh heavenly Father, through the grace and mercy of our Lord Jesus Christ. Forgive us the multitude of our sins and put far from thee the remembrance of our transgressions that we may approach thy courts with gladness. As we wait before thee, do thou now fill us with thy Word and Holy Spirit, which are to us the Bread of Life. Where we have hungered—feed us. Where we thirst, give us to drink from the waters of eternal life that once again we may become the living church of our Lord Jesus Christ. Amen.

## The Church: Its Composition

In seeking to understand the composition of the church, we are interested in its makeup—the manner of the combination of its elements. The apostle Paul drew an analogy of the church as being in a mystical union with Christ—of being in a mystical marriage with him. The meaning is that the church's spiritual union with Christ is vital because from this union emerges the energy-infusing impulse of her life and mission.

Paul wrote of the divisions within the church—the head and body. As a body, the church is composed of the faithful in Christ Jesus, a group of believers who look to God as their heavenly Father and to Christ as their Savior and Lord. We are the body; Christ is the head and Lord.

Our Lord's cross and person are central in worship. Ideally, his mind and Spirit would be that of the church and his likeness the image toward which we move. The church should carry out our Lord's mission of reconciliation, for in its vital spiritual union with Christ, the church is God's agency and representative on earth. With this composition, the church can make an impact on its society, and it can have a redemptive impact in all realms of life. Be the local church large or small, it is still our Lord's redemptive agency in that place where it is situated. Let us look at the early church from another perspective. One might be inclined to ask, "What were they among so many?"

## What Were They among So Many?

The Gospel, in essence, tells us that God loved us. There is nothing very difficult to understand about this. In fact, we like to hear it preached. The New Testament writers, one and all, wrote about a love so great that God sent his Son to a cross to redeem us and reconcile us to himself. Please bear with me, for St. Paul wrote that on occasion we may sound as though speaking as the foolish ones. But here at the cross is where all the trouble begins. Even the apostle Paul admitted to a difficulty here when he raised the question, "Why should God send a good man, his Son, to die for those who are potentially bad?"

This is a question of the Christian religion and its reasonableness. When Paul looked at the cross through the eyes the Roman Empire's contemporary society, he confessed that it looked as so much foolishness. To the wisdom of the world, the concepts of the early church were stumbling blocks—a barrier to its acceptance. Who ever heard of *dying unto self*? Of loving one's enemies? Of blessing the poor? Little wonder that the apostle was accused of madness.

Salvation through the cross was enough to drive away an educated Roman. To the wisdom of the old orient, "the faith of the Crucified Enchanter" was a new thing, a thing of yesterday, and it could never last. To the Greek Sophist, the propagators of the new religion were nothing more than babblers, rude of speech, and lacking the refinement of their cultured universities. Any intelligent, rational person of that era, viewing the simplicity of the new religious movement and also viewing the hostility of mind and spirit that surrounded it, would logically conclude that it was doomed. It lacked the thunderclap of Zeus, the light of Apollo, and the wisdom of the oracle of Delphi. In short, it lacked the blessings of the gods. Just what could these few mendicant babblers accomplish? What could they possible be among so many?

## They Were Nothing

Undoubtedly, there were many people who questioned the reasonableness of being a Christian in the Apostolic Age. What possible chance did these few Galilean peasants and fishermen have against the wisdom of the world? What could they have expected to gain against the might of Imperial Rome? They were uneducated and always in poverty and had to beg for their food. How could they possibly attract people to their new faith? They didn't even wash their hands before they ate, and their grooming left much to be desired. If anything definite could be said about them, it was that they repelled. They were a coarse lot.

If one really took time to analyze them, he would discover that they were bewildered, frightened, and confused. Their prophet from Nazareth had been crucified, and later, a certain James, one of their leaders, was beheaded. Who was there to guide them and lead them? Who was to teach them those things which they had to know? Where would they acquire half the needed strength and fortitude to carry out their mission? The powers had smitten the Shepherd and the flock had scattered. There was more hope for a camel to pass through the eye of a needle than for this tiny group to achieve anything that would be lasting or worthwhile. Reasoning from the view point of the wisdom of the world, one would be compelled to conclude that the Nazarene had erred greatly when he had gathered this rabble together.

What were they among so many? They were nothing, and the propaganda they sought to disperse was also nothing. It was nothing but foolishness. Meek and mild: this was nonsense. Love thy neighbor? Madness! Forgive one another? More foolishness! The good Roman sword was what they needed. The world is a jungle. It goes to the most ruthless, the most savage, and the strongest. It was an eye for and eye and a tooth for a tooth. This love philosophy would never conquer the earth or the meek ever inherit its substance.

And if this were not enough, look at the rabble to whom they spoke—not many powerful, not many wise, and hardly any one of influence. Somebody ought to explode this Jesus myth. When one really looked into this matter and looked at these people as they were, they were really not very much. What were they among so many? Hardly anything at all.

## The Gentleness of Jesus Made Them Great

Yet the centuries have passed. The great Augustus is gone. Nero died by his own hand. Caligula, the madman, fell beneath the daggers of the Praetorian Guard, and the great Trajan and Titus have evolved the way of all flesh. The mighty empire of ancient Rome is also gone. But the faith evoked by the Galilean Carpenter lives on. Simple faith and trust in "the Crucified Enchanter" has stood through the Christian centuries as the visible demonstration that the things of God are eternal. It has lived on in spite of what the powers of earth may have done to quench it. And the Christian faith has done more for the salvation of humanity than any other faith known to have existed.

The Christian faith has elevated women from the position of chattel to one of dignity and grace. It has sought to break down all barriers between the peoples of the earth. It has held marriage and family sacred. It has esteemed the worth of a soul to be incalculable in the sight of God. It has been the moving power behind every reform and mass movement. It was the first to bring healing, teaching, and education to the backward people of the world, and it has sought to renew men's souls.

How could these simple men of long ago have given this faith roots so profound and deep that it has refused to die and has refined itself in persecution? How could men who were as nothing in the sight of the world have accomplished this amazing task with their leader gone? The answer is self-evident: Jesus Christ, whom they came to love and worship, made them great. His Spirit made new men out of them and made them great in his service. They, who had been as nothing among so many, became missionaries of a new and living faith. Anyone who took the time to look could plainly see the effects of the Master's Spirit upon them.

Who ever heard of James and John or of Andrew and Peter before the Master of Galilee called them to his service? Nobody. They would have lingered on with an unfulfilled dream in their hearts, living half a life, and would have died in obscurity had not Jesus of Nazareth called them out from among the many fishermen that plied the Sea of Galilee. From a purely human point of view, who would have seen anything of value in Simon Peter, the big, impulsive fisherman? He had two left feet, always spoke before he gave his words much thought, and loved to boast. He acted bravely when far removed from danger and kept running away from reality. He tended strongly toward vacillation, and when loyalty was demanded, he denied his Master. Who would have chosen Simon Peter? None of us.

The Lord saw all these faults in the big fisherman, and still he named Peter "the Rock." The Lord Jesus saw the new man that the Spirit of grace and the love of the Father would create in Simon Peter. From the first to vacillate, he would be changed into an immutable rock—the very foundation of the Kingdom. Only Jesus Christ could do a thing like that. And the other disciples, who were at one time as nothing, did great things because they had been with Jesus. By doing those things that the world thought foolish, God used them as he had never used men before.

What had happened to them? They learned to die to self, which was probably the hardest thing for any man to do. And in spite of the rivalry that once existed among them, they came to love one another. They learned to carry one another's burdens and to share the load of sacrifice and sorrow. They renounced the hidden things of dishonesty, of evil, and ungodliness and became ministers of mercy and grace. They were ambassadors for Christ and constrained by is love. It was expressed by St. Paul, "They which live should not henceforth live unto themselves, but unto him which died for them, and rose again" (2 Corinthians 5:15). Their motive was love of God. They maintained that "all things were of God, who reconciled us to himself by Jesus Christ, and hath given to us the ministry of reconciliation" (2 Corinthians 5:18).

To be constrained to the work of faith through love of the Son of God, revealed their dedication to the kingdom of God. They labored, and bore patiently the abuse heaped upon them, and yet they were gentle, kind, meek, and considerate one of another. In truth, the Savior's gentleness had made them great. It is little wonder that their enemies exclaimed, "These Christians love each other even before they are acquainted!" The love of Christ changed them, who in the eyes of the world were as nothing, into ambassadors of a new and triumphant faith.

## What Is Today's Church among Its Society?

Since time immemorial, we have heard the critics deride the church of Jesus Christ. It has been criticized for its divisions, fratricide, and for its power or lack of it. Regardless of what the world may think or say, it is still the church of Jesus Christ. It carries within its bosom the eternal Gospel of reconciliation. The only thing that really matters is what the church is among its society today. What is the nature and extent of its impact and moral influence? Among the many forces and power plays that contend in this world, does the church carry a forceful impact for justice, honesty, and noble living it once did? Among the pulling trends of a struggling society, does the church maintain its high moral standard? Is the redeeming influence of the church exerting itself in the world? What is the influence of the church among so many or among so few?

Are we not better educated than those humble fishermen Jesus called to be his disciples? Western culture for hundreds of years has accumulated behind us. We have every advantage of a modern civilization at our disposal. We should be able to do as well or better than those simple fishermen, unless of course we have never been constrained by the love of Christ and have never known the meaning of self-sacrifice.

"Love of Christ," said Francis of Assisi, "sets my heart ablaze." But even more to the point, Bernard of Clairaux wrote, "What we love, we shall grow to resemble." This is one of the most simple and yet deepest secrets of life. Do we love the church? Perhaps, but we must also love the holy and righteous things that she stands for. Have we learned to die unto self? Have we sought God's Kingdom first and with our whole hearts? Is it possible that twelve uneducated and uncultured fishermen discovered a secret of life that ever eludes the cultured and refined generation? Quite evidently, they did, and it made them great. They loved Christ and his Kingdom, and they came to resemble, in part, the image of him whom they loved and served. The apostle Paul expressed the same thought when he wrote in his second letter to the church in Corinth. "All we with open face beholding as in a glass the glory of the Lord, are changed into the same image, from one degree of glory to another, even as by the Spirit of the Lord" (2 Corinthians 3:18). It was true than, and it is true today that "what we love, we will grow to resemble."

A people, a church constrained by the love of Christ, receive their sufficiency from the grace of God. It may be troubled but not in distress. It may be perplexed but never in despair. As we look always to the presence and power of our Lord, who then shall separate us from the love of God which is in Christ Jesus? Are we not more than conquerors through him that loved us?

> For we are persuaded, that neither death, nor life, nor angels, nor principalities, nor powers, nor things present, nor things to come; nor heights, nor depths, nor any other creature, shall be able to separate us from the love of God which is ours in Christ Jesus our Lord.
>
> Romans 8:38-39

## The Church: Its Structure

Generally, the church is organized in either a sacerdotal hierarchy or in evangelical form. The sacerdotal has a priesthood arranged in order of rank, such as the Anglican or the Episcopal and the Roman Catholic Church. The evangelical, in theory, maintains the parity of the ministry. Even though equal in rank, superintendents and conference ministers serve as area administrators. We hold that both structures are of equal validity. Generally, bishops, superintendents, and conference ministers do the same thing. But the sacerdotal rests more direct authority on its bishops.

# The Church: Its Mission

Justin Martyr addressed his *First Apology* to Marcus Aurelius, the ruling emperor at the time of his writing (sometime prior to 160 AD). In it he gave the purpose for which God became man.

> The Father of the universe has a Son, who, being the first-begotten word of God, is also God. Of old he appeared in the shape of fire, and in the likeness of an angel to Moses and to other prophets. But now, in the time of your empire, he has become man by a virgin, according to the Father's design, *for the salvation of those who believe in him.*
>
> *First Apology*—Justin Martyr

## Redemption

Our Lord's purpose in coming to earth was "for the salvation of those who believe in him." This is the main reason for the existence of the church, the major object of its mission, to redeem individuals from spiritual death and to restore them to fellowship with God the Father. "God," wrote the apostle Paul, "was in Christ reconciling the world unto himself...and hath committed unto us the word of reconciliation" (2 Corinthians 5:19). This is the primary mission of the church, the ministry of reconciliation, the reconciliation of man, and the society of which he is a part.

"Preach my Gospel," said Jesus to his disciples. "Reach out to all the nations of the world, teaching them all the things I have commanded you." This is the same commission Jesus gives to his church today. Men and women are created in the image of God, and our Savior believed that their souls and spiritual welfare were supremely worth dying for. The church must respond to people who hunger for a kingdom of righteousness and peace. The ministry of reconciliation is the church's response to men and women in need of grace. The church ministers to those who seek the hand of God in their uncertainty. And the church will extend to them our Savior's compassion, sympathy, and reception. This is what the church is—a spiritual fellowship witnessing to our Savior's grace and proclaiming his Gospel.

## Edification

> And he said to him for the third time, Simon, son of John, do you love me? And Peter was grieved because he said to him the third time, "Do you love me?" And Peter replied, "Lord, you know everything: you know that I love you." Then Jesus said to him, "Feed my sheep."
>
> John 21:17

By preaching the Gospel by its ministry and worship, the church is to nourish the soul of its people. It is to feed them with the Bread of Heaven—to instill in them the spiritual application and principles of our faith. It is to educate them in the knowledge of Christ, bring up the little ones in the faith, and lead them to a godly life.

As a spiritual force, the church must influence society for good. It is the leaven—the salt of the earth. The main thing is the impact of the church in the community, its spiritual strength and steadfastness, its witness to Jesus Christ, and the exertion of its moral influence. The local church and its ministry make an impact in two directions—inwardly among its members and outwardly as a moral influence in the society of which it is a part. It stands for faith, honor, justice, and righteousness, and it opposes evil, oppression, injustice, and inhumanity.

# The Kingdom of God Is Within

When the Lord Jesus met the woman at Jacob's well, she questioned him as to where and how God was to be worshipped. Jesus replied,

> The hour cometh, and now is, when the true worshippers shall worship the Father in Spirit and in truth; for the

Father seeketh such to worship him. God is a Spirit: and they that worship him must worship him in Spirit and in truth.

John 4:23-24

The spiritual nature of God is seen in the nature of his Kingdom and in the nature of its worship. Through his birth, life, and mission, our Savior founded his spiritual Kingdom. The reign of his love, righteousness, and peace was meant to rule in our hearts. The small church and the large and beautiful cathedral are all secondary. The Kingdom of God is a spiritual force, and it is within us. For those who confess Christ as Savior and Lord, the Holy Spirit is manifested in his presence with the believer.

Jesus said to the women at the well, "If thou knewest the gift of God, thou wouldst have asked of him and he would have given thee living water" (John 4:10). The church is endowed with the Holy Spirit as a special gift of grace from God the Father. It is the gentle, compelling grace of the Holy Spirit who turns the heart and mind to faith in the Lord Jesus. It is the leading of the Holy Spirit that gives growth to the kingdom and growth in grace to the believer.

"And I will pray the Father, and he shall give you another Comforter, that he may abide with you for ever: even the Spirit of truth. And you know him; for he dwelleth with you, and shall be in you" (John 14:16-17).

What is the kingdom of God like? This is what it is like. It is a spiritual kingdom, and our Savior's Spirit reigns in our hearts. The rule of the Spirit is revealed in the incidents of our spiritual expression of life. "...which are, love, joy, peace, long suffering, gentleness, goodness, faith, meekness, temperance; against such there is no law" (Galatians 5:22-23). The men and women of the Kingdom can acquire a character not originally their own but that is shaped and molded by the silent working of the Holy Spirit. This is what the men and women of the Kingdom can be like when touched by the Spirit of the living God.

### The Visible Form

We also have the Kingdom of God in visible form in the local churches spread throughout the world. The structure is merely a symbol and a form. The local church is not really a building made with hands. It is composed of people who have turned to the Lord Jesus. We are a fellowship of believers who have confessed our faith in Christ. In the apostolic salutation in his letter to the Ephesians, the apostle Paul wrote, "Paul, an apostle of Jesus Christ…to the saints which are in Ephesus, and to the *faithful in Jesus Christ*. Grace be to you and peace from God our Father, and from the Lord Jesus Christ" (Ephesians 1:1-2).

This is the body, the heart of the local church—the faithful in Jesus Christ, a fellowship of believers. We walk in a fellowship of grace with him who has promised us his comfort, presence, and power.

## The Growth of the Kingdom

> Then said he, "Unto what is the Kingdom of God like? and whereunto shall I resemble it? [Its growth] It is like a grain of mustard seed, which a man took, and cast into his garden; and it grew and waxed a great tree; and the fowls of the air lodged in the branches of it."
>
> Luke 13:18-19

The growth of the Kingdom is like the growth of a mustard seed growing in a garden. The mustard seed is the smallest of seeds, and yet its growth is large. The growth of a local church can be like a flower that a man planted in a garden. In keeping the garden well watered and cultivated, one flower becomes many, and the flowers may grow into a beautiful garden. Any church may grow like a garden of the Gospel of grace. But its love, faith, and patience must be cultivated. You cultivate faith by using it by trusting on the promises of God. The concern and compassion for the strength and growth of our Savior's Kingdom ought ever to be a foremost objective of our faith.

The Church of Christ is commissioned to cast its seed abroad to sow the seeds of love, mercy, and grace. The Church is to work for the redemption of the poor in spirit to preach to the humble of heart and to contend for those who look for the hand of the living God. And it is a good sign of the Kingdom when the Gospel is preached to the poor. Between seed time and harvest lies the unseen work of the Holy Spirit. The little seed, the word of grace, a kindness done with love, patience, and faith, will wax like a great tree. Those seeking the kingdom of God will come and lodge therein.

## Though Smitten, a Church Can Live

> And to the angel of the church of Smyrna write: These things saith the First and the Last, which was dead, and is alive; I know thy works, and thy tribulation, and thy poverty, and I know the blasphemy of them which say they are Jews, and are not, but are a synagogue of Satan. Fear none of these things which thou shall suffer…Be faithful unto death, and I will give you a crown of life.
>
> Revelation 2:8-11

The divine author was filled with sympathy and love for this church and filled with warm affection for its body of believers. Though it was smitten near unto death, in faithfulness to Christ the church yet lived. There are many present-day churches that appear smitten near unto death, and in time, for many of these congregations, the appearance will have become real. One by one, the members of the body drift away. The church will disintegrate, and all that is left is an empty sanctuary. But it need not be so. It was not so with the church of Smyrna. In spite of all its heartbreaking ordeals, it was very much alive. The Lord of the church said that though it was small and appeared weak, it was really triumphant and adorned with a crown of life.

"And again he said, 'Whereunto shall I liken the Kingdom of Heaven? It is like leaven which a woman took and hid in three measures of meal, till the whole was leavened'" (Luke 13:20-21).

The illustration is that the good leaven of the Gospel has been planted deep in the hearts and minds of the fellowship of believers. The life of the church is hidden in Jesus Christ. It has a strong vitality of life that overcomes death and that rises victoriously from apparent dissolution. Though poor in the eyes of the world, it was rich in the grace of our Lord Jesus Christ. If a church is committed to the Gospel, than that good leaven of the Spirit, planted in the hearts and minds of the church members, will rise up into life.

## The Church: Endurance

For the church to endure, she must abide in the presence. Our Lord proclaimed:

> I am the true vine, and my Father is the vine dresser... Abide in me, and I in you; as the branch cannot bear fruit by itself, unless it abides in the vine: and neither can you, unless you abide in me...I am the vine, you are the branches. He who abides in me, and I in him, he it is that bears much fruit, for apart from me you can do nothing.
>
> John 15:1-5

Jesus told his disciples that the branch drew its life and existence from the vine. Apart from the vine, the branch could never bear fruit. We are interested in the spiritual implication of what Christ said. He declared that he alone is the true source of spiritual life of all who believe in him. He is the spiritual source for the Church, which bears his name. Our Savior was speaking of how necessary it is for us to remain aware of his presence. This is our belief, our faith, and our hope; in spite of what may occur now or in the future: as long as the church abides in the presence of the Lord, it shall endure.

## Abiding

To abide means to stand fast in, and to remain in. On occasion, we speak about the "abiding presence," and we mean that in keeping with his promise to be with us always, our Lord's presence continues without change. His presence is enduring and everlasting. This is the promise which the Lord gave to his church. And what a beautiful refrain it has remained. "Lo, I am with you always." David Livingstone wrote, "In a land whose people were hostile to me, and whose language I did not know, and among whom I endured much suffering; do you know what sustained me? It was his Promise—'And lo, I am with you always, even unto the ends of the earth.'" (Matthew 28:20) Our Savior's presence, like his Word, never fails. It is abiding and enduring.

Mark Rutherford, after a night in prison for being a dissenter, said, "Last night, Jesus came into my prison, and every stone shone like a ruby." David Livingstone and Mark Rutherford were speaking about the abiding presence and what it meant for them when most needed. They could say with the apostle Paul, "Though all men forsook me...Notwithstanding, the Lord stood with me, and strengthened me" (2 Timothy 4:16-17). The Lord Jesus manifested his grace and presence to these faithful servants, and they knew that he loved them. The promise is not only that our Savior abides with us but that we also abide with him. Spiritually, we are united to him as the branch is united to the vine.

> And, ah, for a man to arise in me
> That the man that I am may cease to be.
>
> —Tennyson

## The Theology of Grace

We who commit our lives to Christ and to his Kingdom come under the mysterious working of the divine vinedresser. Through our experience, joys, sorrows, and through life and death itself, our Lord removes those things in our lives that keep us from being fruitful for him. As we be come aware of in whom we abide, the man that I am will cease to be. The dying of the old and the rising of the spiritual man go hand in hand, for as in a moment, they are undistinguished one from another. And through it all,

> He works desires you may never forget;
> He shows you stars you never saw before;
> He makes you share with him forever more
> The burden of the world's divine regret.
>
> —Tennyson

Many years ago, John Bunyan wrote, "A church is not measured in greatness by the beauty of its architecture, or even by the ability of its ministry, but by its people, who live truly and serve faithfully, that for which she stands." So much of the success of our churches depends on the spiritual heart of our people. To live truly and to serve faithfully, the things for which the church stands, we must rest in our Lord. We must receive him as he is presented to us in the Gospels, and we must permit his grace and Spirit to cross the threshold of our lives. It is the Savior's grace that can fill us, his Spirit that can possess us, and his love that can constrain us to live truly and serve faithfully the things for which the church stands.

A communion of our historical churches within the Protestant expression of the Christian religion, in the Netherlands, has adopted a phrase from the book of Exodus as the concept for their continuity. "Nevertheless, it was not consumed." The phrase refers to the burning bush that appeared to Moses in the wilderness of Midian. Unknown to Moses, as he walked on holy ground, he had come into the presence of the Lord. To Moses, it was an amazing sight because the bush was burning but not being consumed by the flames.

Though burning in the midst of the fire, the bush was not consumed because our Savior-God was manifested by his presence to be in the midst of it. This was a redemptive presence because God revealed himself as the Redeemer and Savior of his people. Today more than ever the church must be aware that Christ is in her midst—bringing to the church his life-giving Spirit and the ministry of reconciliation. Through him flow its power, glory, and saving grace. And while Christ is in the midst of his church, it will not be consumed, come what may.

In his great work entitled *The City of God*, St. Augustine traced the history and development of the church. He portrayed her as rising out of the ruins of the passing civilizations of the world. The church is seen surviving disasters and catastrophes to rise one day never to fall again. The church is seen bringing to the world the everlasting Kingdom of justice, righteousness, and peace. Even with us today, we must hold our distant vision there through all the dark hours of the world's convulsions. Though it has suffered loss, hardships, tragedies, and pain, nevertheless, the church shall not be consumed—for the Lord God is in the midst of her.

## The Church: Its Ministry

The ministry of the Church is a service of ministering and, ideally, self-sacrifice. Whether or not he is aware of it, the minister, priest, or bishop is both a prophet and a priest. He leads the people in worship and speaks the Word of the Lord to them. He administers the sacraments and is a pastor and spiritual counselor. Let us look at the ministry through the work of the apostle Paul as a pastor and shepherd.

### The Heart and Motive of a Pastor

The apostle Paul, who served as a missionary, evangelists, and builder of churches, was also a builder of men. Included in his function as a prime builder of the kingdom, Paul exercised the offices of a pastor and shepherd. In these offices, Paul sought to be like the Lord Jesus, who is the great Shepherd of the sheep. He tended the flock. His work was to gather, feed, guard, and defend those who chose to follow Christ. In his willingness to give his life for the cause of Christ, we see the heart and soul of a pastor. He conceived his ministry as a "work of faith and a labor of love." Having cast his lot with the Gospel of Christ, Paul never looked back. To him, it was unthinkable that he could serve two masters. He embraced only one Lord and served him with all of his heart, soul, and mind. He had but one goal, one drive, one duty, and one Lord to whom he devoted all he possessed.

Paul's joys were those of the soul and mind, of the glory of the Spirit, and of the grace of God. His delight was in the life of the inner man, where the human soul mingled with the Spirit and grace of our Lord Jesus Christ. He became an advocate for the cause of Christ, for his Church, and for his ministers. He was a bold and daring theologian. Yet he was tender and gentle with new converts. He laid out the theology of the Church in penetrating and massive strokes, and his writings are still a challenge to the heart and mind.

## Paul's Counsel to Pastors

As a counselor of pastors, the apostle was their practical and spiritual overseer. He wrote, I have counseled you, to arouse that love in you, which comes from a pure heart, a clear conscience, and a genuine faith... Remember that you must offer prayers and thanksgiving for all men. And lest the pastor's own vineyard not be kept, he advised them to feed themselves spiritually on the word of faith, not neglecting the spiritual gift that was within them when the prophets spoke and the elders laid their hands on them. Paul also counseled pastors about their conduct toward the congregations they served. "Do not rebuke an older man, but appeal to him as if he were your father...Treat younger men as brothers, the older women as mothers; and the younger women as sisters, with all purity" (1 Timothy 5:1-2).

To authenticate his counsel, the apostle Paul advised his young fellow workers to follow his conduct as they also followed his teaching, purpose, faith, patience, and love. How necessary this is for the true pastors of Jesus Christ. They are attentive to those whose spiritual welfare has been entrusted to their care. He visits the people in their homes, attends to their spiritual needs, and leaves them with the Word of God. He visits the sick and brings them the fellowship of the Spirit. And in the very glory of his calling, the pastor ministers in the name of Christ the sacraments, baptism, and Holy Communion. In Christ's stead, he ministers confirmation and performs the marriage ceremony. Whether he is aware of it or not, in all his ministry, by reason of his calling, the pastor brings the presence of Christ to his people. The very thought of this concept makes the pastor wonder at the grace that has been given him in Christ Jesus our Lord.

Every time a pastor enters a home on the call of the ministry, he brings to the recipient the presence of Christ. Like the Master whom he serves, he will speak as to the slow of heart. He will speak with grace, compassion, sympathy, and understanding; for he serves one who can be touched with the feelings of our infirmities. And like his Master, the pastor will never seek to offend even one of the least of these little ones. Paul said of the congregation to whom he ministered, "I hold you in my heart." With such a concept for the souls with which he has been entrusted, no pastor can go far wrong.

## The Church: The Sacraments

We who have been made new through Christ dedicate ourselves to God.

> They are brought to where there is water. And we are born again, in the name of God, the Father and Lord of all; and

in the name of our Savior Jesus Christ; and of the Holy Spirit, and they receive the washing with water.

*First Apology*—Justin Martyr

Justin Martyr also gave the reason for the sacrament of baptism. "At birth we were born without our knowledge or consent; but… now, we become children of free choice and knowledge, and may obtain through the water of forgiveness" (*First Apology*—Justin Martyr). In the military forces of ancient Rome, in the legion, a Roman soldier took an oath, pledging to obey his commander and not desert his standard. This oath was called a sacrament and was interpreted as a ceremony involving an obligation.

A sacrament of the church is a religious ceremony with sacred and spiritual meanings. Traditionally, a sacrament has been defined as an overt, visible sign of inward and spiritual grace. It is a good definition. As a means of grace, a sacrament has divine approval and imparts spiritual growth, strength, and blessing. It has redemptive significance. It is also a sign and seal of our relationship with Christ and his church. A sacrament may also be said to have been instituted by Christ, engaged in by Christ, and approved by him as a means of grace and spiritual blessing.

## Baptism

Generally we agree with Justin Martyr that baptism is a religious ceremony wherein our relationship to Christ is publicly acknowledged and ratified. Through baptism, we proclaim to all the world that we acknowledge Christ as Savior and Lord. The water signifies a spiritual rebirth and a new spiritual awakening. Since Old Testament times, water also symbolized a spiritual rededication and turning to God with the whole heart; a spiritual cleansing and healing were implied.

Paul wrote that by being buried with Christ in baptism, we were also included with him in his death on the cross, and through him we have also risen to a new spiritual life. The rite performed by John the Baptist was limited to the element of water and its symbolic significance. Our Lord does more: he baptizes with the Holy Spirit. He seals us with the presence of the Spirit as the Holy Spirit of promise. His Spirit within kindles a flame of sacred love, leading us to an exercise of faith and spiritual growth. With all that it implies, baptism is the overt act by which we cross the threshold into the Kingdom of Heaven. And as an initiating act of the Kingdom and spiritual blessing that ensues from baptism. "The promise is to you and to your children forever" (Acts 2:39).

The concept of volition leads some communions of the Protestant religion to lean away from infant baptism; instead, they dedicate the children to God. But as for the infant, the implications are identical with the practice of the major Protestant denominations. Most administer the sacrament to infants with the pledge of the parents that the child will be nurtured in the faith. We hold this to be the better practice though either form or concept is deemed equally valid.

## Holy Communion

Holy Communion imparts redemptive significance. As a means of grace, it effectuates the love of God in us. It implies our union with Christ, our worship of him, and our rededication to the Lord Jesus. It is both a memorial and a testimony to our Savior's love and sacrifice and much more. In Holy Communion, the Presence is encountered. And our spiritual life is renewed and kept strong. Our Lord promised the church his presence and power. We sense and believe in our Lord's spiritual presence during this sacred ceremony. In this sacrament, we believe that our Lord's presence is more acute than in any other service or ministry of the church.

The question has arisen: do the bread and wine become more than the mere symbols of our Lord's body and blood? We believe so. The church doctrine of the Immanence of God applies to all persons of the trinity. As God is, so is our Lord Christ

Jesus, and so is the Holy Spirit; they are actively manifested in a living and operative presence throughout the universe. In Holy Communion, that operative presence is a manifestation of redemptive grace since the Holy Spirit applies the grace of our Lord Jesus Christ to all who partake of the consecrated bread and wine. The presence of Christ can be felt in our hearts, sensed in our souls, and acknowledged in our minds.

The elements of bread and wine are more than mere symbols, and the sacrament of Holy Communion is more than a mere memorial. It is an active, spiritual encounter with our risen and living Lord. It is that moment of Spirit and truth where we receive grace for grace, and where our Lord comes to us with all his redemptive love and spiritual power. If we apply our intellect just a little, we are led to acknowledge that a mere symbol by itself can never be an outpouring of redemptive, spiritual grace. Symbols move us and awaken images of spiritual realities in our minds, but they work no transport of spiritual grace. This is work of the Holy Spirit: he awakens and applies the reality of the indwelling presence to our lives. Thus, in partaking of the elements of bread and wine, grace is applied to our hearts, souls, and minds.

When we come to this sacrament, we come amidst holy things; we come into the presence of our Lord's body that was broken for us and into the presence of his blood that was shed for many and for the remission of sins. As the Spirit calls us, and as our hearts would lead us, we come into our Redeemer's presence with absolute trust and with faith unfeigned. We come seeking as of old the Bread of Heaven. Like the heavy laden, we come seeking rest for our souls and peace for our hearts, for here the weary are at rest.

We come to feel that our souls have been washed in the soul-cleansing blood of the Lamb. We come to sense our spirits up-lifted by the grace of renewal and regeneration. While we are in the presence of his body and blood, together we stand in the presence of a great body of unseen witnesses. We come to embrace the reality of our faith, and to acknowledge that our lives are hid of God in Jesus Christ. Because of God's grace, this is true in spite of all our faults, failures, and sins. Christ our Lord has covered us over with his righteousness through his passion and atonement on the cross.

## The Sacrament: Ever Old, Ever New

The sacrament of Holy Communion is a saving grace where we stand in the presence of the Father of our spirits and in the presence of Christ. We come to strengthen our spiritual union with our Lord, and we come to this sacrament because he has commanded us to do so. We unite, in worship amidst these elements of bread and wine as have all who have walked in the way of the Lord in every generation. In so coming, we discover once again that God's mercy is new every morning. Once again, through our strengthening and renewal, the grace that is ever old and ever new will reveal itself to us, and our Lord will also reveal himself to us.

God reveals himself through the affections of our minds and the moving of our souls. Thus, we come to the bread and wine to be touched by God and to be in fellowship with him in a true spiritual sense. In this sacrament in which we remember Christ's sacrifice for us, we come to the "awakening and to the enlightenment" (*First Apology*—Justin Martyr) that our faith is to believe in God. In these elements, the redemptive reality of the cross of Christ is applied to our souls. Having been fed with the Bread of Heaven and the Word, we confess that the Son of God became incarnate, was crucified, and was raised again for our salvation. Then whenever we partake of Holy Communion, in the mysterious working of God's curious design, our faith is fed and kept strong by the sacrament and the Word.

## Marriage: A Sacrament

Baptism and Holy Communion we hold to have been acknowledged by Christ and personal incidents in his ministry. Both are for the edification of the church and the believer. The concept "instituted by Christ" is a valid criterion for the acknowledgement of a sacrament. We also believe that "instituted by God" is also an equally valid authentication of a sacrament. Our faith and our belief affirm that the estate of marriage is an honorable estate and is to be held in esteem by all men and be "instituted by God" for the proper relationship of husband and wife.

Male and female created he them, and for this cause shall a man leave his father and his mother and shall cleave unto his wife. God bestows his blessing upon the marriage estate and looks upon it with favor, and the union between Christ and his church is portrayed as a mystical, spiritual marriage. As with baptism and Holy Communion, the marriage of a believer is a religious ceremony. The Gospel of Jesus informs us that the marriage ceremony was beautified and adorned by the presence of Christ in Cana of Galilee where he performed his first miracle and turned the water into wine.

Because marriage was instituted by God for the proper relationship between a man and a women, and because God blesses the marriage community, and because the marriage vows implying mutual fidelity and obligations are made and exchanged in the names of the Father, Son, and Holy Spirit, the marriage estate is a means of grace. When the vows of mutual fidelity and obligation are undertaken within the church and the ceremony is performed by an ordained minister or priest, we hold marriage to be a sacrament.

Heaven help us, for we must still reason with men, and like the disciples at the announcement of the resurrection, we must look to the women of our faith. Knowing in their hearts, all the above, the women of our faith have always wanted their marriage performed within the church. They do so because they want God's blessing and favor on their marriage, and they want the world to know that they have united in the marriage estate to express their love as directed by God the Father. They wish to have their marriage beautified and adorned by our Savior's presence—as he did at the marriage ceremony in Cana of Galilee. And they desire that the Holy Spirit seal their marriage with his promise. They seek his grace and favor. To women of our faith, marriage is a sacrament in their hearts.

When the community of marriage is such a necessary and vital part of our society, why should an overly cautious mental attitude, stemming from the Protestant Reformation, exclude marriage from the grace, glory, and redemptive significance of being a sacrament? No particular church made marriage a sacrament. God did that, and he did it at the beginning of creation. The Roman Catholic Church simply had the good, common, theological sense to acknowledge it as such. Marriage is a sacrament. We believe that marriage was the very first sacrament established by God in the Garden of Eden—that it was "instituted by God"—at the beginning of creation?

## Confirmation: A Sacrament

Confirmation is also a sacrament and is supplemental to baptism. It is generally administered to children who have reached the age of discretion. It confers upon the participant the full privilege of church membership that is gained through baptism and their nurture in the church. The Eastern Orthodox and the Roman Catholic churches consider it a sacrament. Again, mostly due to mental reservations growing out of the Protestant Reformation, most Protestant churches fail to acknowledge confirmation as a sacrament. We believe them to be in error, and we would allay their fears. Acknowledging confirmation to be a sacrament will not corrupt the church or make it a synagogue of Satan.

Confirmation is the high point of the religious experience for those who have been nurtured in the church. It is that moment in their religious growth when a fuller relationship to Christ their Savior and to his church is realized and accepted by them. This moment is also acknowledged and accepted by the body of Christ. When I was a child, I thought as a child, I spoke as a child, and I acted accordingly. Now, by the grace of God, I would put away childish things. I have reached the age of discretion, and I would acknowledge my faith in Christ my Savior. We would take our place in our church as young men and women, for we have reached the years of understanding.

An overt, visible sign of inward spiritual grace? Could anything be more visible than the ceremony of confirmation? Could any other religious ceremony for a young man or woman more clearly display the gift of inward spiritual grace? Does anything more clearly lead to the building up of the church? Confirmation leads to a more acute awareness of the youth's spiritual relationship to Christ, to God the Father, and to the Holy Spirit, and the Holy Spirit blesses that awareness. The Holy Spirit blesses that hour, that moment, when a young man or woman embraces the spiritual realities of our faith for themselves. The years of Sunday school attendance and the completion of the confirmation class reach their climax in this religious ceremony. If any religious ceremony of our church is an overt and visible sign of inward spiritual grace, it is confirmation, and this makes confirmation a sacrament.

## Prayer

Eternal Savior, oh thou who has redeemed my soul, be attentive to our petition, we pray thee. Protect and defend thy church. Strengthen it with thy Spirit. Open our eyes that we may be aware, that as long as thy grace and Spirit be with us, we are thy church militant, thy church victorious, and thy church triumphant. And both in Heaven and in earth, we are thy church glorious. Amen.

# Eschatology: The Doctrine of the Last Things

We conceived Christianity to be a revealed religion. Its mission is that of redemption and restoration to fellowship with God the Father. Christianity is also an eschatological religion. Through all the changing scenes of human history, it moves triumphantly to a glorious consummation. The vindication of the Christian religion does not lie in the past or present or on thin air. It moves forward with the power of the Spirit to a victorious end. In the life of the believer, the Holy Spirit moves him to the fullness of the image of Christ. And while it so moves, the spiritual influence of Christianity serves to preserve the society in which we live.

In Christ our Lord, through all her trials, sufferings, and tribulations, the victory of the church is assured. To the church, Christ is all in all, and his glorious appearing will be the final vindication of the faith and love that repose in Christ Jesus. We do not stress the hereafter to the neglect of what our faith can do and is doing now in the lives of its people and for the society of which we are a part. The eschatological teachings of our religions and the second advent of our Lord are the concluding segments of the Gospel of Jesus Christ.

We will not touch on all aspects of Eschatology that theologians usually touch upon. We will deal conceptually in this field with broad strokes, leaving adequate room for discussion. We note that the Revelation of St. John is typical of Scriptural passages that deal with the teachings of the last things. In this final book of the New Testament, the teachings come in signs, symbols, and figures of speech that are found in Ezekiel, Daniel, and Isaiah. Many parts appear hidden in a symbolic cloud of obscurity, and others are vague at best. Hence, we will deal with the plain, simple language found in Scripture, and we will also deal with our Lord's interpretation of some of these passages.

There are phrases in Scripture that seem offensive to many people. One is the "eternal lake of fire." This is found in the Gospels and was used by Christ during his earthly ministry. It was also used by the disciples of our Lord and the early church fathers. They used it in reference to the Last Judgment. When we come to a literary discussion of the Last Judgment, we will deal with it as a historical doctrine in the concepts of the early church. We have no intention of avoiding any difficulty this concept may present to the modern mind.

## Introduction to Justin Martyr

We will begin our discussion on Eschatology with some thoughts and beliefs held by an early church apologist Justin Martyr. He wrote around 160 AD. Justin was well educated and a brilliant early defender of Christianity against the assaults of the pagan world and against persecution of Christians by the Roman civil authorities. Justin defended his faith when the church, as of yet, did not have a fully thought-out theology. He had to contend against the best thoughts of his day, and he did it well. In the afterglow of the resurrection and the writings of the disciples of our Lord, the early church was highly eschatological. In defense of his religion, Justin expressed the beliefs commonly held in this field by the early church.

Prior to his conversion to Christianity in adult life, Justin was a Syrian philosopher of Greek parentage. Under Marcus Aurelius, he died rather than to deny his faith and his Lord. (Marcus Aurelius ruled the empire from 161 to 180 AD.) Justin had traveled throughout the empire as a student of philosophy. He sought for knowledge of reality and perception of the truth. He studied all the great schools of philosophy of his era—the Stoics, Aristotelians, Pythagoreans, and Platonists. With all this behind him, he was deeply impressed by the courage and fortitude of the early Christians. He was attracted by the moral and intellectual appeal of Christianity. He wrote that a flame was kindled in his soul for this new faith, together with a love of the prophets and of those who were the friends of Christ.

Justin Martyr turned to the Lord Jesus about 132 AD. He was the first thoroughly trained philosopher to be won to the Christian religion. He put his intellectual ability to work for the cause of Christ, which he came to embrace. Christianity and the Christ whom he served became a possessing, inner reality with Justin Martyr. Our interest in him lies in his nearness to the disciples of our Lord and their immediate successors, the apostolic fathers, and in Justin's perceptive ability.

Even though Justin was a brilliant intellectual, we note the simplicity of his doctrinal concepts and the language used to express them. In his *First Apology,* he did not intend to write a theology of the church as such. His purpose was to defend his faith and to seek reasonable justice for the Christians who were persecuted and put to death for the simple reason that they confessed the name of Christ.

However, in defending his faith and fellow Christians from persecution, Justin was compelled to state some of the cardinal teachings of the church and to state its current practices and beliefs. Hence, we get pure, unadulterated concepts of his beliefs, which were those of the early church. In this instance, we are interested in his eschatological concepts. He wrote.

> Now the prophets have proclaimed two advents of Christ: the first which is already past, when he came as a dishonored and suffering man; the second advent, when according to their prophecy, he shall come from Heaven with glory, accompanied by his angelic hosts; and also when he shall raise the bodies of all who have ever lived, and clothe those of the worthy with immortality. And he

will send those of the Wicked One, endued with eternal consciousness into everlasting fire with the wicked devils.

*First Apology*—Justin Martyr

Justin Martyr touched on the eschatological doctrines of:

(1) Immortality

(2) The resurrection of the body

(3) The second advent of Jesus Christ

(4) The final judgment

We will also include in our discussion the concept of the new heaven and new earth. This was the circle of thought in which the eschatological concepts of the early church moved. Justin Martyr expressed the belief in a conscious and continued existence of the soul after the dissolution of the body. He wrote about who taught these things to the church.

> To the utmost of our power we praise him by services of prayer and thanksgiving for all the things with which we are supplied. For we are taught that the way to honor him worthily is not to destroy by fire what he has framed for our sustenance, but to use it for ourselves and those in need; and to offer him thankful prayers and hymns in gratitude for our creation, and for all the means of health, and for the varied qualities of different species of things, and the changing seasons; and to present him our souls for a second and incorruptible life through faith in him. Our Teacher in these things if Jesus Christ, who was born for this end, and who was crucified under Pontius Pilate, the procurator of Judea, in the time of Tiberius Caesar.
>
> *First Apology*—Justin Martyr

## Immortality

In the *Declarations of Forgiveness and Assurances of Pardon*, we petition that our heavenly Father have mercy upon us, pardon and deliver us from all our sins, confirm and strengthen us in all goodness, and bring us to everlasting life through Jesus Christ our Lord. Amen. We pray in this manner because our citizenship is in Heaven.

> Our citizenship is in Heaven; whence we wait for our Savior, the Lord Jesus Christ: who shall recreate this body of our humiliation that it might be conformed like unto his own glorious body, according to the might working whereby he is able to subdue all things unto himself.
>
> Philippians 3:20-21

In the Gospel of John, our Lord said, "I am the resurrection and the life: he that believeth in me, though he were dead, yet shall he live: And whosoever liveth and believeth in me shall never die" (John 11:25-26).

What a beautiful thought and what a lovely promise our Savior has given us. With heart and soul we respond:

> O Thou who makest the stars and turnest the shadows of death into morning: we render unto Thee, O Lord, the tribute of praise for this day, for the everlasting hope that rises within the human heart, and for the Gospel which has brought life and immortality to light.
>
> *Pilgrim Hymnal*—Prayers For Morning

St. Paul's letter to the church in Corinth expressed the same thoughts as those taught by our Lord.

> For this corruptible must put on incorruption; and this mortal must put on immortality. Then will be brought to pass the saying: Death is swallowed up in victory. Where

the, O Death, is thy sting? And where then, O Grave, is thy victory?.Thanks be unto God who giveth us the victory through Jesus Christ our Lord.

1 Corinthians 15:53-57

When God created man and breathed into his nostrils the breath of life, man became a living soul, and the soul was meant to be immortal. Immortality means life beyond the physical death as we know it in our limited experience. A new creation and conception of the body will evolve and unite us with the Lord. We believe that the presence of our soul with Christ is immediate upon our death. We believe that immortality is implied in the sovereignty of God and in the resurrection of Christ as the first fruits of them that slept. As Christ is the first fruits, then we who claim him as Savior will follow in his train. As we have born the image of the earthly, we shall also bear the image of the heavenly, and this mortal will have put on immortality. That the soul is immortal has never been doubted in the history of the Christian church. The concept of immortality is expressed in many hymns of the church.

## Still, Still with Thee

"How precious also are thy thoughts unto me, O God! How great is the sum of them: If I could count them, they are more than the sand: when I awake, I am still with thee" (Psalm 139:17-18).

The thought of immortality has always been accepted by our people and cherished. For us and all believers in those quiet moments of prayer and in our times of devotion, we open up our hearts and minds to thoughts of God. In the stillness of the morning or in the quietness of evening, we shut out the world for moments of worship. We look to that communion where spirit to spirit speaks, where our souls reach out to touch the Spirit of the Most High.

We are still with thee, oh Lord, when the morning breaketh. We awaken to awareness that we may walk daily in the presence of our Savior. If we have known him, then whether in the early dawn before the breaking of the day or on that occasion when night shall fall no more, the sense of the presence remains. The shadows of night fly away, for thy mercies, oh Lord, are new every morning. But far lovelier is the thought that when the night has passed and we awake, we are still with thee—we are still abiding in thy presence. Our hearts and souls give witness to our faith that when we shall have passed through the portals of death, we shall awake to find we are still with thee. The consciousness will dawn that we have crossed the threshold into immortality with thee.

And yet, in the ebb and flow of our spiritual life, the days come when our souls are faint. Our spiritual sensitivity grows dim. We feel as though our souls slumber like a feeling of spiritual depression. So many things we are unable to explain, and we feel it in the stillness and darkness of the falling night. What is this sweet mystery of life? We shall trust thee, oh Lord, to whom there is no mystery, for we have taken shelter under the wings of the Almighty. God knows the way we take, and our destiny is in his keeping. And we shall awake to find thee there.

On our appointed hour, we shall stand on the threshold of eternity. We glory in the thought that our immortality begins in the new Heaven and new earth with our Lord. Many have no hope when life's shadows flee and death claims their bodies. For them, physical death ends all. But for those who love the appearing of the Lord Jesus, when the soul seeks God in prayer, that prayer will be answered. Our immortality and our mystery of life are resolved in God the creator of life. We look to our risen and living Lord to lead us as we follow in his path, and we look to him to assure us that God is behind both the darkness and the light of life. "Yea, the darkness hideth not from thee; but the night shineth as the day: the darkness and the light are both alike to thee" (Psalm 139:12). Christ in us is our hope of glory and our hope of immortality, for when we are awake, we are still, still with thee, oh Lord our God.

## In The Sequel of Death

In a symposium compiled by Doran Antrim on immortality, Helen Keller of the American Foundation for the Blind wrote:

> To me there is no such thing as death, in the sense that life has ceased. As I wander through the dark, encountering difficulties, I am aware of encouraging voices that murmur from the spiritual realm…I am conscious of the splendor that binds all things of earth to all things of Heaven. Inured by silence and darkness, I possess the light which shall give me vision a thousand fold when death sets me free.

When death sets us free, what then? What becomes of us when we pass beyond this life that we know? A cardinal teaching of the Christian religion is the belief in the continued, conscious existence of the soul after death and the dissolution of the body.

## Immortality in the Old Testament

Dust thou art and to dust thou shall return, but the soul shall return to God who gave it.

> And many of them that sleep in the dust of the earth shall awake; some to everlasting life, and some to shame and everlasting contempt. And they that be wise, shall shine as the brightness of the firmament: and they that turn many to righteousness, shall shine as the stars for ever and ever.
>
> Daniel 12:2

Justin Martyr pointed out that the prophets had a strong belief in immortality and in the continued, conscious existence of the soul after the physical death of the body, and so did the early church. The present day church also holds to this belief. The thought of immortality runs throughout the Old Testament. By retaining his faith and belief in God amidst the sufferings of this world, Job uttered, "Though worms destroy this body, yet in my flesh shall I see God." The prophet Isaiah wrote, "Thy dead shall live together with my dead body, and they shall arise. Awake and sing, you that dwell in the dust of the earth, for my dew is as the dew of the herbs, and the earth shall cast out her dead" Isaiah 26:19).

Even though we have quoted from only a few passages of scripture, without a doubt, the faith of the Old Testament embraced the belief in immortality.

## Immortality in the New Testament

The New Testament is full and running over with the concept of immortality and the future life. Was it not Christ who brought life and immortality to light for all those who believe in him? In his apology before King Agrippa, the apostle Paul wrote, "And now I stand…at the bar…and am to be judged for the hope of the promise made of God unto the fathers. For which hope's sake, King Agrippa, I am accused of the Jews. Why should it be thought a thing incredible with you, that God should raise the dead" (Acts 26:6-8).

If we believe on the Lord Jesus Christ and his Word, we should not think it incredible that the souls of believers at their death pass immediately into paradise. Their bodies, being united to Christ, rest in their graves until the resurrection. "Today," said our Lord to the penitent thief, "thou shalt be with me in paradise." He made this statement from the cross when our Lord knew he had paradise before him. Our belief in immortality is no idle hope, and it was expressed in the words of eternal life by the Lord Jesus. His most poignant remarks on this were "Because I live, you shall live also" (John 14:19).

Here lies the whole of the matter: within the teachings of the final consummation of the Christian religion, we must believe in risen and living Savior to embrace the hope of immortality.

This belief that is strong in our hearts will give us strength and fortitude for the struggles of today and the unknown things of tomorrow. It can move within us like a strong energizing impulse of the soul. It comes to us from the throne of grace of that life that is to come.

## The Resurrection of the Body

Again quoting from the *First Apology*, Justin Martyr wrote, "For we expect to receive our bodies again, though they be dead and cast into the earth, for we declare that with God nothing is impossible." The *Apostles' Creed* expressed the belief of the early church. "I believe in the resurrection of the body and the life everlasting."

In developing his concept on the resurrection of the body, the apostle Paul based that expectation on the resurrection of Jesus Christ. "But now is Christ risen from the dead and become the first fruits of them that slept. Since by man came death, by the man Christ Jesus came also the resurrection of the dead" (1 Corinthians 15:20-21).

In Adam, as a type and figurehead of the human race, the body is subject to death. But in Christ Jesus, the Second Adam, the body will be resurrected. "For as in Adam all die, even so in Christ shall all be made alive. Christ being the first fruits; and afterward they that are Christ's at his coming" (1 Corinthians 15:22-23). When Christ appears in his second advent, that is when the resurrection of the body of those who sleep in him shall occur. The apostle developed his theme on immortality by using the illustration of a seed: as a seed is sown in the ground, the seed dies, and from it new life emerges.

> So also is the resurrection of the body. It is sown in corruption; and it is raised in incorruption. It is sown in dishonor, and raised in glory; it is sown in weakness: it is raised in power. It is sown in a natural body; and it is raised

in a spiritual body. For the first Adam was a living soul; and the last Adam is made a quickening Spirit.

1 Corinthians 15:43-45

In the development of his theme, the apostle proceeds step by step, writing in opposition as each step moves higher and higher. Like the seed that is sown in the ground, the old body of our humiliation will die, but the death of the seed brings new life. All the attributes inherent in the natural body die with it: its corruption, dishonor, weakness, and mortality. The new creation will be raised in incorruption in glory and raised in a spiritual body. It will be like unto our Lord's own glorious body. "For as we have born the image of the earthly, we shall also bear the image of the heavenly." Paul wrote that he revealed a mystery to the church, which he received by revelation. "We shall not all sleep, but we shall be changed" (1 Corinthians 15:51).

When the apostle Paul began his discussion of the resurrection of the body, he gave his reason for doing so. "That you not be like those who have no hope" (1 Thessalonians 4:13). Those who refuse to believe in a personal God and in the historical tenets of the Christian religion have no hope beyond this world. They may be unaware that they leave nothing to themselves beyond the concept that they are born in futility and will die in despair. We quote from one writer who presented the best thought of his day.

> Brief and powerless is man's life; on him and all his race the slow, sure doom falls pitiless and dark…The life of man is a long march through the night, surrounded by invisible foes, tortured by weariness and pain, towards a goal that few can hope to reach, and where none may tarry long. One by one, as they march, our comrades vanish from our sight, seized by the silent orders of omnipotent death.
>
> *Mysticism and Logic,* p.56—Bertrand Russell

## The Theology of Grace

Our universal hope lies in the expectation of immortality that is taught to the church by the Lord Jesus Christ. In the eschatological teachings of the church, immortality is joined with the resurrection of the body in a glorified and new spiritual entity. Expressing this tenet of our religion, our committal service is one of comfort and hope:

> Unto Almighty God we commend the soul of our brother departed, we commit his body to the ground: earth to earth, ashes to ashes, dust to dust; in the sure and certain hope of the resurrection unto eternal life, through Jesus Christ our Lord; at whose coming in glorious majesty to judge the world, the earth and the sea shall give up their dead; and the corruptible bodies of those who sleep in him shall be changed, and made like unto his own glorious body: according to the mighty workings whereby he is able to subdue all things unto himself.
>
> *Committal Service*—Book of Common Prayer

We do not fear death, and the expectations we express in immortality are found in the hope and comfort of the Scriptures.

> God is our refuge and strength, a very present help in trouble. Therefore we will not fear, though the earth be removed, and though the mountains be carried into the midst of the sea; and though the waters thereof roar and be troubled, though the mountains shake with the swelling thereof…We can be still…even in the face of death…and know that thou art God.
>
> Psalm 46

In the Revelation of St. John, we read, "And I heard a voice from Heaven saying unto me, write, Blessed are they which die in the Lord from henceforth; yea saith the Spirit, that they may rest from their labours; and their works follow them" (Revelation 14:13). In the knowledge of our blessed hope, we can let our forbearance be known unto all men. And in nothing need we be anxious, not even in approaching death. We can be thankful for the life we have received. In everything by prayer and supplication we can let our request be made known to God. And the peace of God, which passes all understanding, shall guard our hearts and thoughts in Jesus Christ our Lord.

## The Second Advent of Our Lord Jesus Christ

The early church looked with expectation and joy on the return of the Lord in his second coming. Once he came in gentleness and grace and ended his tenure on earth in humility and shame. Once he came as the suffering servant of God who was rejected by his people. Many were unable to understand or accept that he came to bear humanity's burdens and nail them to his cross. He suffered judgment and condemnation by sinners, though he had done no wrong. Long ago, he died in shame and dishonor that those who believed in him might live in the glory and honor of God.

In our Lord's second advent, he will come in strength and unimaginable power. With his angelic host, he will come in all his glory and majesty, and all eyes shall look upon him who was pierced for the remission of their sins. He shall come to claim and raise his own. He shall appear and all things shall be subdued unto him. God the Father has given the Son dominion over all. For Christ shall come as the exalted Lord of glory—the crown Prince of the Godhead. He shall come as the sole judge of the quick and the dead, and who then shall stand when he appears?

The delineations of Christ's Second Advent are more numerous and more explicit than those of his first advent. This was the belief of our Lord's disciples. It was the belief of the early church, of the Apostolic Fathers, the early church bishops, and the early church apologists. The belief in the Second Advent is found in all the Christian literature of the early church writers, and it was a cardinal doctrine of all the Protestant Reformers. Had not the eternal Son of God come in his first advent to inherit a body like ours and to be identified with us in his humanity, we surely would have lost him in the vastness and splendor of the universe. And out of the vastness of the created universe, he has promised to come again.

## The Spiritual Expectation of the Second Advent

During the time of his first advent when our Lord came as a baby to a manger, there was a warm expectation in the hearts of all the people. It was a spiritual expectation. And when our Lord walked among the people during his earthly ministry, it was the expectation of the soul that his presence awakened in every heart that came to know him. The intensity of the eschatological aspect of the early church and its people was centered on the promised second advent of our Lord. The thought of his coming filled their souls, hearts, and minds with expectation, and they chose to die in the arena rather than to forsake their faith or deny their Lord.

The belief of the Second Advent held by the early church moved them deeply. It enhanced their spiritual awakening; they lived and breathed in the aura of its occurrence. A strong belief in the Second Advent of our Lord always enhances the spiritual vitality of the church, and this belief comes endued with a deep spiritual faith. This deep spiritual faith brings to the people certitude of our religion. We see in our Lord, who is the source and strength of our spiritual life, the exceeding greatness of his power and the unending riches of his grace.

There is a season in the church year, the advent season, when the expectations aroused by Christ's coming once more become acute. In our Christian symbols, the figure of the dove signifies the presence of the Holy Spirit. In the Christmas season, the anniversary of our Lord's first advent, now long past, the presence of the Holy Spirit is felt, pervading the season. This season also serves as a prelude and reminder of the promised Second Advent, and its awareness stirs the deep, inner realities of our souls. Even so we must forebear and not permit things to draw our thoughts away from the significance of the advent season. We must discern between those things that awaken our souls, drawing our consciousness toward God, and those things that tend to turn our thoughts away from the expectation of the Savior's coming.

In these times of acute spiritual awareness, there are moments when we can be still and know that the sense of God's presence can fill our souls with peace. We can await our Lord's coming in perfect tranquility, looking "unto the patient waiting for Christ." To keep the equilibrium of spirit and truth in the present reality of our daily lives, we will retain our souls in trustful security. Advent is always the anniversary of our Savior's coming—and of his coming again.

## Christ and the Millennium

The millennium generally refers to the thousand years mentioned in the twentieth chapter of the book of the Revelation of St. John, at the end of which the Kingdom of Heaven becomes triumphant. In this period of time, Christ rules as Lord of both the physical and spiritual realms. The reality of immortality and the resurrection of the body center in the second advent of Christ. The Last Judgment also centers on the Second Advent. Two main questions have arisen that ought to be discussed.

(1) As we move toward the end or toward the consummation of the societies of men, will the moral aspect of the human race become better or worse?

(2) Will the Second Advent be pre-millennium, post-millennium, or a-millennium?

## The Theology of Grace

### Better or Worse

From the view-point of human history, most great, ancient civilizations did not last. And it appears that they did not last because they had the seeds of self-destruction inherent within them. They fell apart through wastage incurred through wars of conquest engendered by greed and through the wastage of internal strife caused by civil wars. In looking at the Roman Empire and its civilization in which our faith was born, we see the slow and steady decline of its allegiance to duty, honor, justice, and morality. Historians have acknowledged that Rome wasted itself in wars of conquest and of internal strife.

But even more important, the moral force of its pagan religions had spent itself. They lost their belief in immortality, in self-sacrifice, honor, duty, truth, and justice. They fell into sensuality, and their civilization decayed and finally disintegrated. By the time of our Lord's first advent, Roman civilization was already in the process of decline. The value of human the soul had lost its worth. And when human lives were slaughtered in the arena simply to entertain the mobs, their civilization was doomed.

It seems that new civilizations must always arise out of the ashes of the old. We trust that our civilization will fare much better. No one can doubt that our nation's morality has dropped drastically from when our nation was founded in 1776 with liberty and justice for all. We believe our religion has a moral and spiritual impact on our society and that it serves as a restraining force against the decline in allegiance to duty, honor, country, God, and morality. We trust that the church of Jesus Christ and its redeeming influence are still the good leaven of our civilization. We believe that if the church does not temporize and conform to the slow and steady stain of the world, it can prevent the complete disintegration of our society.

If our present civilization does not destroy itself in a nuclear Armageddon, then our concept lies with that of St. Augustine, the society of moral disintegration, and the society influenced by the church of Jesus Christ will grow hand in hand, and they shall do so through all the changing phases of history. The church has always revived itself, and it has done so time and time again—and therein lies the hope of humanity. Its moral influence and spiritual force will prevent the total disintegration of our civilization. And it will do so in spite of the strong anti-Christian sentiment in many institutions of our society.

As to the Millennium, we believe that the Millennium denotes a time of the present, physical reign of Christ on earth. If this is a physical reign, then Christ would be present. We hold that Christ's present physical reign begins at the coming of his second advent. Our view then of the Second Advent is premillennial. The postmillennial view would set the personal reign of Christ in his second advent—after a thousand years of peace.

Our criticism of the post-Millennial view is this: it would seem illogical to conceive of a reign on earth for one thousand years if the Second Advent were to occur after the period stated. Hence, we hold to our conception that our Lord's Second Advent would coincide with the beginning of the millennial period. And on the amillennial view, our criticism is just as brief. We believe that it is an intellectual avoidance of the problem. The statement "a thousand years will not matter much in eternity" is hardly an academic presentation on the subject.

## The Final Judgment

Again we seek for the church's historical concept on this matter as held by the early church. Even though it may be subject to some modification, we will start here. We begin with some passages from Scripture.

> (1) How you have turned from idols to God to serve the living God and to wait for his Son from Heaven whom he raised from the dead even Jesus Christ *who delivered us from the wrath to come*? (1 Thessalonians 1:9-10)

## THE THEOLOGY OF GRACE

(2) Who shall punish with everlasting destruction from the presence of the Lord and his glory forever? (2 Thessalonians 1:9)

(3) "And I saw a great white throne, and him that sat on it; from whose face the earth and Heaven had fled away. And I saw the dead...standing before the throne; and the books were opened; and another book was opened and it was the book of life: And the dead were judged out of the things which were written in the book, according to their works. And the sea gave up the dead that were in it. And if any was not found in the book of life, he was cast into the lake of fire" (Revelations 20:11-15).

Apart from the epistles of Paul and the writing of the disciples of our Lord, we have the concept of the final judgment as expressed by Justin Martyr. Even though Justin wrote in the defense of the Christian religion, his concepts were also those of the early church.

> And we have learned that it is better to believe even what is beyond the power of our nature, and beyond the power of any man, than to be unbelieving like the rest of the world. For we know that our Master, Jesus, said: "What is impossible with man is possible with God." And our Master also said, "Fear not them that kill you, and after than can do no more; but fear him who after death is able to cast both body and soul into hell. Hell is that place where those are punished who have lived wickedly, and do not believe in the certainty of the things which God has taught us in Christ."
>
> *First Apology*—Justin Martyr

Again we quote from Justin Martyr:

> But if you ignore our prayers and sincere explanation, the loss will not be ours, since we believe, or rather are

persuaded, that every one will suffer punishment in eternal fire according as his deeds deserve it, and will render account of the power he once received from God.

*First Apology*—Justin Martyr

In the Pauline quotation from 1 Thessalonians, we believe we are correct in understanding the phrase "Who does deliver us from the wrath to come" to mean that all who are in Christ Jesus are delivered from the final judgment. Paul's writings affirm this to be so when he wrote, "Therefore now, no condemnation to those who are in Christ Jesus" (Romans 8:1). The phrase "wrath to come" refers to the final judgment from which believers are absolved.

The concept of the final judgment was a cardinal element in the eschatology of the early church. The second Pauline quotation "Who shall be punished with everlasting destruction from the presence of the Lord" has been used by many as an alternative form of final judgment, and we believe the use a valid alternative. "Eternal destruction from the presence of the Lord" is the opposite of everlasting life in the presence of the Lord, which is the promise to those whose life is hid of God in Christ Jesus.

The simple reasoning of the human mind leads us to believe that after death there can be only two alternatives. There will be complete and eternal extinction, and that will be the end of all individuals—no more sorrow, or suffering, or pain. Or alternatively, the body will be raised and again joined with the soul to a conscious existence and made to stand before the final judgment. This latter alternative was the belief of the early church as expressed by Justin Martyr. Whether it was portrayed as a figure of speech or as a future event through prophetic description, St. John in his Revelation gives the conception that all will be raised, stand before the throne of Judgment, and be judged according to his works.

To be raised in the body and made to stand in the final judgment before the throne of Christ is indeed beyond the power of man. And we, like Justin Martyr, have learned that it is better to believe even that which is beyond the power of men than to be unbelieving like the rest of the world. For truly our Master said, "What is impossible for man is possible with God." And it is only God who is behind all that is possible either in this present world or in the world which is to come.

In summary, the Eschatological concepts as expressed by the early church are as follows. There will be a final judgment. Disposition will be made by Christ Jesus who has been appointed by the Father as the sole judge of both the quick and the dead. It is conceived by St. John in his Revelation that the thousand years reign by Christ is an era of peace. During this era of peace, Satan will be bound and his evil power will have been stayed. At the conclusion of the thousand years, Satan will be loosed for a short period, and a time of tribulation will come.

A gigantic battle will be fought, and the power of evil will be defeated forever. The final judgment will take place, and Lucifer and all his fallen angels will be cast into that place called hell. The redeemed, those justified by grace and whose life is hid of God in Christ Jesus, will be forever with the Lord. The condemned will be consigned to the hell of darkness and of eternal separation from the presence of God forever.

## The New Heaven and the New Earth

"I am Alpha and Omega, the First and the Last, the Beginning and the End...I, Jesus, have sent mine angels to testify unto you these things for the churches. I am the Root and Offspring of David, the Bright and Morning Star" (Revelations 22:10).

> And I saw a New Heaven and a New Earth: for the first Heaven and the first earth are passed away. And I saw the Holy City, the New Jerusalem, coming down out of Heaven from God, made ready as a bride adorned for her husband. And I heard a great voice, like the sound of many waters, out of the Throne saying, Behold, The Tabernacle

of God is with man; and he shall dwell with them, and he shall be their God. And he shall wipe away every tear from their eyes; and death shall be no more; neither shall there be any mourning, nor crying, nor any more pain: for the first things are all passed away. And he that sitteth on the throne said: Behold, I make all things new.

Revelations 21:1-5

I do not believe that mere words can add anything to the above passage of Scripture; we let it rest with St. John. "Thanks be unto God who always causes us to triumph in Christ Jesus our Lord." Amen.

# GRACE FOR SUCCESSFUL LIVING

The soul is the core of our spiritual life. It gives impulse to our thoughts and desires. A close affinity to our Lord leads to a deepened spiritual life. Celsus, a critical writer of the early first century, made a literary attack on the Christian religion. He wrote: "The root of Christianity is the excessive valuation of the soul; and the absurd idea that God takes an interest in man." While it may be absurd to many, Christians accept as true that God takes an interest in man and the condition of his soul. In the eighth Psalm, the writer is startled by the realization that God takes an interest in man. It staggers his imagination. Looking to the vast expanse of the heavens, his words express his thoughts: "What is man that thou art mindful of him?"

We acknowledge the validity of his question. God could well have been lost to us in the immensity of the universe. But had he not taken an interest in man, God the Son would not have left the splendor of heaven to assume the form of a man and come down to us: "For the grace of God that bringeth salvation hath appeared to all men [in Christ Jesus]" (Titus 2:11). All we have written in the previous chapters about the grace of God is in order that God's love and salvation may be applied to the life of the individual believer. And how is this done? Look at the words of the verse below.

> I will both lay me down in peace, and sleep: for thou, Lord, only maketh me to dwell in safety (Psalm 4:8).

> We can let this concept flood over our minds. God gives good gifts to men and women and these gifts come on the wings of the Spirit. His gifts include love, knowledge of his presence, and care of the soul. All our fears and anxieties can be swept away in God's never ending gifts of grace. We look to the nearness of God and to the sense of his

presence. We can think on this: "God has not given us the spirit of fear; but of power, of love, and of a sound mind" (2 Timothy 1:7). We can repeat this verse until its power becomes part of our mental image. And while we may have to wait on his presence, we do so with expectation.

I waited patiently for the Lord: and he inclined unto me, and heard my cry. He brought me up out of the horrible pit, and out of the miry clay, and set my feet upon a rock, and established my going. And he hath put a new song in my mouth (Psalm 40:1-3).

## Grace in Our Daily Lives.

There are days when we ask ourselves, why do we have difficulty dealing with some situations that others seem to manage so well? Why do we feel so down? What has occurred is that we have come to that point where we have lost part of our ability to cope with things that matter to us. And our inability to cope with matters that affect us causes us to feel down. "Oh, Lord!" we cry. Christians will look to their faith for help in times of need, but many are not too sure they will find help there. It touches us deeply when we question why our religious lives seem ineffective. The truth is that there is a beating pulse, and also a pause, in the intensity of our religious lives. We cannot always move on the highest plane of our religious experience. And we have to deal with things that diminish our spiritual lives. Nevertheless, we believe that our faith enables us to deal better with all the harsh realities of life. And life does not always move on an even keel.

Our inner resources are drained by the things we must do to keep our little worlds going: getting the children ready for school, worrying about the one away at college, tending a sick family member, and checking on the welfare of our parents. There is a constant demand on our time, ability and physical energy. And then there are the bills to pay at the end of the month. The resolution of difficulties and tasks do not come easily to a tired mind. But it is still a world of give and take. Taking all things into consideration, we get our fair share of the breaks. The solution is that we are need of rest and spiritual renewal.

## Grace and Our Spiritual Life

There are times when we are discontented and ill at ease. We feel estranged from the strong religious impulse we once experienced and knew was a part of us. We wonder. "What happened to our faith? Did it also drain away?"

This world never stops turning, and it takes a toll of our religious life. The steady strain of the world came upon us slowly. It came as though hidden in the darkness of the night. It came unseen and unfelt. There was no immediate sense of the loss when our moral and spiritual strength began to lessen. The impulse of spiritual things became weaker with no sense of pain. We may have been inattentive to the perseverance of our spiritual lives and the care of the soul. In these unguarded moments we may have failed to replenish our moral strength or make amends for what had gone out of us. In the strength of our past deep encounters with Christ, we thought we could go on for ever. But the attrition of our spiritual lives by the world is relentless. Our saving hope is that God's mercies are new every morning. And in looking to the Lord Jesus there is more than sufficient grace to help in time of need. We need inner renewal as much as our bodies need rest and recreation; and we need inner renewal constantly. To replenish our inner, spiritual strength, we must look to our Lord's presence and power.

For grace to be a factor in our lives, we must appeal to the Lord Jesus. We look to him as more than a saving Christ. We look to him as the Lord of life. When we feel the need for strength, we pray for the Holy Spirit to empower us. When we sense the need for patience, we ask the Lord to calm us with his perfect peace. When we wish to be free from anxiety, we draw near and ask Christ to banish all our fears. When we doubt our ability to manage a difficult situation, we pray for our Lord's grace to restore our confidence. We can be refreshed by a sense of well-being formed in our minds by our Lord's presence and spiritual aura.

## Grace and Inner Renewal.

Having confessed Christ as the mediator of our peace and Savior of our souls, we ought not to fear in seeking his grace to help in time of need. There will be times when we will need all our patience, mental powers, and spiritual force to enhance our ability to get through a situation. The grace of Christ always enlarges the area of appreciation. In our mental attitudes, he broadens sympathies and expands our understanding. Christ's spirit moves us with energy and creative urge for the things we must do. But we must cease giving all things priority over the tenor of our spiritual life. Inner renewal touches on our emotional well-being, on our physical abilities, and our mental processes. We contend best when we are relieved of anxiety and do not have to think with a tired mind. We can find inner strength in a few moments of personal devotion. We can unburden our mind of worry and turn our thoughts to things above.

Michelangelo saw beautiful images, shapes, and forms in his mind before he painted them on canvas or in a fresco. All forms, hopes, and ideas that we perceive fall into our imagination, and there we give them meaning and expression. We ought not to forget that we are created in the image of God. We are endowed with the capacity to respond to spiritual things. We can give meaning and expression to our expectations, and we can retain creative hope when we have suffered a loss.

Thought-awakening images that move in our imaginations are meant to stir our souls. We can see them in our minds' eyes; use them when we are tempted to be apathetic. We have the ability to conceive persons, scenes, or situations which are beneficial to us. The mental images we create in our minds come with a feeling, an impulse for good, and lead to the sense of possible achievement.

## The Theology of Grace

The thought awakening images that stir the soul, and the hope they create in us, remind us that we stand forth as witnesses to the essential unity of God's creation.

And turning our thoughts, hopes, and imagination to our trust in God can bring a resurgence of all our expectations. They can be as strong and as real as we dare to believe.

Our faith embraces belief in Christ as our Redeemer, God's gift of the Holy Spirit, and Christ's Spirit present in the life of the believer. In our theology of grace, we have encouragement for a meaningful existence—in the ultimate reality of our religious beliefs. How meaningful and uplifting is the very thought of it—*our Savior's presence*. From the days of early youth to the days of diminishing strength, we are confronted by difficulties and unforeseen obstacles.

But we will discover that difficulties will be overcome, and obstacles will fade away like a bad dream receding in the night.

Our era has unleashed a power of such vast destruction that sane men—contemplating its destructive power—are shackled in a paralysis of hopelessness and dread. To this age of desperation, looking in fear to the future the most uplifting fact in this world is that the living Christ has graced it with his presence. Through his Spirit, Christ is in the midst of this world here and now. He does not remain hidden and remote from human experience. Our faith proclaims that his is a living, active, and operative presence throughout the universe. Our Lord is sympathetic to our needs of body and soul, and is responsive to our appeals.

We declare to every individual soul that the most inspiring reality about life is that it can be lived in a transforming aura of redeeming grace. Every human being can live in a fellowship of one who came in humility, suffering, and death, and who has promised to come again in wondrous glory. This concept has the testimony of the Christian centuries. Our Savior's presence is the most marvelous fact of this or any other era in human history. God's grace in our lives comes through our Savior's living presence.

Although we may not always sense the Savior's presence, we can trust his promise to be with us always: "And, lo, I am with you always" (Matthew 28:20). We can pray the Holy Spirit to give us an awareness of our Savior's presence. In confessing him as Lord, each may experience a personal encounter with the Christ of the cross. Each may know how deeply significant and enriching a personal affinity with our Lord Jesus can be.

Wherever our pilgrimage through life may lead us, whatever obligations our duty may impose upon us, and whatever tragedy may befall us, we have the *Presence* come alongside to help. Jesus will be there to uphold, encourage, and sustain us. The apostle Paul wrote: "*We are more than conquerors through him that loved us*" (Romans 8:27). Listen to the wonder and glory of this verse, to its loveliness and power: We as individual believers are more than conquerors through him that loved us. [Excellent.] What an absolutely beautiful thought. What good encouragement for every individual believer: the living presence of Christ with his people. How uplifting the very thought of it. Amen.

(Martin Angelo Recio 01-22-1986)